FAMILY OF FAITH
LIBRARY

Economics of social issues

FAMILY OF FAITH
P. O. 2
Shawnee, OK 74804-1442

Family of Faith Library

Economics of social issues
third edition

RICHARD H. LEFTWICH

ANSEL M. SHARP

Both of the
Department of Economics
Oklahoma State University

1978

BUSINESS PUBLICATIONS, INC. Dallas, Texas 75243

Irwin-Dorsey Limited Georgetown, Ontario L7G 4B3

© BUSINESS PUBLICATIONS, INC., 1974, 1976, and 1978

All rights reserved. No part of this publication may be
reproduced, stored in a retrieval system, or transmitted,
in any form or by any means, electronic, mechanical,
photocopying, recording, or otherwise, without the prior
written permission of the publisher.

ISBN 0-256-02082-5
Library of Congress Catalog Card No. 77–91322

Printed in the United States of America

1 2 3 4 5 6 7 8 9 0 ML 5 4 3 2 1 0 9 8

Preface

In this third edition of *Economics of Social Issues* we have brought our data, supplementary readings, and, we hope, our discussions up to date. We have tried throughout the book to improve our organization, our exposition, and even our economic analysis.

The objectives and the orientation of the book have not been changed. Our experience, together with many comments that we have received from users of the book, strongly support the usefulness of the issues approach in introducing economics to students. The objectives are (1) to create student interest in the study of economics and its application to current social issues and (2) to provide a framework of basic analytical tools that are useful in the analysis of social problems or issues. To accomplish these objectives, first we introduce an issue. Next we develop the elementary economic concepts important in the analysis of the issue. Finally, we apply the concepts to the issue to see what light they can shed on the resolution of the issue. The sequence of the issues in the book has been planned to provide a logical development of basic economic concepts and to reinforce understanding of those concepts through repeated use and application of them.

We have had advice from many quarters that has been valuable to us in this edition. We are especially grateful to the following persons who have furnished us with detailed comments: E. Victor Maafo, North Carolina Central University; Harold M. Seeberger, Heidelbert College; Gary L. Stone, Winthrop College; Sydney Hicks, Florida State University; Edward J. Deak, Fairfield University; David E. R. Gay, University of

Arkansas; Professor George H. Hand, Southern Illinois University; and Clair E. Morris, United States Naval Academy. Also Howard D. Leftwich, Oklahoma Christian College; Willard W. Howard, Phoenix College; Michael Sattinger, Miami University; Philip F. Warnken, University of Missouri; Harry L. Cook, Southern Oregon State College; John Neal, Lake-Sumter Community College; and Michael W. Babcock, Kansas State University.

We absolve them from the responsibility for any mistakes that may remain.

January 1978   ANSEL M. SHARP
                                                  RICHARD H. LEFTWICH

Contents

PART TWO
DISTRIBUTION OF INCOME

PART THREE
STABILIZATION

Introduction

Chapter 1

POPULATION GROWTH

CHECKLIST OF ECONOMIC CONCEPTS

Economic activity
Insatiability of wants
Scarce resources — natural
Labor — human
Capital — non-human
Technology process of production
Gross national product (GNP) econ's annual output of goods & services in final form
Production possibilities curve pic. of what soc. cld. do if they used all res.
Per capita GNP GNP ÷ by pop.
Economic growth

1

Population growth
Can the earth hold us all?

Peter was happy to see the wild afternoon come to a close so he could escape from the people who swarmed the supermarket where he worked as a stockboy. They seemed to hold him personally responsible when the market ran out of the popular sizes of several different items. So he breathed a sigh of relief as he walked toward the bus stop where he would catch the No. 6 bus for his home.

Peter was not the only one waiting for the No. 6 bus. He squeezed on when it stopped, but he was lucky. The seats and aisles were full, and when the doors closed a sizable group was left to wait for the next bus. Peter stood in the aisle, hanging onto the back of a seat for the hour-long ride home.

Peter's home neighborhood was crowded and dirty. Kids playing ball in the street ran into him as he walked from the bus stop to his home. There was not much yard space around the apartment houses in which the hordes of youngsters could work off their excess energy, so the only place where Peter, his two brothers, his three sisters, and the neighbors' kids had elbow room was in the streets. The family's cramped apartment provided little more than a place to eat and sleep.

It often occurred to Peter (as it has to many of us) that there may be too many people running around in this world.

WHAT ARE WE AFRAID OF?

General concern over population problems is of fairly recent origin. There have been some persistent worriers for a long time, dating at least back to the late 1700s, but they were in the minority until World War II. In fact, many people—especially those in state governments—looked with great favor on population growth prior to that time. The post World War II emphasis on economic development seems to have brought about some changes in thinking. Newspapers, telecasts, magazines, books, and everyday conversation refer to the "population problem" time and again. In all these media, at least three main fears about population growth surface: (1) it strains the capacity of the world to provide adequate food supplies, (2) it creates ever-increasing environmental problems, and (3) it causes crowding or congestion problems.

Pressures on food supplies

Population pressure on the food supply has evoked the most concern over time. We are told persistently that the world's capacities to produce food cannot keep pace with its growing population, that the day of reckoning is at hand, and that massive famines are in the offing unless we mend our reproductive ways.[1] These dire predictions are not new. In the late 1700s a British clergyman-sociologist-economist, Thomas Robert Malthus, was voicing the same set of ideas.[2] He presented the issues logically and systematically, and his analysis is well known today as the Malthusian theory.

Malthus believed that the world's population tends to increase faster than its food supply, keeping the bulk of the population at the verge of starvation or subsistence. He argued that an unrestrained population tends to increase in *geometric* progression; that is, in the series 2–4–8–16–32 . . . The food supply increases in *arithmetic* progression 2–4–6–8–10 . . . This being the case, living standards can never rise far above subsistence levels because of constant population pressure on the food supply.

Malthus pointed to two sets of checks or restraints that operate on the total population. The first consists of *natural* checks—starvation, disease or pestilence, and war. All of these are the natural outgrowth of population pressure on the food supply and serve to limit the size of the total population. The second is made up of *positive* restraints that humans can use to limit population growth. Chief among them are celibacy, late marriage, and birth control. Do these ideas seem to have a familiar, modern ring?

---

[1] Paul R. Ehrlich, *The Population Bomb,* rev. ed. (New York: Ballantine Books, 1971).

[2] Thomas Robert Malthus, *On Population,* ed. Gertrude Himmelfarb (New York: Modern Library, 1960). Originally published 1798.

Environmental problems

Concentrations of population are expected by many to affect the environment adversely—at least in the immediate vicinity of the concentration and sometimes well beyond it. As people produce and consume goods and services, they create wastes. These must be disposed of, and the environment—land, atmosphere, and water—serves as the wastebasket or the sewer. Biochemical processes work on the wastes, transforming some of them back into usable forms. But if a growing population increases the rate at which wastes are dumped into and on the environment above the rate at which it can process them, pollution problems are created. The air becomes smoggy; the rivers and lakes lose their capacities to support aquatic life; and the land may be stripped of valuable resources, to say nothing of the destruction of its beauty.

Crowding

There can be no doubt that crowding and congestion are commonplace throughout the world. Try going home at 5 P.M. in Los Angeles, New York City, or Stillwater, Oklahoma. Drive through the ghetto of any major U.S. city, walk through the bazaar areas in Old Delhi or Hong Kong, or ride a train through the Japanese countryside. Any of these experiences will provide ample evidence of crowding and congestion. They often are cited as examples of the adverse effects of population growth.

POPULATION AND ECONOMICS

The expressed fears have a common theme—that continuing population growth affects living standards adversely. Clearly, population pressure on the food supply, if it occurs as predicted, will result in lower living standards than we now enjoy in the United States. Increases in pollution levels result in deterioration of the quality of life—some even go so far as to say pollution will eventually destroy life. Similarly, increasing levels of crowding and congestion are expected to reduce the quality of life. This is an economic theme—it sums up what the study of economics is all about.

An explicit understanding of the foundations of economic activity is essential to an analysis and assessment of population problems—whether or not population problems really exist and, if they exist, where they are and how serious they are. Consequently, in this section we shall sketch out the fundamental aspects of economic activity and of economics as an intellectual discipline.

Our insatiable wants

Economic activity springs from human wants and desires. Human beings want the things necessary to keep them alive—food and protection from the elements of nature. They want a great many other things, too, and the fulfillment of these wants and desires is the end toward which economic activity is directed.

As nearly as we can tell, human wants in the aggregate are unlimited or insatiable. Why? Because once our basic needs are met, we desire variety in the way they are met—variety in foods, in housing, in clothing, and in entertainment. Additionally, as we look around, we see other people enjoying things that we do not have (ten-speed bicycles, for example) and we think that our level of well-being would be higher if we had those things, too. But most important of all, want-satisfying activity itself generates new wants. A new house generates wants for new furnishings—the old ones look shabby in the new setting. A college or university education opens the doors to wants that would never have existed if we had stayed on the farm or in the machine shop. To be sure, any one of us can saturate ourselves—temporarily, at least—with any one kind of good or service, but almost all of us would like to have more than we now have and better quality in our purchases than we now can obtain.

Our limited means

The fundamental economic problem is that the means available for satisfying wants are scarce or limited relative to the extent of those wants. The amounts of goods and services per year that the economic system can produce are limited because (1) the resources available to produce them cannot be increased by any great amount in any given year and (2) the technology available for production is also subject to a limited degree of annual improvement.

An economy's *resources* are the ingredients that go into the making of goods (like automobiles) and services (like physical examinations). Production is a bit like cooking. Resources (ingredients) are brought together; technology is used to process these resources in certain ways (stir and cook them); and then out comes a good or service (a cake, perhaps). Some outputs of production processes are used directly to satisfy wants. Others become inputs for additional production processes. The resources available in an economy are usually divided into two broad classifications: (1) labor and (2) capital.

Labor resources consist of all the efforts of mind and muscle that can be used in production processes. The ditch digger's output as well as that of the heart surgeon and the university professor are included. There are many kinds and grades of labor resources; their main common characteristic is that they are human.

Capital resources consist of all the nonhuman ingredients that go into the production of goods and services. They include land which provides space for production facilities, elements that enable it to grow crops, and many useful mineral deposits. They also include buildings and equipment that have been built up over time, along with the economy's stock of tools. In addition, all of the raw and semifinished materials that exist in the economy at any given time and that are available for use in production are capital resources. Sheets of steel and grocery store inventories are examples of semifinished materials.

Resources are always scarce relative to the total amounts of human wants. Consider the U.S. economy. We have a population of over 200 million persons wanting more of all sorts of things than they now have. Can the economy increase next year's production enough to fulfill all of these wants? Obviously not. The labor force available from the present population cannot be increased substantially. Its quantity can be increased slowly over time by increasing the population, but this increases total wants, too. The stocks of buildings, machines, tools, raw and semifinished materials, and usable land are not susceptible to rapid increase, either, but are accumulated slowly over time.

Technology refers to the known means and methods available for combining resources to produce goods and services. Given the quantities of an economy's labor and capital resources, the better its technology, the greater the annual volume of goods and services it can turn out. Usually improvements in technology in an economic system result from increasing the scope and depth of its educational processes and from an ample supply of capital that provides, among other things, a laboratory for experimentation and practice.

The capacity of the economy to produce

Gross national product. The value of an economy's annual output of goods and services in final form is called its *gross national product,* or GNP. For any given year the upper limits of GNP are determined by the quantities of resources available to the economy and by the level of technology that can be utilized. A picture of the economy's performance over time—whether it is expanding, contracting, or remaining stationary—is provided by GNP data for the appropriate series of years.

Production possibilities. Given an economy's available stocks of resources and its level of technology, there are any number of combinations

FIGURE 1–1
Production possibilities curve for an economy

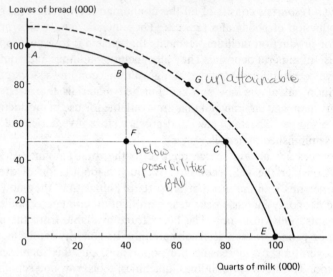

Loaves of bread (000)

Quarts of milk (000)

Line *AE* shows all combinations of bread and milk that the economy's available resources and techniques of production can produce annually. Combinations such as *F* imply unemployment of resources or inefficiency in production. Those such as *G* are not attainable.

of goods and services that can comprise its GNP. For simplicity suppose that it produces only two items—bread and milk—and that all of its resources are devoted to the production of these two things. The line *AE* in Figure 1–1 represents all possible combinations of bread and milk that can be produced. It is appropriately called the economy's *production possibilities curve*. Thus, GNP may consist of 100,000 loaves of bread per year as shown by point *A,* or 100,000 quarts of milk per year as shown by point *E*. Or it may consist of any combination on the curve, such as *B,* containing 90,000 loaves of bread and 40,000 quarts of milk, or *C,* containing 50,000 loaves of bread and 80,000 quarts of milk, or some combination under the curve such as *F*.

If an economy's GNP is a combination of goods and services such as *F,* which lies below its production possibilities curve, the economic system is not operating efficiently. Some of its resources may be unemployed, used in the wrong places, or wasted. It also may not be using the best available techniques of production.

Combinations of goods and services such as *G,* lying above the production possibilities curve, are not currently attainable. The economy does not have sufficient quantities and qualities of resources and/or good enough techniques of production to push its GNP out to that level. Over time, perhaps, it can accumulate enough resources and/or improve its techniques and press its production possibilities curve outward to the dotted line. Then combination G would become a feasible level of GNP.

For the combinations of bread and milk making up line AE, all of the resources of the economy are employed and the best possible techniques are used. If all resources were used to produce bread and no milk were produced, the result would be the 100,000 loaves per year shown at point A. If some milk is desired, some resources must be withdrawn from the production of bread and used to produce milk. Suppose, for example, a decision is made to produce 40,000 quarts of milk. Bread production must be reduced by 10,000 loaves in order to release enough resources to produce the milk. The new combination of milk and bread is represented by point B on the diagram. By giving up 40,000 more loaves of bread, an additional 40,000 quarts of milk can be produced, leaving the economy with the 50,000 loaves of bread and the 80,000 quarts of milk shown by point C. At point E all of the economy's resources are being used to produce milk.

Living standards

Gross national product data alone indicate little about how well an economy can provide for its inhabitants. If the economy's GNP is divided by its population for any given year, the result is *per capita* GNP. This concept is a rough measure of an economy's performance potential. For any one country, per capita GNP for a series of years is indicative of whether or not the performance of the economy in terms of the average well-being of its inhabitants is improving. Among countries, the comparative per capita GNPs are indicative of the comparative economic performances of the countries.

Per capita GNP is a measure of an economy's standard of living, but it is in no sense a perfect measure. It fails to take into account such things as the distribution of the economy's output among the population. If a few people get the bulk of the output while the masses are at a subsistence level, per capita or average figures provide a distorted picture of individual well-being. But by and large, they are the best measure currently available.

It should be obvious now that concern over population growth is to a very large extent economic in nature. Given a country's GNP, the larger its population the lower its average standard of living, as measured by per capita GNP, will be. If a country's living standards are to improve over time, its GNP must increase at a faster rate than its population.

HOW POPULATION GROWTH IS MEASURED

Demographers, who study population characteristics, have developed a standard set of concepts for measuring and analyzing population growth. The most important ones for our purposes are (1) the rate of natural increase, (2) the net migration rate, (3) the rate of population increase, and (4) the fertility rate.

The rate of natural increase

Measurements of a country's population growth usually start with the concept of the *crude birth rate,* or CBR. The CBR is defined as the number of babies born per year per 1,000 people in the country's population. In Table 1–1, column 2 shows the crude birth rate for the United States from 1935 through 1975.

TABLE 1–1
Measures of population growth in the United States, 1935–1975 (annual rates per 1,000 of midyear population)

(1) Period	(2) Crude birth rate	(3) Crude death rate	(4) Rate of natural increase	(5) Net migration rate	(6) Rate of population increase	(7) General fertility rate
1935–39	18.8	11.0	7.8	0.4	8.2	77.6
1940–44	21.2	10.8	10.4	0.8	11.4	87.5
1945–49	24.1	10.1	14.0	1.6	15.7	103.1
1950–54	24.8	9.5	15.2	1.8	17.1	113.1
1955–59	24.8	9.4	15.4	1.8	17.2	120.7
1960–64	22.6	9.4	13.2	1.9	15.1	113.2
1965–69	18.3	9.5	8.8	2.1	10.9	89.9
1970	18.2	9.4	8.8	2.1	10.9	88.0
1971	17.2	9.3	7.9	1.9	9.8	81.9
1972	15.6	9.4	6.2	1.6	7.8	73.3
1973	14.9	9.4	5.5	1.6	7.1	69.3
1974	14.9	9.1	5.8	1.5	7.3	68.4
1975	14.7	8.9	5.8	2.1	7.9	66.8

Note: Numbers may not total due to rounding.

Sources: U.S. Department of Commerce, Bureau of the Census, *Estimates and Projections,* Current Population Reports, Series P–25, no. 481 (April 1972) and no. 632 (July 1976); *Statistical Abstract of the United States, 1972,* p. 10, and 1974, p. 11; U.S. Department of Health, Education, and Welfare, National Center for Health Statistics, *Vital Statistics Report,* vol. 21, no. 11 (January 30, 1973), vol. 23, no. 12 (February 28, 1975), and vol. 23, no. 13 (May 30, 1975).

The CBR of a country is determined by a complex of forces. The percentage of the population that is composed of women in the childbearing age bracket, generally defined as ages 15 through 44 years, is very important. So is the economic value of children to the family; for example, the advantages of more hands to work the farm in a rural area, or the drag of more mouths to feed in an urban setting. Add in the social beliefs or values of the population—attitudes toward early or late marriages, sexual permissiveness, children born out of wedlock, abortion and birth control, working wives, and a variety of other attitudes. Religious beliefs are also important; witness the birth rates in the predominantly Catholic Latin American countries. Then, certainly, the level of technical knowledge of birth control and the facilities available for dispensing birth control information, medicines, and devices are critical. All of these factors work together in determining the CBR.

Next we consider the country's *crude death rate,* or CDR, which is the number of deaths per year per 1,000 of the country's population. U.S. CDR data for the years 1935 through 1975 are shown in Table 1–1, column 3.

The crude death rate of a country also is influenced by a complex of forces. Perhaps the most important one is the society's level of medical and sanitary knowledge, together with the facilities available for putting that knowledge into practice. Where these are at low levels, infant mortality rates are high and life spans are short. Another important factor will be the productivity of the country's economy: Can it produce enough goods and services to provide an adequate diet? The country need not be agriculturally oriented, but it must be productive enough to grow or trade for an adequate supply of food. Social beliefs and values also affect the CDR. They help shape the diet that the population eats and the exercise regimen it follows—and these contribute importantly to the general state of health. They also influence the kinds of medical and sanitary practices that are acceptable. For example, it is widely accepted in one part of the world that fresh cow manure is good medicine for an open sore.

A country's CDR is subtracted from its CBR to obtain its annual *rate of natural increase,* or RNI. The RNI for the United States from 1935 through 1975 is shown in column 4 of Table 1–1. The measurements are obtained by subtracting column 3 from column 2 for each group of years. For example, in 1970 the CBR was 18.2 and the CDR was 9.4 per 1,000 persons. Consequently, the RNI was 8.8. Some can see more readily what this means if it is put in percentage terms—the RNI is divided by ten to make this conversion. In 1970 the *percentage* rate of natural increase was 0.88. Certainly it looks less startling this way.

The net migration rate

If we want to know how fast a country's population is growing, we must take its *net migration rate* as well as its RNI into account. First its *crude in-migration rate,* the number of persons coming into the country per year per 1,000 of its population, is considered. Then its *crude out-*

migration rate, the number per 1,000 population leaving annually, is determined. The difference between the two is its net migration rate, or NMR, which may be either positive or negative. For the United States, as column 5 of Table 1–1 shows, it was positive for the years indicated.

The rate of population increase

A country's RNI and its NMR are added together to obtain its annual *rate of population increase,* or RPI. The RPI of the United States from 1935 through 1975 is presented in Table 1–1, column 6. It also can be converted to percentage terms by dividing it by ten. Thus in 1970 the population increase was 1.09 percent. The rate of population increase as a measurement concept is most useful for describing what has been and is now occurring with respect to a country's population. In other words, it is a better device for recording events than for predicting them.

The fertility rate

The measurement concept most useful in predicting the future course of population growth is the *fertility rate.* This concept is defined as the number of births annually per 1,000 females in the childbearing age—that is, 15 through 44 years of age. The annual fertility rates for the United States for the years 1935 through 1975 are shown in Table 1–1, column 7.

Fertility rate trends of a country provide valuable information for forecasting total population trends over time. Suppose, for example, that the annual fertility rate of a country has been stable over a series of years, and then it falls. This does not affect the number of women of childbearing age immediately; in fact, it will be 15 years before it does so. Consequently, the immediate effect is on the number of children being fed into the population from the potential mothers already living. Eventually the lower fertility rate also causes the number of potential mothers to be lower than it would otherwise be, thus augmenting its effects on population growth.

The annual fertility rate figure can be converted easily into the average number of children born per woman during her childbearing years. Consider the 1971 fertility rate of 81.9 children per year per 1,000 women. Dividing by 1,000 indicates that each woman has 0.0819 children per year. When this is multiplied by 30—the years comprising ages 15 through 44— it can be determined that the average number of children borne by each woman during her life span is 2.457.

Population experts estimate that an average of 2.1 children per woman will result eventually in a *zero population growth,* or ZPG, abstracting from net migration. Two children would replace the parents, and the 0.1 child makes allowance for those who die before reaching adulthood.[3]

POPULATION GROWTH FROM THE ECONOMIC VIEWPOINT

In examining the prospects for future population growth and the economic implications of those prospects, we shall consider first the impact of population growth on living standards. Then we shall turn to the crowding and pollution aspects of population growth. Finally, we shall consider the possible impact of zero population growth on economic activity.

World population growth

Is population growth a serious threat to living standards? Has it kept them from rising, or does it seem to be a significant factor in holding down their rate of increase? Is there any evidence that it has caused them to deteriorate? Per capita GNP data over the years should provide important clues to the answers to these questions.

To analyze the effects of population growth around the globe, a sampling of countries can be classified according to their levels of per capita GNP.[4] We will arbitrarily classify those with per capita GNP below $1,500 per year as *lesser developed* countries, or LDCs, and those with per capita GNP above $1,500 as *developed* countries. A random sample of countries in each classification is shown in Table 1–2.

Lesser developed countries. The sample of lesser developed countries shows substantially higher rates of population growth than does the sample of developed countries. Most of the countries show growth rates in the 2.5 percent to 3.5 percent per year range. But high population growth rates are not in themselves sufficient to demonstrate that overpopulation is a serious problem—population densities, per capita GNP, and growth rates in per capita GNP must be considered also.

In the samples of lesser developed countries, India, Korea, and the Philippines show relatively high population densities. India and the Philippines also show low levels of per capita GNP and relatively low per capita GNP annual growth rates. Korea has been experiencing relatively high

---

[3] Charles F. Westoff, "The Populations of the Developed Countries," in *The Human Population* (San Francisco: W. H. Freeman and Co., 1974), p. 70.

[4] Actually the correct term is per capita gross domestic product, a concept used by the United Nations in gathering data on the output of different countries. The differences from per capita GNP are not significant for our purposes, however, and we will use the latter term.

TABLE 1–2
Population trends and per capita GNP for selected countries

Country	Population estimate 1974 (millions)	Annual rate of population increase 1970–74 (percent)	Population density, 1974 (per square kilometer)	Per capita GNP* (1974)	Percentage annual growth rate of GNP per capita (constant prices)	
Lesser developed						
Bolivia	5.5	2.6	5	341	1960–70	3.1
					1970–75	2.5
Ethiopia	27.2	2.6	22	98	n.a.	
Kenya	12.9	3.6	22	207	1964–70	3.4
					1970–74	1.9
Philippines	41.5	3.0	138	359	1960–70	2.1
					1970–74	3.3
Tanzania, United Republic of	14.8	2.7	16	152	n.a.	
Korea, Republic of	48.9	2.0	222	504	1960–70	6.4
					1970–74	9.1
India	586.3	2.1	178	130†	n.a.	
Chile	10.1	1.8	14	731	1960–70	2.0
					1970–74	0.5
Southern Rhodesia	6.1	3.5	16	532	1965–70	2.7
					1970–73	4.7
Mexico	58.1	3.5	29	1,119	n.a.	
Thailand	41.0	3.2	80	323	1960–70	5.0
					1970–73	2.3
Developed						
Argentina	25.1	1.3	9	1,954	1960–70	2.8
					1970–72	2.6
Canada	22.5	1.3	2	6,463	1960–70	3.7
					1970–74	4.2
France	52.5	0.8	96	5,067	1960–70	4.6
					1970–74	4.3
Italy	55.3	0.8	184	2,706	1960–70	4.6
					1970–74	3.0
Israel	3.3	3.2	159	4,029	1960–70	5.9
					1970–74	5.5
Japan	109.7	1.3	295	4,152	1960–70	9.4
					1970–74	5.5
Singapore	2.2	1.7	3,819	2,389	1960–70	6.2
					1970–73	10.5
Sweden	8.1	0.4	18	6,876	1960–70	3.7
					1970–74	2.4
United Kingdom	56.0	0.2	229	3,375	1960–70	2.2
					1970–73	3.2
Venezuela	11.6	3.1	13	2,542	1960–69	2.3
					1965–69	1.1

TABLE 1–2 *(continued)*

Country	Population estimate 1974 (millions)	Annual rate of population increase 1970–74 (percent)	Population density, 1974 (per square kilometer)	Per capita GNP* (1974)	Percentage annual growth rate of GNP per capita (constant prices)	
West Germany	62.0	0.6	250	6,198	1960–70	3.5
					1970–74	2.6
United States	211.9	0.8	23	6,597	1960–70	3.3
					1970–73	4.1

* At market prices ($ U.S.).
† 1973.
n.a. = not available.
Source: United Nations, *Statistical Yearbook, 1975,* pp. 67–78, 684, 687, 700–702.

per capita GNP annual growth rates. Several countries with low population densities—Bolivia, Kenya, and Chile—also have relatively low per capita GNP annual growth rates. Population pressures may impede increases in living standards in *some* of the LDCs, but obviously we must look elsewhere for the basic causes of low per capita GNP and slowness in its growth.

Developed countries. The sample of developed countries shows uni- formly low population growth rates in the countries that comprise it. But note the population densities that exist in Italy, Japan, Singapore, the United Kingdom, and West Germany! Only India and the Philippines among the lesser developed countries exhibit densities in the same ballpark. Yet, the levels of per capita GNP are substantially higher in these developed countries, and the per capita GNP annual growth rates of Israel, Japan, and Singapore are much higher than those of the LDCs.

Summary. The data of Table 1–2 are consistent with generally accepted demographic theory.[5] In premodern poor societies, death rates were high and, for such societies to survive, it was necessary that their birth rates be high too. In modern times the lesser developed countries are succeeding—often with the help of the developed countries—in reducing their crude death rates. Better medical knowledge and health facilities, improvements in sanitation, and higher levels of nutrition are the responsible factors; and these are generally welcomed by the countries in question. But measures to reduce birth rates do not receive the same social approval as those that reduce death rates. Reductions in the birth rate lag behind reductions in the death rate, and it is during the lag period that so-called

[5] Paul Demeny, "The Populations of the Underdeveloped Countries," in *The Human Population* (San Francisco: W. H. Freeman and Co., 1974), pp. 105–15.

population explosions occur. But, as the sample of developed countries indicates, the birth rate eventually falls and the rapid increase in population subsides. Greater affluence and higher educational levels help bring the birth rates down.

The available evidence does not indicate that population pressure—population density and a high rate of population growth—is *the* fundamental economic problem in the underdeveloped and moderately developed countries. It may be a contributing factor in some, but we must look elsewhere to determine why it is that so much of the world's population lives in misery.

U.S. population growth

Suppose we take a closer look at population growth and living standards in the United States. Data on population growth are shown in Table 1–3 and on per capita income (as measured by GNP) in Table 1–4.

The population growth trends in the United States are far from frightening; they contain no hint of a population explosion. Three estimates of population growth patterns to the year 2025, based on different assumptions as to what the fertility rate will be from now until that year, are shown in Table 1–3.

The medium Series II projection appears to pick up the trend evidenced through 1974, carrying it through the year 2025. This projection is based on the assumption that each woman by the end of her childbearing period will have had 2.1 children. The actual fertility rate for 1974 was 68.4, which converts to 2.004 children per woman and is slightly below the assumed fertility rate for the Series II projection. If the medium projection is more or less correct, the United States will eventually reach a zero population growth rate. This would occur during the last half of the 21st century at a population level between 300 and 400 million.

Fertility rates can be volatile over time, but much evidence points toward permanence of the assumed rate or to a rate even lower. We noted previously that the rates of population growth tend to be much lower in the developed countries of the world than in those that are less developed. In the United States a number of factors point in the direction of lower fertility rates: later marriages, higher divorce rates, an increasing number of women in the labor force, improvements in contraceptive techniques, and liberalization of abortion laws.

Effects on living standards. There is no evidence that population growth, either experienced or projected, has had or is likely to have adverse effects on United States living standards as evidenced by per capita GNP. Trends in per capita GNP are shown in Table 1–4. The effects of inflation or rising prices have been removed from the data by quoting the

TABLE 1–3
U.S. population trends

| | Population | | Projected population* | | | | | |
| | | | High (Series I) | | Medium (Series II) | | Low (Series III) | |
Year	Millions	Average annual increase†	Year	Millions	Average annual increase†	Millions	Average annual increase†	Millions	Average annual increase†
1800	5.3	%	1980	225.7	1.1	222.8	0.9	220.4	0.7
1850	23.2	—	1985	241.3	1.4	234.1	1.0	228.4	0.7
1900	76.0	—	1990	257.7	1.4	245.1	0.9	235.6	0.6
1950	152.3	—	1995	272.7	1.2	254.5	0.8	241.2	0.5
1960	180.7	1.9	2000	287.0	1.0	262.5	0.6	245.1	0.3
1970	204.9	1.3	2005	303.1	1.1	270.4	0.6	247.9	0.3
1971	207.0	1.0	2010	322.0	1.2	278.8	0.6	250.2	0.2
1972	208.8	0.9	2015	342.3	1.3	287.0	0.6	251.7	0.1
1973	210.4	0.8	2020	362.3	1.2	294.0	0.5	251.9	0.0
1974	211.9	0.7	2025	382.0	1.1	299.7	0.4	250.0	−0.1
1975	213.5	0.8							
1976	215.1	0.7							

* High, medium, and low projections are based on assumptions of 2.7, 2.1, and 1.7 children, respectively, for each woman in the population at the end of her child-bearing age.

† Computed.

Sources: U.S. Department of Commerce, Bureau of the Census, *Statistical Abstract of the United States, 1972*, p. 10; Current Population Reports. Series P–25, no. 481 (April 1972), Current Population Reports, no. 541 (February 1975), no. 700 (April 1977).

TABLE 1–4
Per capita GNP in the United States, 1950–1976

Year	Per capita GNP (1972 prices)	Rate of annual increase (percent)
1950	$3,503.0 ⎫	1.6
1960	4,077.5 ⎬	
1970	5,247.9 ⎭	2.9
1971	5,350.2	1.9
1972	5,608.7	4.8
1973	5,862.2	4.5
1974	5,713.2	−2.5
1975	5,580.7	−2.3
1976	5,879.0	5.3

Sources: U.S. Department of Commerce, *Survey of Current Business,* vol. 56, no. 1 (January 1976), part I and part II; *Statistical Abstract of the United States, 1976.*

value of per capita output of goods and services for each of the years in terms of 1972 prices. During the 1950s per capita income growth was relatively low. This was not due to population growth but rather to recessions or periods of slack economic activity following the Korean War and again in the late 1950s. Through the 1960s the growth rate of per capita GNP was substantially higher, although the population growth rate did not slow appreciably until the end of the decade.

Forecasting vary far into the future is an uncertain business, but in general the outlook is certainly not dismal. The population projections referred to above indicate an eventual leveling off of the total population at around 350 million persons—not even double the present population. At this point the population density would still be less than 40 persons per square kilometer, which is relatively low as compared to many countries with similar or higher per capita GNP growth rates.

Crowding. How serious are the crowding problems engendered by population growth? Population density is the usual measure of the extent to which crowding occurs, but the density levels at which crowding can be said to occur differ, depending upon who is defining the term. Daniel Boone felt crowded when he could see the smoke from a neighbor's fire, but many people who live in New York City are not happy in more sparsely populated environments.

Many countries have a population density that far exceeds that of the United States. The population density of West Germany, for example, was 250 persons per square kilometer in 1974. In Japan it was 295 persons per square kilometer. In both countries people are accustomed to living in close quarters. Is it likely that they *feel* more crowded than do people in the United States where population density is only 23 persons per square kilometer?

Crowding and congestion occur in some places—particularly in urban areas—but not in others. A flight over New Mexico, Arizona, Colorado, or Utah will reveal thousands of square miles of empty land. In Texas, Oklahoma, Kansas, Missouri, and almost any other state there are vast areas with ample elbow room. Similarly, around the world there are vast areas that are sparsely populated. Why do people put up with crowding? All things considered, they apparently believe their living standards are higher in the more densely populated areas than they would be in the more sparsely populated areas.

Pollution. Population concentrations have always had adverse effects on the environment in which the concentration occurs. Anthropologists have speculated that the abandonment of old Indian cities like Chichén Itzá in Yucatán and Machu Picchu in Peru may have resulted partly from waste accumulations. Terrible pollution problems existed in the cities of Asia, Europe, and Africa in ancient and medieval times, resulting in plagues and epidemics that wiped out thousands of persons.

Pollution can also be observed in the crowded areas of the United States, and we sometimes confuse the pollution problem with population problems. Certainly the more people that occupy a given area, the more wastes there will be to dispose of. But the amount of pollution that occurs also depends upon the means available to dispose of wastes. We shall treat the pollution problem in detail in a later chapter. At this point, we can say with some degree of confidence that intolerable levels of pollution of the environment are not the inevitable consequences of the population growth projected for the United States in the foreseeable future.

Some economic implications of zero population growth (ZPG)

Although a zero population growth situation is not expected to occur in the United States before 2050, its economic implications are interesting. These implications follow primarily from the changes in the age distribution of the population as we move toward zero population growth.

Age distribution of the population. It is possible to project what will happen to the number of people in different age brackets as the population grows to its zero growth rate level. First, there will be little growth in the number of people under 25 years of age. Second, there will be a marked increase in the number between 25 and 65, as well as in the number over 65. The median age of the population will rise from about 28 to 37 years.

Growth of GNP. Gross national product will continue to increase, both while the population is growing and after it reaches its stationary level. Since the proportion of the population between the ages of 25 and 65 will be increasing, the labor force will tend to increase faster than the population as a whole. In addition, the economy can be expected to continue accumulating capital resources both while the population is increasing and after it becomes stationary. After the population becomes stationary, GNP will continue to grow as capital is accumulated and as the quality of the labor force is improved—if it is improved.

Changes in the pattern of demand. The demand pattern of the population will change as its age composition changes. For example, a ZPG fertility rate means that the diaper and pacifier industries will cease to grow. The lower growth rate of the school-age population means that the demand for school facilities will grow relatively more slowly than demand in general, soon tapering off to a zero rate of increase unless educational efforts become more intensive. Presumably, as the proportion of the population over 65 increases, demand for medical facilities, drugs, nursing homes, travel, and leisure-time activities will increase more rapidly than demand in general.

These changes in demand patterns are no cause for alarm. Demand patterns are always changing over time as new inventions and innovations come to the market. The changing age distribution of the population will be gradual enough so that it will not bring about sudden changes in demand. In fact, the demand changes stemming from the changing age distribution are likely to be swamped or hidden by those that occur in the normal course of events over time.

THE ROLE OF GOVERNMENT

What, if anything, should governments do to influence population growth? Public opinion in the United States and in other countries is not unanimous in answering this question. Most people agree that governments can take steps that will reduce fertility rates and, eventually, population growth; but questions of what is ethical, what is moral, and what is socially acceptable cause divided opinions with regard to what should be done. We shall consider two alternative courses of possible government action. The first consists of positive programs to influence of coerce people to limit family size. The second consists of programs for birth control education and action in which final judgments are left to the individuals concerned.

Programs to influence family size decisions

A government may use its taxing powers to induce people to limit their family size. It could, for example, levy a heavy tax on each minor child over and above some specified number, say two children. The costs of additional children could be made heavy enough to induce many to seek out and use birth control information, devices, and methods.

Such a tax would place poor people at a disadvantage in relation to rich people. The incentives *not* to have children would tend to be greater for the poor than for the rich if the tax on all children in excess of two were the same for everyone, because the tax on a child would constitute a larger proportion of the income of a poor person than that of a rich person. Some unintended pregnancies and births over and above the limit are likely to occur, and taxation of these would thus place a greater burden on the poor than on the rich.

Subsidy payments provide another means of governmental influence on fertility rates. The government of India, for example, has been paying a subsidy to each male who undergoes a vasectomy, provided he has fathered two children. An interesting facet of this program is that a like subsidy was paid to any individual who induced another to have a vasectomy, so a supply of procurers of patients was developed. Subsidies can also be used to encourage females to be sterilized. Again, the primary incidence of efforts to reduce the fertility rate will be on the poor.

Programs for birth control education and action[6]

Population experts estimate that some 20 percent of total births in the United States are unwanted, an unwanted birth being defined as one in which either contraception failed or, in the absence of contraception, there was no intent that the woman become pregnant. Most of these result either from an absence of knowledge on the part of those engaging in sexual intercourse or from the unavailability at the time of intercourse of reliable contraceptive devices. Obviously, if every birth were the result of deliberate informed choice the fertility rate would be below its present level, and progress toward zero population growth would be more rapid than it is now.

The ultimate objective of birth control education and action programs is precisely that of making every birth the result of deliberate, informed choice. At a minimum, birth control education would be aimed at providing information on the causes and consequences of childbearing and on the availability and reliability of contraceptive devices and techniques, but it by no means needs to be limited to these areas. It would be universal and introduced before young people reach the childbearing age.

Education would be supplemented by birth control clinics, which would make reliable contraceptive devices available to all who want them. They would be staffed by trained medical personnel capable of rendering sound medical advice on the pros and cons of different means of contraception.

---

[6] This section is based on Ansley J. Coale, "Man and His Environment," *Science* 170 (October 2, 1970): 132–36.

They would also be available for all of the routine medical examinations necessary for effective contraceptive practices.

For every birth to be indeed a matter of deliberate choice, it would be necessary to use abortions as a last resort to terminate unwanted pregnancies, some of which would occur despite widespread dissemination of birth control information and use of contraceptive practices. The moral issues raised by abortion are without doubt more pronounced than those raised by any other means of preventing unwanted births. Until very recently most states have had antiabortion laws, but antiabortion sentiment is changing. Some state antiabortion laws have been declared unconstitutional, and others have been made less stringent. Some states—New York, for example—make abortion a private matter between the doctor and the patient.

The appropriate course

Unfortunately, the appropriate course of action for all governments to take in influencing population growth is not clearly evident. The impact of population growth is not the same for all countries. Within any given country a web of moral, ethical, and social values will determine what is feasible at any given time. There will seldom be unanimity among the population of a country; we consider the alternatives and make our choices. Then we engage in discussion with our fellow citizens to try to come to a meeting of the minds on what courses of action to take or, perhaps, on whether no action at all should be pursued by the government.

SUMMARY

Many people are concerned about population growth because they fear it will reduce living standards, raise pollution levels to unbearable levels, and cause excessive crowding. These fears are to a large extent economic in nature, and a knowledge of the nature of economic activity is essential to their analysis.

Economic activity is generated by the wants of human beings, which seem to be insatiable in the aggregate. The means available in any economy for satisfying the wants of its population are scarce. They consist of the economy's resources—its labor and its capital—along with its available technology. The supplies of resources, together with the level of technology available, determine the maximum GNP that the country can turn out to satisfy wants. Dividing a country's GNP by its population yields its per capita GNP, which is a rough measure of its standard of living. Thus an assessment of the impact of population growth over time on living standards is largely an assessment of whether or not it has any appreciable impact on the growth of per capita GNP over time. The population growth rate of a country, or its rate of population increase, is made up of two components, the rates of natural increase and net migration. Predictions of the future population growth rate hinge on the country's anticipated fertility rate.

There is not much evidence that population growth by itself has impinged significantly on the living standards of most countries around the world. A limited few countries may be exceptions. Developed countries have already achieved very low population growth rates.

Neither does population growth appear to be a serious problem in the United States. Fertility rates are now and should continue to be low enough to result in zero population growth at less than twice the present population level. Meanwhile per capita GNP continues to grow at a very satisfactory rate. Crowding is a problem only for those who choose to make it so. Pollution is not an inevitable outcome of foreseeable population growth in the United States.

As zero population growth is approached in the United States, the distribution of population among age brackets will shift upward. Gross national product and per capita GNP should continue to grow, but demand patterns will change. These will likely be swamped by "normal" changes in demand patterns.

Governmental policies and actions may be used to influence fertility rates and population growth rates. They may be aimed at influencing directly family size decisions or disseminating birth control information and techniques. Whatever course of action the government pursues will most certainly be surrounded by controversy, for this is a morally sensitive area.

SUPPLEMENTARY READINGS

Bogue, Donald J. *Principles of Demography.* New York: John Wiley & Sons, 1969.

A comprehensive book covering the entire field of population studies, written to be comprehensible to all levels of college and university students. Each chapter is more or less self-contained and thus can be read and understood independently.

Coale, Ansley J. "Man and His Environment." *Science* 170 (October 2, 1970): 132–36.

A thoughtful treatise on population growth and environmental problems. Coale is a population expert who understands economic principles. His treatment of appropriate governmental policies relative to human fertility is especially good.

Ehrlich, Paul R. *The Population Bomb.* Rev. ed. New York: Ballantine Books, 1971.

A scare book written by a biologist with little understanding of economics. It is an important book, however, worthy of the attention of anyone seriously concerned with population problems.

Enke, Stephen. *"ZPG:* Good or Bad for Business?" *Wall Street Journal,* Tuesday, May 18, 1971, p. 20.

A report on some of the findings at Tempo, General Electric's center for advanced studies at Santa Barbara, Cal. The impact of a zero population growth fertility rate on GNP and the structure of demand is examined.

Human Population, The. San Francisco: W. H. Freeman and Co., 1974.

A compilation of articles published in the September 1974 issue of *Scientific American.* The authors provide a balanced informative look at the human population—its history as well as current demographic and food problems.

"Population Heads for a Zero Growth Rate." *Business Week,* October 24, 1970, pp. 102–4.

The possibility of zero population growth is discussed, and its consequences for the economy are projected. The article then considers possible governmental policies to reduce the fertility rate.

PART ONE

Resource allocation

Chapter 2

GOVERNMENT CONTROL OF PRICES

CHECKLIST OF ECONOMIC CONCEPTS

Price floors minimum price, good for seller
Minimum wages 1938, Labor unions, help poor
Price ceilings maximum price, Vinflation, help the poor
Market
Competitive markets
Monopolistic markets
Demand
Changes in demand
Change in quantity demanded
Supply
Changes in supply
Change in quantity supplied
Equilibrium price
Surplus
Shortage
Price elasticity of demand
Income distribution
Unemployment

2

Government control of prices

A boon to the poor?

The winter had not been quite as bad as old Joe Henderson had expected. The cattle had wintered well. There was adequate wheat pasture and the really cold spells were of relatively short duration. He had been able to get the tractor overhauled and, hopefully, would raise a good corn crop. But it was the wheat situation that caused him great irritation. Price supports had been removed under the previous Administration. Sizable increases in outputs by wheat farmers coupled with lagging foreign sales had driven the price down to levels at which wheat growers could no longer cover their costs of production. Surely farmers are entitled to a better shake than that. Maybe the new price support law of this Carter fellow would help give farmers what they deserve.

Apart from the money crops, things weren't too bad. Sally's garden continued to provide plenty of vegetables for current use and canning. In addition, there was plenty of meat from the two hogs and the beef they had butchered. The milk and egg money more than covered the groceries they had to buy. But one thing bothered them. Their cooking, heating, and air conditioning equipment were all operated by natural gas. The price was supposed to be regulated, but the ceiling was constantly being raised. Now there was talk that the price regulation would be removed entirely. Doesn't the government care about ordinary people—especially farmers—anymore?

WHY DO GOVERNMENTS CONTROL PRICES?

Governments engage in price fixing for selected items from time to time. Sometimes they set floors under the prices of certain goods and will not let them be sold at less than those prices. Sometimes they set ceilings on the prices of certain goods and will not let them be sold at more than those prices. Usually, selected price controls are intended to benefit specific special interest groups in the economy.

Price floors

When price floors or minimum prices are fixed for particular items, the intent of the government usually is to increase the incomes of those who sell them. Under what circumstances are price floors likely to be set? If there are groups of sellers whose incomes are relatively low, those sellers may be able to convince legislatures or Congress that price floors are in order. Or, if there are groups of sellers that are politically strong, they may be able to get the idea across with equal effectiveness. Two classic cases come to mind.

The first case is that of agricultural price supports. From the 1920s to the 1970s, per capita farm income was below per capita nonfarm income. In addition, the agricultural sector has had great political clout. Consequently, from 1933 through 1974, farm prices supports were a major fact of life in the operation of the U.S. economy. After a two-year lapse they are back in the picture again.

The second case is that of minimum wage legislation. The Fair Labor Standards Act of 1938 established the first federal minimums for workers in designated industries. Over the years, its coverage has been extended greatly and the minimum rates have been increased substantially. In addition, many state governments have enacted minimum wage legislation to cover workers not covered by federal minimums. Minimum wages have had wide support throughout the United States. They apply, of course, to workers at the lower end of the income scale. They have generally been pressed politically by labor unions and by persons in this country who profess a strong social conscience.

Price floors on certain items may come about in ways other than through direct legislation. In the barbering trade in many states, barbers of each county or city may get together and establish a minimum price for haircuts and other services. Once determined, these joint decisions have the force of law. Labor unions, through government-approved collective bargaining procedures, may be able to establish price floors that are as effective as legislated ones. In these and other cases, the analysis of the nature of and the effects of price floors is not much different from that of the two classic cases.

Price ceilings

Price ceilings or maximum prices have been put into effect from time to time in the United States for two primary purposes. They have been established across the board at some points in time to hold inflation in check. They have also been used on a selective basis to keep the purchase of certain items within reach of those at the lower end of the income scale. This latter purpose sometimes has an anti-inflationary intent also. Across-the-board price ceilings in the United States have been confined largely to wartime periods except for the 90-day wage-price freeze of August 1971; but selective price ceilings have been used in specific markets at other times. We shall concern ourselves in this chapter with selective price ceilings, using as illustrations rent controls and ceilings price on natural gas.

Rent controls have been used in metropolitan areas to hold down housing costs for low income groups. The outstanding example is undoubtedly that of New York City, which has had rent controls in effect since World War II. On a much smaller scale, we often find a similar situation on the university campus when a university sets rental rates for university apartments at relatively low levels to help alleviate problems encountered by low income students.

The control of natural gas prices at the wellhead dates from 1954 when the Supreme Court ruled in *Phillips Petroleum Co.* v. *Wisconsin* that the Federal Power Commission should regulate the price of gas that moved in interstate commerce. The FPC moved slowly and laboriously in putting controls into effect. By the early 1960s the efforts of the Commission began bearing fruit. Since 1968 it has had the price of natural gas moving in interstate commerce effectively controlled. Intrastate sales of gas are, however, exempt from FPC controls.

SOME USEFUL ECONOMIC CONCEPTS

Price floors and price ceilings have been enacted in response to specific problems of certain groups of people. Generally, they have been enacted by legislative groups in good faith and in the expectation that they would help alleviate the problems to which they were addressed. Almost invariably, the results have been unsatisfactory. The price controls have tended to generate more problems than they have solved. Why has this been so? What has gone wrong?

To analyze and assess the impact of price controls, some economic concepts beyond those developed in Chapter 1 are required. These new concepts are (1) market structure, (2) demand, (3) supply, (4) market price determination, and (5) elasticity of demand. We shall develop these in turn.

Market structure

When the buyers and sellers of a product interact with one another and engage in exchange, a *market* exists. The geographic area of any one market is simply the area within which buyers and sellers are able to transfer information and the ownership of whatever is being exchanged. Some markets are local in scope; others are national or international.

The degree of competition that exists in markets is important in economic analysis. At one end of the spectrum, markets fall into the purely competitive classification. At the other they are classified as purely monopolistic. The markets of the world range all the way from one end of the classification system to the other.

Competitive markets. For a market to be purely competitive it must exhibit three important characteristics. First, there must be enough buyers and sellers of the product so that no one of them acting alone can influence its price. To illustrate this point consider the individual consumer buying a loaf of bread in a supermarket or an individual farmer selling wheat at a grain elevator. Second, the product price must be free to move up or down with no governmental or other kinds of price fixing impeding its movement. Third, buyers and sellers must be mobile. This means that any buyer is free to move among alternative sellers, and can buy from whomever will sell at the lowest price. Similarly, sellers are free to move among alternative buyers and can sell to whomever will pay the highest price. Few markets are purely competitive in the sense of rigorously fulfilling all three requirements, but some may be almost so. Agriculture provides an example.

Monopolistic markets. A purely monopolistic selling market, by way of contrast, is one in which there is a single seller of a product. The seller is able to manipulate the product price to its own advantage. It is able to block potential competitors out of the market—frequently with governmental help. The telephone company serving a given area provides an example of a market that approaches pure monopoly.

Demand

The demand for a product refers to the quantities of that product that consumers or buyers will purchase. These quantities are expressed in rates per *time period,* like 10,000 bushels of wheat per month. It makes little sense to say that demand is 10,000 bushels unless the time span during which that amount would be taken is specified. Further, the amount taken per month, or per year, or whatever the specified time period is will depend on the price per bushel that buyers will have to pay. It will also depend on (1) the *prices of substitutes* and of *complements* for wheat, (2) *the purchasing power of buyers,* (3) buyers' psychological *tastes and preferences,* and (4) the *number of buyers* in the group under consideration.

Definition. Demand for a good or service is defined as the set of quantities per time period that buyers are willing to take at various alternative prices of the item, *other things being equal.* We can think in terms of a scientific experiment in which the "other things being equal" are the given conditions of the experiment. These are the factors (other than the price of the good) that were enumerated in the preceding paragraph. When these factors are held constant, how much will consumers take at each of various alternative price levels?

If we could actually consult all consumers of wheat, for example, we could devise a table something like Table 2–1, which is called a *demand schedule* for wheat. This demand schedule is plotted as a demand curve in Figure 2–1 (page 36). Both illustrate a fundamental characteristic called the *law of demand*—the lower the price of the product, the more consumers will take, and the higher the price, the less they will take.

TABLE 2–1
A demand schedule for wheat

Price (dollars)	Quantity (bushels per month)	Price (dollars)	Quantity (bushels per month)
$10	1,000	$5	6,000
9	2,000	4	7,000
8	3,000	3	8,000
7	4,000	2	9,000
6	5,000	1	10,000

Changes. Since demand refers to an entire demand schedule or demand curve, a *change in demand* means a shift in the position of the entire curve. The shift results from a change in one of the "other things equal" that would cause consumers to take more of the product at each possible price or less of the product at each possible price. Suppose, for example, that an increase in consumers' purchasing power causes them to take an additional 1,000 bushels of wheat at each possible price. In Figure 2–2, (page 37), the demand curve shifts (increases) from DD to D_1D_1. An increase or decrease in quantity taken in response to changes in the price of the product, like the movement from A to B in Figure 2–2, is called a *change in quantity demanded.* It is not called a change in demand.

FIGURE 2–1
A demand curve for wheat

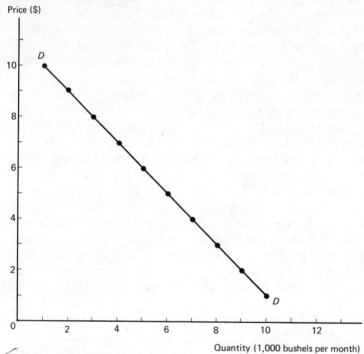

The numbers of Table 2–1 plotted graphically are points forming the demand curve *DD*. The demand curve shows the quantities that all consumers will take at alternative prices, other things being equal.

Supply

Definition. The *supply* of a product refers to the quantities per time period that sellers are willing to place on the market at alternative prices of the item, *other things being equal.* In the case of supply, these "other things" are (1) resource prices, and (2) techniques of production.

If the suppliers of wheat were asked how much per unit of time they would place on the market alternative price levels, their answers would provide the information for a *supply schedule* or *supply curve* of the product, as illustrated in Table 2–2 and Figure 2–3 (page 38). Ordinarily, suppliers would be expected to place more on the market at higher prices, so most supply curves slope upward to the right. There are two reasons for this. First, since it is more profitable to produce at the higher prices, each individual supplier is induced to place more on the market. Second, the greater profits earned from higher prices induce new producers to enter the market.

FIGURE 2–2
A change in demand

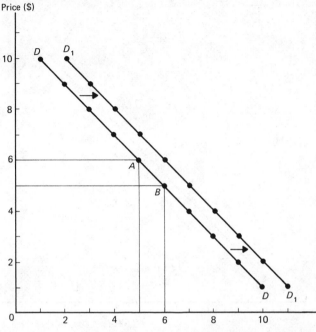

Quantity (1,000 bushels per month)

A change in demand means a shift of the entire demand curve
from one position to another—say from *DD* to *D₁D₁*. A movement
from *A* to *B* is not called a change in demand. Rather, it is called
a change in quantity demanded because of a price change.

TABLE 2–2
A supply schedule for wheat

Price (dollars)	Quantity (bushels per month)	Price (dollars)	Quantity (bushels per month)
$1	2,000	$ 6	7,000
2	3,000	7	8,000
3	4,000	8	9,000
4	5,000	9	10,000
5	6,000	10	11,000

Changes.   The same distinction is made between a *change in supply*
and a *change in the quantity supplied* because of a price change as was
made for the corresponding demand concepts. In Figure 2–4 (page 39) a
shift from *SS* to S_1S_1 is a change in supply, and a movement from *F* to *G* is

FIGURE 2–3
A supply curve

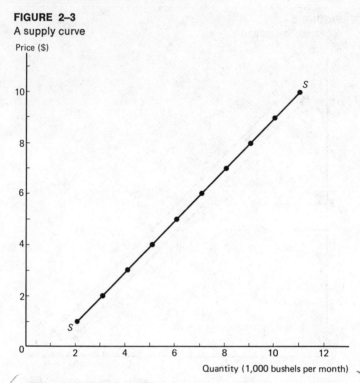

Price ($)

Quantity (1,000 bushels per month)

Prices and quantities from Table 2–2 are plotted as points forming the supply curve SS. The supply curve shows the quantities that
all suppliers will place on the market at alternative prices, other
things being equal.

a change in quantity supplied. An improvement in techniques of production that makes it possible for each output level to be produced at a lower
cost per unit causes an increase in supply, since it also makes it possible to
produce more at each possible price level than before.

Competitive market price determination

Equilibrium price. The price of a product in a competitive market
is determined by the interaction of buyers and sellers—or, as economists
like to say, by the forces of demand and supply. How this comes about is
shown in Figure 2–5 (page 40). The supply curve shows that at a price of
$5 per bushel sellers want ot sell 6,000 bushels of wheat per month. The
demand curve shows that at this price, 6,000 bushels per month is what
buyers want to buy. The price at which buyers want to buy the same
quantity that sellers want to sell is termed the *equilibrium price.*

FIGURE 2–4
A change in supply

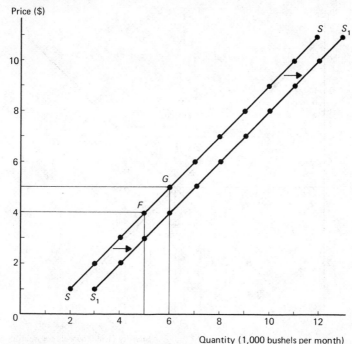

Quantity (1,000 bushels per month)

A shift in the supply curve from *SS* to S_1S_1 is called a change in supply. A movement along *SS* from *F* to *G* is called a change in quantity supplied because of a price change.

Effects of a price above equilibrium. If the price is not at the equilibrium level, market forces are set in motion that move it toward that level. Suppose, for example, that the price of wheat in Figure 2–5 were $7 per bushel. Sellers would want to place 8,000 bushels per month on the market, but buyers would be willing to buy only 4,000 bushels. Thus, there would be a *surplus* of 4,000 bushels per month. Any of the many individual sellers not able to sell all supplies would have an incentive to cut price a little below that at which the others sell. The price advantage would enable the seller to dispose of its surplus. As long as surpluses exist, sellers have incentives to undercut one another. When the price has been driven down to $5 per bushel, no seller is caught with a surplus, and the undercutting stops.

Effects of a price below equilibrium. On the other hand, if the price were $4 per bushel, buyers would want 7,000 bushels per month but sellers would be willing to place only 5,000 bushels on the market. A *shortage*

FIGURE 2–5
Competitive market price determination

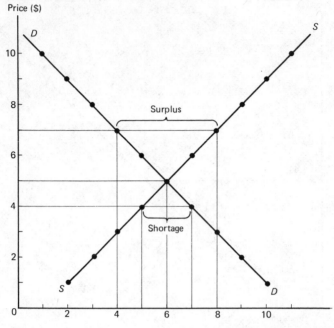

The demand curve and the supply curve together show how the equilibrium price for a product is determined in the market. If the price is above the equilibrium level, surpluses occur, and sellers undercut each other's prices until the equilibrium price is reached. If the price is below the equilibrium level, shortages occur, and buyers bidding against each other for available supplies drive the price up to the equilibrium level. At the equilibrium level there are neither surpluses nor shortages.

of wheat would exist. Individual buyers wanting more than they can get at that price will bid up the price in the attempt to alleviate their shortages. An incentive exists for them to increase their offering prices as long as shortages occur. When the price reaches the $5 equilibrium level, there are no shortages, and the upward movement of the price will cease.

Price elasticity of demand

A question that comes up frequently in economic analysis is how responsive the quantity taken of a product is to a change in its price, given the demand for the product. The measure of such responsiveness is called the *price elasticity of demand*. It is computed by dividing the percentage change in quantity taken by the percentage change in price.

The computation of elasticity is illustrated in Figure 2–6. Let *DD* and *SS* be the original demand and supply curves. Now suppose an improvement in technology shifts the supply curve to the right, to S_1S_1. The equilibrium price was originally $5, but with the increase in supply a surplus exists at that price, causing the equilibrium price level to move downward to $4. The quantity exchanged rises from 6,000 bushels to 7,000 bushels, which is a 17 percent increase. Price falls by 20 percent. So elasticity of demand for the price change is 17/20, or 0.85, meaning that a 1 percent change in price generates an 0.85 percent change in quantity taken.

FIGURE 2–6
A price change, demand elasticity, and total receipts

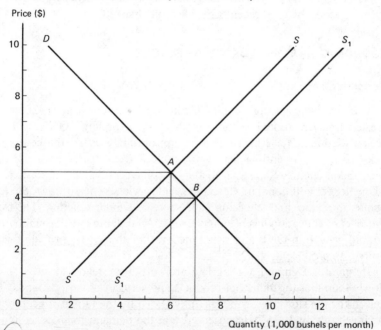

Elasticity of demand for a price change is computed by dividing the percentage change in quantity by the percentage change in price. In this example the percentage increase in quantity is outweighed by the percentage decrease in price. Demand is inelastic, and total receipts fall.

The elasticity measurement may turn out to be greater than 1, less than 1, or equal to 1, depending upon the demand curve under surveillance and on the part of the demand curve for which elasticity is measured. If it is less than 1, as it was in the foregoing example, demand is said to be *inelastic*. If it is greater than 1, demand is said to be *elastic*. If it is equal to 1, demand has *unitary elasticity*.

The magnitude of elasticity provides information on what will happen to the total receipts of sellers (or the total expenditures of buyers) if the price of a product changes. Consider the original equilibrium situation at point *A* in Figure 2–6. Total receipts of sellers, found by multiplying the quantity sold by the price, are $30,000. After the increase in supply and the decrease in price, total receipts are $28,000. This will always be the case for a price decrease when demand is inelastic—total receipts of sellers will fall because the percentage increase in quantity taken is less than the percentage decrease in the price. Similar reasoning leads to the conclusion that a price decrease when demand is elastic will cause total receipts of sellers to rise. When demand is of unitary elasticity, a decrease in price leaves the total receipts of sellers unchanged.

ECONOMIC ANALYSIS OF PRICE FLOORS

Agricultural markets

The relatively low per capita incomes of farmers from 1920 to the present time are rooted in the growth of the economy's GNP over that period of time. The 20th century is appropriately called the century of innovation and invention. The automobile and electricity have not only been made commercially useful, but they have provided the basis for a whole host of additional new products and services. The airplane, the telephone, the radio, and television have served a similar function. The average level of education has been increasing. All of these have brought about a rapid growth in GNP and rising incomes for those who provide the resources to produce it.

Demand.   Demand for agricultural products tends to grow more slowly than that for industrial products and services of various kinds. The reason for the slower growth was aptly stated by the father of economics, Adam Smith, in 1776.[1] He observed that the demand for food is limited by the size of the human stomach. Demands for food and for fiber for clothing depend to a large extent on the number of people to be fed and clothed, especially after GNP has become large enough to provide a relatively nutritious diet and a reasonable degree of protection from cold and from heat. The demands for manufactured goods and for services seem, on the other hand, to expand without limit as incomes grow.

---

[1] Adam Smith, *The Wealth of Nations,* Cannan Edition (New York: Modern Library, 1937), p. 164.

Supply. While demand for agricultural products has been increasing more slowly than demand for manufactured goods and for services, the supply of agricultural products has kept pace with the growth of supply in the other sectors of the economy. Continuous improvements in the levels of technology, invention, and innovation have occurred in the agricultural as well as the nonagricultural sectors.

Price. The impact of the relatively slower growth of demand for agricultural products on the prices of those products is represented in Figure 2–7. Suppose wheat is representative of agricultural products and that

FIGURE 2–7

Differences in the rate of growth of demand and supply for wheat and automobiles

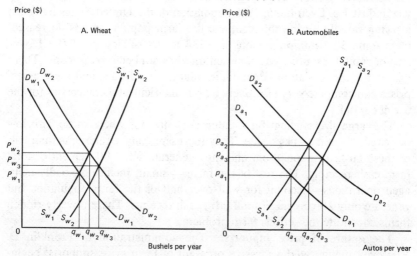

Growth in GNP and income increases demand for all normal goods and services, but the demand for agricultural products such as wheat increases proportionally less than the demand for nonagricultural products such as automobiles. Prices and profits increase relatively more in nonagricultural production, thus raising the incomes of nonagricultural persons relative to those in agriculture and providing an incentive for resource owners to shift some of their resources into nonagricultural production. The shift has not occurred rapidly enough to eliminate the farm/nonfarm per capita income differential.

automobiles are representative of manufactured products. Let $D_{w_1}D_{w_1}$ be the initial demand curve and $S_{w_1}S_{w_1}$ be the initial supply curve for wheat. The initial market price is P_{w_1}. Let $D_{a_1}D_{a_1}$ and $S_{a_1}S_{a_1}$ be the initial demand and supply curve for automobiles, making the equilibrium price P_{a_1}. There is no implication that the price scales of the two diagrams are identical. Let P_{w_1} be \$4.00 per bushel and let P_{a_1} be \$4,000 per automobile. Now, suppose that over time the demand for automobiles increases faster than the demand for wheat while the relative supplies of the two products increase at about the same rate. The price of wheat rises to P_{w_3}, or \$4.50. The price of automobiles rises to P_{a_3}, or \$6,000.

The relatively greater demand and price increases for nonagricultural products over time makes their production more profitable than the production of agricultural products. This is reflected in the differences in incomes of those who live on the farm and those who do not. In more specific economic terms, labor and capital become worth more and are paid better prices in nonagricultural pursuits.

The differences in resource prices and in individual incomes between agricultural and nonagricultural production activities provide incentives for resources to move out of agriculture and into manufacturing and service industries. Even though the population of the United States has been growing rapidly during this century, the farm population has decreased, from some 32.3 million persons in 1934 to 9.4 million in 1971.[2] Diversion of capital resources out of agriculture has not been so dramatic. There has been a consolidation of capital into larger size farms, and these enterprises can compete very effectively with nonagricultural enterprises for the use of capital.

The large size efficient farm enterprises are not where those with low per capita farm incomes reside. They represent considerably less than half of the total farm population, and they generate some 90 percent of total farm cash receipts. The rest of the farms—small, inefficient, badly-managed operations—account for well over half of the farm population but generate only 10 percent of total farm cash receipts. These poverty-ridden farms constitute the serious farm problem.

The nature of price supports.   The administration of Franklin D. Roosevelt inaugurated a massive program of farm price supports, beginning with the Agricultural Adjustment Act of 1933. The thinking of the administration—and Congress—seemed to be that, if prices of agricultural products could be raised relative to other prices, farmers' incomes would also increase relative to nonfarm incomes. Farm price supports were effective from 1933 until 1974; then, after a two-year lapse, they were reinstated in 1977.

Agriculture price supports are put into effect for the most part through a storage and loan program. The government determines a support price level for a given product, such as wheat. At harvest time any farmer can place wheat in government-approved storage facilities and obtain a loan from the government equal to the support price on each bushel stored.

---

[2] U.S. Department of Agriculture, Economic Research Service, *Farm Income Situation,* July 1972, p. 49.

When the loan falls due, the farmer has the option of paying it off or of letting the government have the stored wheat in repayment.

Under the program wheat farmers are given an incentive to store wheat and to borrow from the government whenever the support price exceeds the market price. When repayment is due, if the market price is still below the support price, the farmer lets the government have the wheat. If, however, the market price is above the support price, the farmer pays off the loan at the support price, redeems the wheat and sells it at the market price. In effect, the government guarantees that the farmer can receive the support level price for the wheat.

A demand and supply analysis of a storage and loan program is presented in Figure 2–8. Suppose the equilibrium price p is less than the support price level p_1 set by the government. At the support price level p_1, consumers will buy only q_1 bushels, but farmers want to place q_2 bushels on the market. But if they do so—if they sell more than q_1 bushels

FIGURE 2–8
Effects of price supports, storage and loan

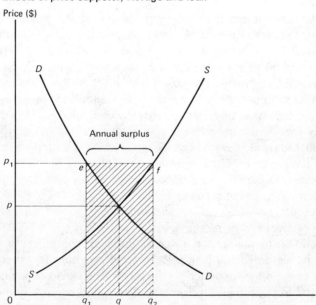

The support price p_1 is above the equilibrium price p. Consumers will purchase quantity q_1 at the support price, but farmers produce quantity q_2. The government purchases the surplus, making total payments to farmers equal to the shaded area q_1efq_2.

—the sales price will necessarily be less than p_1. Rather than sell the excess over q_1 they will store the surplus wheat—quantity q_1q_2—obtaining loans for it. Unless the market price exceeds p_1 when the loan is due, farmers will let the government have the wheat in repayment of the loans. In effect, then, when the government sets a support price above the equilibrium price level, consumers buy the quantity they want at that price, and the government buys the surplus wheat.

Economic effects of the program. A most obvious result of a storage and loan program is that if the support price for a product is effective it must result in the accumulation of surpluses of the product by the government. If a support price is set at or below the equilibrium price level, the equilibrium price level will prevail and the support price will not be effective. To be effective the support price must exceed the equilibrium price, and when this is the case the accumulation of surpluses of the product is inevitable. This is exactly what has happened but, instead of being expected by most people in the government and most of the general public, it is taken to mean that the program is in some way not being operated properly.

As the government accumulates surpluses of the product, pressure builds for the establishment of special surplus disposal programs. These take several forms. Surpluses may be sold abroad by the government at less than support prices—like the large sales to the Soviet Union in 1974. They are used to provide low-cost school lunches. They are used to expand food stamp programs. Some are left to deteriorate in storage.

Probably the most important consequence of surplus accumulations is that they provide incentives for supply or acreage restriction programs to be established by the government. To qualify for price supports, individual farmers have been required to restrict their planting in order to shift the supply curve to the left, and reduce the annual surplus. But the cost of this to consumers in the economy is that some quantities of the economy's scarce resources—land—are left idle, with a consequent reduction in gross national product and living standards.

In addition to the surplus disposal problem, consumers are harmed directly by a storage and loan price support program. It causes them to buy less of the price-supported product than they would otherwise choose to buy and to pay a higher price for it than would be the case under free market conditions. In Figure 2–8, without price supports consumers get q bushels at price p per bushel. The imposition of the support price raises the price to p_1 and reduces the amount they purchase to q_1. This makes consumers worse off than they would be in the absence of the support.

Also, the direct costs of a storage and loan program must be met by taxpayers. These direct costs are of three kinds. The first is the cost of governmental purchase of the surplus; it amounts to the number of bushels of surplus product multiplied by the support price. In Figure 2–8 this amount is q_1q_2 multiplied by p_1, or it is the area of the shaded rectangle q_1efg_2. It represents a shift of purchasing power from taxpayers to the farmers who receive the support-price payments. The second is the costs of storage, handling, and disposal of surpluses. These costs, too, are incurred by the government and paid by taxpayers. Third, in addition to the acreage restriction required for participation in a storage and loan plan, further reductions in planting have been sought through direct payments to farmers for leaving additional land idle. Again transfers of purchasing power from taxpayers to farmers are involved.

Another important consequence of farm price supports is that they result in much larger government payments to large, wealthy farmers than to small, poor ones. The smaller the output of the farmer—the poorer one is—the less the amount of government payments the farmer receives. The greater the output of a farmer—the richer one is—the greater the payments received. These are the direct results of supporting *prices* rather than *incomes.* As a means of combatting poverty, a price support program is an upside-down welfare program providing much welfare for the rich and little for the poor!

Labor markets

The establishment by law of minimum hourly wage rates is looked upon favorably by a large majority of those comprising our society. Most of the general public see minimum wage rates as a means of helping those at the lower end of the income scale raise their wage rates and thereby raise their incomes. A widespread impression exists that low wage rates and low incomes occur because of employer exploitation of unskilled workers and that minimum wage rates will stop the exploitation. It would be wonderful if it were that simple!

Demand. The demand of employers for labor depends upon what workers can contribute to the revenues of the employers. Employers will hire workers if they expect them to contribute more to their total revenues than it costs to hire them.

Suppose, for example, that in Figure 2–9 we are dealing with unskilled labor. Each hour of labor up to 100 person-hours per week for all employers will contribute more than $3 each to employers' total revenues but that each hour can be had for a wage rate of $3. Obviously, it pays to hire 100 person-hours. If additional hours beyond 100 per week will each add less than $3 to employers' total revenues, it is just as obvious that at a wage rate of $3 per hour it will not pay to hire them. However, if the wage rate were $2 per hour and another 200 person-hours of work will each add more than $2 to employers' total revenues, it would pay to ex-

FIGURE 2–9

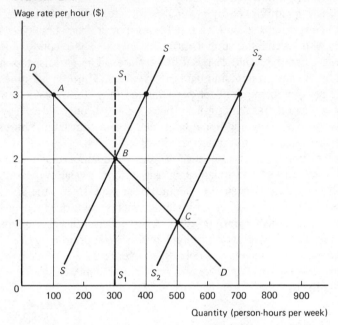

The demand curve and the supply curve for labor are *DD* and *SS*, respectively. The equilibrium price of labor is $2 per hour and the quantity employed is 300 person-hours. There is no un-employment. If a minimum wage of $3 per hour is established, unemployment of 300 person-hours will result. At that minimum wage level, unemployment would be 200 person-hours if the supply curve were S_1S_1. It would be 600 person-hours if the supply curve were S_2S_2.

pand employment up to the 300-hour mark. If additional hours beyond 300 would each add less than $2 but more than $1 to total revenues, they would not be hired—unless the wage rate were lowered to $1. If another 200 person-hours of work fall in this category, a wage rate of $1 per hour will induce employers to hire 500 hours—but no more than that. Given the above information about how much additional person-hours will add to employers' total receipts, we have located three points on the demand curve for unskilled labor, *A, B,* and *C.*

Ordinarily, we would expect the law of demand to apply to the demand curve for unskilled labor; that is, the higher the wage rate the less employ-ers would want to hire, other things being equal. In Figure 2–9, suppose that the wage rate is $1 per hour and that 500 person-hours can be hired, each of which contributes $1 or more to employers' total receipts. The number of person-hours that will add $2 or more each to employers' total receipts must be less than the number that would add $1 or more. So, at a $2 per hour wage rate, fewer hours—say 300—will be employed. The number that will contribute $3 or more each to employers' total revenues must be still less—say 100. Consequently, at a wage rate of $3 per hour, only 100 person-hours would be hired.

Oddly enough, most people fail to remember that the law of demand applies to labor as well as to goods and services. The general public—and Congress—apparently believes that an increase in wage rates *will not* reduce employment. Yet, upon reflection, we all know that it will. For example, there is some wage rate low enough to induce me to hire eight hours of yard work per week on my yard; all that is necessary to bring this about is that I value the contribution of each such hour to my well-being at more than the wage rate. But an increase in the wage rate will induce me to reduce the hours that I hire. I will work a little bit myself and, in addition, will let the lawn and flower beds look a little more ragged. I will hire labor to do only the more important things that add more to my well-being than the higher cost of the wage rate. There is, of course, a wage level that prices me out of the market altogether. As a matter of fact, this level has already been reached, much to the regret of my neighbors.

Supply. Ordinarily, the supply curve of unskilled labor would be expected to slope upward to the right as Figure 2–9 illustrates. More person-hours of work are likely to be placed on the market at $2 per hour than at $1 per hour. At $3 per hour, still more probably will be forthcoming. The reason that more labor will tend to be forthcoming at higher than at lower rates is quite simple. People have alternative uses for their time. The higher the wage rate they can obtain by working the more expensive it is for them to devote hours to pursuits other than work—and the less they are inclined to do so. These points are reflected in supply curve *SS.*

Whether or not the labor supply curve slopes upward to the right is of no great importance for our present purposes. It could be—and many people think it is—vertical as is S_1S_1 in Figure 2–9. The supply curve would be vertical if the quantity of labor placed on the market is not responsive to the level of the wage rate. If there are 300 person-hours of labor available and if all of it would be placed on the market regardless of the wage level, then S_1S_1, instead of *SS*, would be the supply curve.

Price. If in Figure 2–9 the demand curve for unskilled labor is *DD* and the supply curve is *SS*, the equilibrium wage rate will be $2 per hour and 300 person-hours will be employed. Note that at the equilibrium wage rate there is no unemployment. Neither is there a shortage of labor. There is no problem of exploitation present.

Suppose that the unskilled labor supply is greater as shown by S_2S_2. The wage rate at which the quantity of labor demanded will be the same as the quantity of labor supplied becomes $1 per hour. Note carefully that the decrease in the wage rate is *not* caused by exploitation. It is caused by the larger supply. Wherever the supply of labor is large relative to the demand for it, wage rates will be low.

The effects of a minimum wage. Suppose now that a well-meaning Congress, concerned about the low income levels of unskilled workers, enacts a minimum wage law requiring employers to pay $3 per hour for labor. If the supply curve were *SS,* the increase in the wage rate would coax an additional 100 person-hours into the labor market for a total of 400 person-hours seeking employment. However, employers would find it profitable to employ only 100 person-hours, so 300 person-hours would be unemployed or surplus.

Alternative positions or slopes of the labor supply curve make no difference in the analysis if the minimum wage rate is an effective one; that is, if the minimum wage rate is set above the equilibrium market level. If the supply curve were S_1S_1, the establishment of the minimum wage rate would still cause unemployment, although the amount of unemployment would be less than if the supply curve were *SS.* If the supply curve were S_2S_2, the effects of the minimum wage would be more horrendous than in the other two cases.

These effects are not what Congress anticipates—or are they? Certainly they are not what the general public anticipates. They may very well be what labor union officials, who are often more knowledgeable about economic relationships than their pronouncements would lead us to believe, expect. The reasoning of Congress and the general public seems to be, "If the minimum wage is put into effect, it will raise the wage rates of those receiving less than the minimum up to the level of the minimum. Therefore, their incomes will be increased." Congress and the public seem to believe that the demand curve for unskilled labor is completely inelastic —that it approaches a vertical slope. They forget the lesson that they teach themselves day in and day out, even with respect to the cereal that they eat for breakfast—the higher the price of an item, the less of it they will buy, other things being equal.

Some people benefit from the minimum wage. First, those who provide the 100 hours that remain employed are better off than they were without it. Second, those who own skilled and semiskilled labor power for which the market wage rate is greater than the minimum wage rate gain. They gain because some of the work formerly done by those made unemployed now becomes available to them—low wage unskilled competition is eliminated by the minimum wage rate. Many union members may fall in this category of gainers.

The economy as a whole and certain groups in the economy lose. First, because some of the labor force becomes unemployed, GNP becomes smaller and consumers in general lose. Second, those who cannot find employment because of the minimum wage lose—they cannot find employment because they are not worth as much to employers as it would cost the employers to hire them. Especially hard hit are groups in the economy about whom much concern is expressed—minority groups, teenage members of the labor force, and females. We are often informed by congressional personnel and by the newsmedia that the minimum wage is designed to *help* these groups. If it is, it is highly likely to miss the mark!

ECONOMIC ANALYSIS OF PRICE CEILINGS

Housing markets

Almost everyone looks with disfavor on slums. In certain areas of any city, one sees housing conditions that are distressing to say the least. Several families may be using the same bath and toilet facilities. Some families live in units that are not well lighted or well ventilated. Two or more families may be living in the same small apartment. The buildings and apartments may be in various states of disrepair. Why do people live in them? They may be all that lower income families can afford. Or, if you have tried to find an apartment in Manhattan recently, you know that they may be all that one can find available. Why do these problems occur? Do the rent controls that have been operative in places such as New York City serve the best interests of lower income groups? An examination of housing demand, supply, and pricing will help us evaluate this approach toward solving the housing problems of the poor.

Demand. The demand for housing originates in households—families and unattached individuals living in the economic system. Within the confines of the incomes available to them and the prices that they must pay for different goods and services, households make their choices as to what goods and services they will buy and how much of each they will take. Presumably, each household moves toward that allocation of its income that will yield it the highest level of total satisfaction. Housing looms large in the array of items that households purchase. For example, for households that rent housing, over half pay rents amounting to 35 percent of their total budgets. Almost one fourth of renters spend over 35 percent of their total budgets for rent.[3]

The demand for housing depends upon the same set of forces that influences the demand for other goods and services. One of these is household incomes. Another is the psychological desires of consumers for hous-

---

[3] U.S. Bureau of the Census, 1970 Census of Housing, *Components of Inventory Change, United States and Regions* (Washington, D.C.: U.S. Government Printing Office, June 1973), pp. 1–21.

ing. Another is the price or rental rate of housing units. Another is the price of other goods and services that comprise households' budgets. Any given household will try to allocate its income among various goods and services in such a way that a dollar's worth of housing contributes the same to consumer well-being as a dollar's worth of anything else the household buys. If a dollar's worth of something else, say food, were more valuable to the household than a dollar's worth of housing, the household would gain by shifting some of its expenditure away from housing toward food. On the other hand, if a dollar's worth of housing were more valuable to a household than a dollar's worth of food, the household would gain in well-being by purchasing less food and more housing with its more or less fixed income.

How does this translate into a demand curve for housing? In Figure 2–10 suppose that the rental rate is r dollars and that when households are spending their incomes so that a dollar's worth of housing makes the

FIGURE 2–10

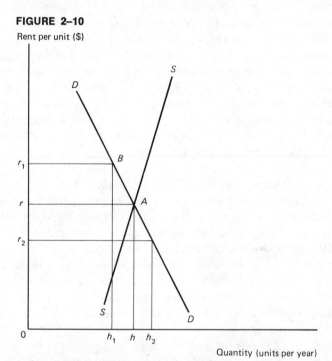

The demand curve for housing DD shows the value of a unit of housing to households at various alternative quantities. If the quantity available were h units per year, the value of a unit to households is r dollars per year. If the quantity available were h_1, the value of a unit to households is r_1 dollars. If h_2 units were available, the value of a unit becomes r_2.

same contribution to household well-being as a dollar's worth of anything else they take h units of housing per year. What would happen to the quantity of housing taken if rent rises to r_1 and there is no change in the prices of other goods, in the household's tastes and preferences, or in households' incomes? At the higher rent level, a dollar's worth of housing is a smaller quantity of housing; consequently, the contribution that a dollar's worth of housing makes to household well-being is smaller than it was before the rent increase. The contribution of a dollar's worth of any other item to household well-being thus is greater than is that of a dollar's worth of housing. Households will shift dollars from housing to other items, reducing the amount of housing consumed to some level h_1. The entire demand curve DD is made up of such points as A and B, at which households consider that they are buying the correct amounts of housing relative to other goods and services.

One more point should be made before we leave the concept of demand for housing. The demand curve DD shows that when households take h units of housing a unit of housing is worth r dollars to them; that is, they believe the amount it (a unit) contributes to their total well-being is the same as r dollars' worth of the other goods and services they consume contributes. Similarly, if only a smaller amount h_1 were available to them, they would value a unit of housing at r_1 dollars. In general terms, the less we have of any given item, the more we value a unit of it.

Supply. The supply of housing available is not very responsive to price and/or rent levels over relative short time spans. The supply curve tends to be sharply upward sloping to the right or rather inelastic as shown by SS in Figure 2–10. The reason for this is quite evident. Most of the housing supply in any given year consists of the stock of already existing units. In the course of a year, the amount by which this stock is likely to be increased or decreased is relatively small. For example, from 1960 to 1970 the total stock of housing changed by 20.3 percent for an average annual change of 2 percent.[4]

Nevertheless, some variation in the quantity supplied will occur in response to price changes. Consider, for example, the entire complex of housing units in New York City. The space that they occupy is highly valuable for business purposes. A decrease in housing rental rates relative to what the space could earn if converted to business uses would cause some conversion to occur and decrease the number of housing units available. This can also work the other way around. An increase in housing rental rates relative to what the space could earn in business uses may result in conversion of some business space to housing units. It may also result in some new construction of housing units.

---

[4] Ibid., pp. 1–17.

Price. Suppose now that in New York City the demand curve for housing is *DD* and the supply curve is *SS* in Figure 2–11. The equilibrium rental rate is *r* and the number of housing units occupied is *h*. Over time economic growth and rising household incomes increase the demand for housing to D_1D_1. In the absence of rent controls, the short-run impact of the increase in demand is a rise in rental rates to r_1 and an increase in the units made available to h_1.

The rise in rental rates will make investment in housing units more profitable, and in the long-run—say a period of five years or more—such additional investment will shift the supply curve for housing to the right.

FIGURE 2–11

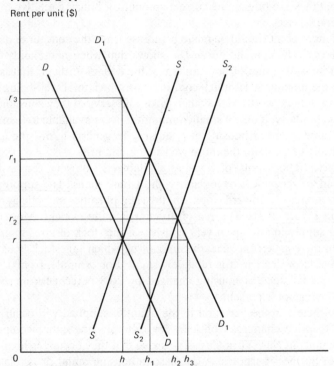

If the demand curve for housing units is *DD* and the supply curve is *SS*, the equilibrium level of rent is *r* and the equilibrium quantity occupied is *h*. An increase in demand to D_1D_1 increases the rent level to r_1 and the quantity occupied to h_1. The increased profitability of providing housing causes the supply curve to shift to S_2S_2 over time, increasing the units occupied to h_2 and lowering rents to r_2. If, however, rent controls had been enacted at level *r*, the long-run increase in housing would not take place. A shortage of hh_3 units would persist over time.

Rental rates will fall to some value r_2 and the number of units rented will rise to h_2. In New York City, because of space limitations and because of the alternative of using property for business purposes, it is highly unlikely that increases in supply can keep pace with increases in demand so the rental rate r_2 will undoubtedly exceed the original rental rate r. In other localities in which space is a much smaller problem and in which business competition for space is much less, r_2 may be very close to r.

The effects of rent controls. Following World War II, New York City elected to maintain rent controls established during the war. These controlled rates were maintained in some degree although over time they have crept gradually upward. The purpose of the controls has been to keep the price of housing within the reach of lower income groups. What are the effects of the controls?

In the first place, they generate a housing shortage. In Figure 2–11, as demand increases from DD to D_1D_1 with the supply curve at SS, if rents are not allowed to rise above r, a shortage of hh_3 units develops. Not all households looking for apartments are able to find them. Not all households desiring to add to their living space are able to do so. Much time is wasted in futile searches for apartments. Those whose employment is in New York City and who cannot find housing there are forced to outlying areas from which they must commute.

In the second place, the cost of housing is not kept down for everyone. In the normal turnover of housing units—some households vacating their apartments and others renting them—it becomes common to make undercover payments to landlords for the privilege of a new lease. For those seeking housing the search time is extended by the shortage, and the value of the extra search time required is a cost to the searchers. Many, if not most, of those forced to commute find their costs increased in at least three ways: (1) higher rents, (2) direct costs of commuting, and (3) the value of time lost in commuting. Only those ensconced in housing before the controls were put into effect and who did not move after they became effective can be sure that the controls will not raise their housing costs.

In the third place, the long-run profit inducements that would shift the supply curve to the right to S_2S_2 are eliminated by the rent controls. The rising household incomes that serve to increase the demand for housing also increase the demand for other goods and services produced in New York City. These are not subjected to price controls. The industries producing them become relatively more profitable than the housing industry in which investors can not capture higher returns from households. Consequently, investors in real estate are provided with profit inducements to increase the space available for business relative to the space available for housing. It is even possible that rent controls may cause the supply curve for housing to decrease in the long run, leaving even fewer housing units available than existed before rent controls were put into effect.

In the fourth place, landlords faced with rent controls tend to allow the quality of their properties to deteriorate. For any given type of good or service, lower quality sold at the same price per unit is equivalent to an increase in the price when the quality is not decreased. So quality deterioration is a disguised means of securing at least some price relief. The enactment of minimum housing standards by a municipality may block landlords from this escape route; however, omnipresent slums indicate they are not always a resounding success.

Finally, the enforcement of rent controls means that for present housing supplies the rental level of housing units is held below households' valuation of those housing units. For example, in Figure 2–11, after the increase in demand to D_1D_1, the quantity of housing supplied with rent controls at r is h units. But for this quantity of housing, the value of a unit to households is r_3. The price of housing is not allowed to reflect the value that households place on a unit of it.

Natural gas markets

Natural gas is one of the most important sources of energy in the United States. The ultimate consumers of it are residential and commercial (business) users, together with industrial users. The gas is discovered and produced by petroleum companies. Pipeline companies such as the El Paso Natural Gas Company and the Southern Natural Gas Company act as wholesalers, buying from the petroleum companies and selling to industrial users and to state and local public utility companies. These latter companies sell and distribute to residential and commercial users.

Petroleum companies engage in exploration and drilling for natural gas as well as for crude oil. Some of what they discover is "associated" gas found with, or rather in, oil pools. They also prospect for and find "nonassociated" gas in reservoirs by itself. Together, the associated and nonassociated gas discovered comprise natural gas reserves. Pipeline companies buy from these reserves.

Demand.   Energy users in the United States secure approximately one third of their requirements from natural gas. The major substitutes for it are coal, petroleum products, nuclear energy, and hydroelectric power. In 1973, for cooking, heating, cooling, and the like, residential and commercial users of energy obtained some 40 percent of their requirements from natural gas. Industrial users fulfilled 45 percent of their needs with gas, the main substitutes being fuel oil and coal. Natural gas provided some 20 percent of the fuel for generating electric power, competing in this area with nuclear power, water power, coal, and fuel oil.[5]

---

[5] Federal Power Commission, *National Gas Survey,* vol. 1 (Washington, D.C.: U.S. Government Printing Office, 1975), p. 123.

One of the major attractions of natural gas to its users is its clean-burning, nonpolluting characteristics; however, the quantity of it demanded will be responsive to its price. An increase in the price of natural gas relative to the prices of other energy sources will induce users to switch to those other sources. A decrease in its relative price will spur its use. We would expect long-run demand to be considerably more elastic than short-run demand because in order to switch to or from natural gas consumers must convert their facilities to use the different energy sources. A representative demand curve is shown by *DD* in Figure 2–12.

The demand for natural gas has expanded rapidly over the last 25 years. Prior to the 1950s, markets were largely local in scope, confined to the areas in which gas was discovered. The technology and plant for long-

FIGURE 2–12

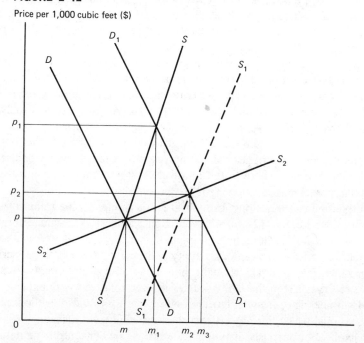

Price per 1,000 cubic feet ($)

Quantity (1,000 cubic feet per year)

Let demand and supply for natural gas be *DD* and *SS* initially. An increase in demand to D_1D_1 increases the price from p to p_1 and the quantity to m_1. Higher profits induce producers to increase exploratory activity and increase supply to S_1S_1. The price falls to p_2 and the quantity sold increases to m_2. The long-run supply curve is S_2S_2. Price controls at price p would eliminate the inducement for the increase in exploratory activity, leaving supply at *SS* and creating a shortage of mm_3.

distance pipeline transmission had not yet been developed. During the 1950s and especially in the decade of the 1960s, interstate pipelines and transmission techniques were developed, opening up a national market for the product. The clean-burning nature of natural gas as compared to the polluting characteristics of coal and fuel oil made natural gas an attractive fuel. The increase in demand is represented in Figure 2–12 by the shift in the demand curve from DD to D_1D_1.

Supply. The key element in the supply of natural gas consists of the discovered reserves that exist. Pipeline companies enter into long-term contracts with the industrial consumers and the public utility gas companies that they serve. In turn, they attempt to assure that they can deliver by making long-term (5- to 20-year) contracts with the gas producers that own the reserves. The time period required for the discovery of new reserves and the tapping of those reserves for production into pipelines may be as long as five years, so pipeline companies making contracts with gas producers are careful to determine that adequate reserves exist to fulfill the contracts.

The short-run supply of natural gas thus tends to be rather inelastic since it is based on current reserves plus the current rate of discovery of new reserves. In Figure 2–12, short-run supply is illustrated by the curve SS. It is not completely inelastic since the reserves that exist—usually a 20- to 30-year supply—can serve as a cushion between price changes and the discovery of new reserves. If the price were to become relatively high, the annual quantity supplied can be increased to some extent by depleting reserves. If the price were to fall relatively low, the annual quantity supplied can be decreased, allowing reserves to build.

In the long run the supply of natural gas is thought to be rather elastic like S_2S_2 in Figure 2–12. At relatively higher prices, exploratory activity will be stepped up eventually resulting in higher levels of reserves. At relatively lower prices, exploratory activity will decline and existing reserves will decline. It is generally thought that the amount of potentially discoverable reserves left in the United States is large relative to annual rates of use. Estimates vary from 851 trillion cubic feet up to 6,600 trillion cubic feet.[6] Annual usage has not yet exceeded 25 trillion cubic feet.

Prices. For purposes of simplicity, suppose we concentrate on natural gas prices at the wellhead; that is, the price at which gas producers sell the gas to pipeline companies. The demand curve for natural gas, then, should be interpreted as the demand of pipeline companies on the gas producers which, of course, reflects the demand of ultimate consumers. The supply

---

[6] Paul W. MacAvoy and Robert S. Pindyck, *Price Controls and the Natural Gas Shortage* (Washington, D.C.: American Enterprise Institute for Public Policy, 1975), p. 5.

curve shows the quantities per year that the gas producers will produce and sell the pipeline companies at alternative price levels.

Natural gas prices were relatively low and more or less stable during the 1920s and the 1930s. Demand during those decades was confined primarily to the producing areas since interstate pipelines were not yet in place. The discovery of reserves was to a large extent a by-product of oil exploration activity. Gas was even considered a nuisance in some areas and was burned off with flares or simply released into the atmosphere.

Price controls at the wellhead on gas transported in interstate commerce were inaugurated in 1954 but were not really effective until 1960. In the meantime, following World War II, the market for and the demand for natural gas expanded rapidly because of (1) the rising affluence of the U.S. population and (2) the development of effective long-range pipeline transportation facilities. Supply did not keep pace with the rising demand; and, as a consequence, prices rose rapidly. Free market pricing on gas sold across state boundaries, or in interstate commerce, gave way to controlled pricing by the Federal Power Commission in 1960.[7] However, gas sold within the state where it was produced was not under the Federal Power Commission's jurisdiction and was therefore exempt from its control.

The effects of price controls.   Figure 2–12 provides us with a basis for predicting the effects of price controls. An increase in demand from DD to D_1D_1 with no increase in supply (a situation analogous to one in which demand is increasing more rapidly than supply) will result in a shortage of mm_3 if the price is controlled at level p.

In the absence of price controls, there would be no shortage. The short-run effects of the increase in demand would be a rise in price to p_1 and an increase in quantity exchanged to m_1. The increase in quantity would come from short-run depletion of reserves. However, the higher price would make the production and sale of natural gas more profitable. Exploratory activity would be increased, and in the long run existing reserves and the quantity supplied would be increased. The price would come down to p_2 and the quantity supplied from the larger reserves would be m_2. With the existing larger reserves, the short-run supply curve will have shifted to the right to S_1S_1. The actual developments in the industry follow the prediction.

The Federal Power Commission has been charged with the dual responsibilities of (1) insuring adequate supplies of natural gas to consumers and (2) holding down the prices that consumers must pay for it. Most economists think these objectives are incompatible; and over the last two decades adherence to the second has, in fact, prevented the first from be-

---

[7] The preceding paragraphs are based on Robert B. Helms, *Natural Gas Regulation* (Washington, D.C.: American Enterprise Institute for Public Policy, 1974), pp. 17–25.

ing achieved. As the Federal Power Commission perfected, increased, and extended its control over the wellhead price of natural gas, shortages began to develop. In the middle 1960s, it became apparent that the quantity demanded of natural gas at controlled prices was exceeding the rate of discovery of new reserves. Initially, reserves were used to cushion the shortages; but as reserves were depleted, it became necessary for pipeline companies to curtail their deliveries to industrial users and local gas utility companies. The gas producers found it unprofitable to provide on a continuing basis the quantities demanded at the controlled prices. In 1973 pipeline companies were forced to curtail the amount supplied their customers by an amount equal to about 6 percent of total natural gas production. In 1974 the shortage was about double that, and these estimates leave out of account potential customers who had to be placed on waiting lists.[8] In the winter of 1976–77, natural gas shortages reached almost disastrous proportions.

Are consumers made better off by the price controls? The weight of evidence and logic is that they are not. It appears that consumers are made worse off.

In the first place, with controlled prices the quantities of natural gas produced and consumed are less than they would be otherwise. Those who want but can not get natural gas at the controlled prices are forced to turn to more costly (less efficient) substitute fuels. All of this tells us that the economy's total output or GNP is held below what it would be in the absence of controls.

In the second place, it is likely that the gas that is produced and consumed is not put to its most productive uses. The Federal Power Commission is authorized to control prices only on gas that is shipped among states; it has no control over the prices of gas sold by producers in a given state to customers in that state. Thus, if shortages of gas occur at controlled prices, where would you expect producers to sell the available supplies? Obviously, they will sell in the intrastate market where the price is not controlled. Once they have sold as much in the intrastate market as it is profitable to sell, the remainder will be sold out of state at the controlled price. Thus, the burden of shortages falls on customers and potential customers in nonproducing states. It is possible—even likely—that some of the gas sold intrastate could be more efficiently used in interstate markets. Gas consumers in the Northeast, North Central, and Northwest areas of the United States have been especially penalized by the shortages. Their supplies were curtailed as shortages developed and potential customers simply found natural gas impossible to obtain.

---

[8] See Patricia E. Starratt, *The Natural Gas Shortage and the Congress* (Washington, D.C.: American Enterprise Institute of Public Policy, 1974), pp. 3–5, 21–23.

SUMMARY AND EVALUATION

Governmental units control the prices on various selected items in the United States. This is usually done for two reasons: (1) to help the poor and (2) to help politically strong special interest groups. The objectives sought frequently are not obtained and, in addition, unanticipated side effects usually result from the price fixing.

Demand and supply concepts are useful in analyzing the effects of price fixing. Equilibrium prices and quantities, at which neither shortages nor surpluses occur, tend to be established in free markets. Price floors established above market equilibrium levels cause surpluses to accumulate. Price ceilings set below market equilibrium levels create shortages.

Price floors have been used extensively for agricultural products. The results have been surpluses. Resources were wasted in producing them and problems were encountered in disposing of them. Initially intended to help a low income group—farmers—they have proven to be an upside-down kind of welfare measure, helping large, wealthy farmers much and small, poor farmers little.

Minimum wage rates set above market equilibrium levels for unskilled workers also result in surpluses—we call it unemployment. The ones that they are supposed to help—minority groups, teenagers, and women—are the ones hurt most. They must bear the brunt of the unemployment effects of the minimum rates.

Rent controls illustrate the effects of price ceilings. When these are set below market equilibrium levels, the result is housing shortages. Incentives to build new units are destroyed and existing units are likely to be permitted by their owners to deteriorate. Rent controls do not appear to provide an avenue to improve housing for the poor.

Price ceilings on natural gas have created substantial shortages. In the process, they have inhibited the discovery of new reserves and have contributed to inefficiency in the use of existing supplies.

It would appear that governmental price fixing ventures usually impose significant costs and problems on households of the economy. They may benefit some special groups, but they are unlikely to benefit all households. In determining whether or not we should have them, we must weigh the costs to the society against the benefits obtained by the special groups.

SUPPLEMENTARY READINGS

Higbee, Edward. *Farms and Farmers in an Urban Age.* New York: Twentieth Century Fund, 1963.

Provides a highly competent, well-reasoned criticism of post World War II farm policies.

Leftwich, Richard H. *Elementary Analytics of a Market System.* Morristown, N.J.: General Learning Press, 1972.

A comprehensive elementary discussion of the nature of a price system and its role in guiding the operation of a private enterprise economy.

MacAvoy, Paul W., and Pindyck, Robert S. *Price Controls and the Natural Gas Shortage.* Washington, D.C.: American Enterprise Institute for Public Policy, 1975.

Explains the structure of the natural gas industry, the evolution of controls by the Federal Power Commission, and examines the effects of those controls. An econometric model is used to predict the impacts of alternative regulatory policies.

Stewart, Charles T., Jr. "The Effects of Federal Minimum Wages on Employment." In *Price Theory in Action,* edited by Donald S. Watson. Boston: Houghton Mifflin Company, 1973.

Expounds the theory of the minimum wage and examines empirical evidence of its impact on employment and incomes.

Chapter 3

ECONOMICS OF HIGHER EDUCATION

CHECKLIST OF ECONOMIC CONCEPTS

Investment in human capital *dev. of human or labor resources*
Social spillover benefits *benefits to non-consumer & non-producers*
Social spillover costs *Costs to people who don't cons. or prod.*
Alternative-cost principle *prod. 1 thing. can't prod. another*
Production possibilities curve
Explicit costs
Implicit costs
Demand
Supply
Equilibrium price
Surplus
Shortage
Transfer payments
Free riders

3

Economics of
higher education

Who benefits and who
pays the bills?

The atmosphere was tense in the Wilson household, but young Doug stood his ground. The problem was not new; it had been brewing all through his senior year in high school. Now that the year was almost over and decisions must be made about where he would go to college, the problem had come to a head.

Doug's parents wanted him to attend State University. It would be much less expensive than Private University where Doug had been accepted and where he desired to go. Tuition at S.U. for instate students was only $600 per year, and at P.U. it was $3,500. With three kids to put through college, the Wilsons considered Doug's desire to go to P.U. unreasonable.

There were some intangibles, too, in the Wilson's thinking. They would be more comfortable with Doug at S.U. It offered good, solid academic work, even though it was overcrowded with students and despite the fact that the legislature never seemed to appropriate quite enough money for its operation. They would feel a little better, too, knowing that the legislature sort of kept an eye on things at S.U. so that nothing very far out—like the teaching of radical economics—was likely to occur.

Doug thought the academic challenge would be greater at P.U. It had a reputation for academic excellence and for flexibility in the programs that students could pursue. Many of its faculty had national and even international reputations in their fields. Doug had been a Merit Scholarship Finalist in high school and had done exceptionally well on his Standard Achievement Tests. He wasn't sure what major field of study to pursue— he wanted to sample several before making up his mind. At P.U. he could major in about anything he wanted to—ethnomusicology, for example. If it were not a standard major, they would help him build a nonstandard one. Doug was ready for P.U.

In addition to the appeal of P.U.'s program, Doug thought college life would be much more enjoyable if he were far enough from home to be relatively independent of his family. There comes a time in one's life to cut the apron strings, and this seemed to Doug to be it. He believed that he was quite capable of making sound decisions on his own.

PROBLEMS IN HIGHER EDUCATION

While students like Doug wrestle with their problems of choice, colleges and universities themselves are going through troubled times. In the 1950s and 1960s enrollments increased rapidly, placing tremendous pressure on their personnel and their facilities. In the 1970s the rate of increase has dropped dramatically, and university administrators talk of retrenchment in both personnel and facilities. Though the riots, strikes, boycotts, and other disruptions of the academic processes that were so common in the 60s have subsided, they remain as potential threats to administrators. Most institutions face serious financial problems. Some say too many degrees are being granted—there is no room for new college and university graduates to work in the fields of their choice. Others say that colleges and universities are too tradition-bound and are not responsive to the needs of society.

All of these issues—and more—call for systematic analysis of the higher education system. The economics of such analyses center around four interrelated questions: (1) what kinds of higher educational services should be provided, (2) how much should be provided, (3) what is the appropriate institutional structure for providing them, and (4) who should pay for them.

What kinds of services?

Society expects higher educational institutions to perform multiple roles. Traditionally they have been learning centers, accumulating and transmitting knowledge of all kinds to students. Universities are expected to engage in research and other creative activities that advance the frontiers of knowledge, and to be at the cutting edge of the intellectual, cultural, social, and technological developments of civilization.

In addition, society has come to expect colleges and universities to provide professional and vocational types of training. These range from the preparation of physicians and lawyers to the training of automobile mechanics and secretaries. In many, if not most, cases, these dual roles of colleges and universities are inextricably bound together.

How much service?

The question of how much college and university educational service the society should provide is a very live issue today. Another name for this problem is "the financial crisis" of higher education. Most administrators, faculty members, and students are convinced that a financial crisis exists —that not enough is being spent for educational services.

Over the years legislative appropriations to public institutions have not kept pace with growing enrollments and rising costs. Tuitions have been increasing in both public and private schools. Many private schools have been operating with deficits, and a number face the possibility of shutting down their operations. Is all this an indication that society is unwilling to support higher education at present levels, or that it believes relatively too much is being spent for higher educational services?

What institutional structure?

The present system of higher education is a dual one made up of both private and public colleges and universities. In both components of the system, there are three types of institutions: (1) junior colleges, (2) four-year colleges, and (3) universities. The public institutions are state owned and operated, except for a growing number of community colleges and a very few municipal colleges and universities.

Is this structure conducive to providing the appropriate kinds and quantities of higher educational services relative to other goods and services desired by the society? Is it flexible? Or is it tradition-bound and susceptible to being a political football for state politicians?

Who should pay?

A related question concerns the extent to which governments (taxpayers) should pay the costs of producing the services of higher education and to what extent the costs should be paid by students and their families. If the government is to pay a substantial part of the cost, how should it go about doing so? Is that state university, with state appropriations for its capital and operating costs, the best way? Or should the state, instead of making appropriations to institutions, make funds available to students themselves, letting them choose their schools and pay tuition and fees sufficient to meet the costs of their educations? Should government payments of the costs of higher education favor poor families? These are some of the questions that bother us.

The economic basis of the problems

The basic issues outlined above are primarily economic problems. The economics of providing higher education services was largely ignored until the 1960s because such services comprised a relatively small part of the gross national product and used small proportions of the nation's resources. In addition, it was somehow thought that education was above mundane things like economic benefits and costs.

The burgeoning enrollments since World War II have changed all that. Those responsible for decision making with regard to higher education—legislators, administrators, faculties, students, and concerned citizens—can no longer ignore the economic consequences of their decisions. The provision of higher educational services requires the use of large quantities of resources, and the resources so used are not available to produce other goods and services. Higher educational services represent one of a great many competing uses for resources.

In this chapter we shall construct an economic framework of the higher education "industry" that should be useful in the decision-making processes concerning it. The present system of higher education will be evaluated within the context of that framework.

THE "PRODUCT" OF HIGHER EDUCATION

Like other producing units in the economy, institutions of higher education use resources and technology to turn out something of benefit to individuals and to society. This "something" can probably best be characterized as *educational services*. To get at what comprises educational services, we can pose the question, "Why are you attending a college or university?" There are at least three answers to the question. First, you expect higher education to improve your capacity to produce and to earn income, that is, to augment the quality of your labor resources. Second, quite apart from improving the quality of your labor resources, you derive direct immediate satisfaction from your present participation in college or university processes and activities—it is in this respect a direct consumption service. Third, you may expect that there will be some benefits to the society as a whole in addition to the benefits that accrue to you from your obtaining higher education. We will look at these facets of educational services in turn.

Investment in human capital

A large part of educational services must consist of the development of the human or labor resource. This is called an *investment in human capital* because in an economic sense it is very much the same thing as investing in machines, buildings, and other material capital. We invest in nonhuman capital whenever we think that the increase will generate enough additional product output to more than repay the investment costs. Similarly, it pays an individual to invest in human capital—additional education—if the increase in education increases the earning power of the person being educated by more than the cost of the additional education. Just as investment in nonhuman capital is expected to increase and expand the capacity of capital resources to produce, so is a large part of the investment in human capital expected to augment the capacity of labor resources to contribute to gross national product.

Investment in human capital is in no sense restricted to the provision of vocational education. Classical education—language and literature, the humanities, the fine arts, philosophy, and the like—broadens and deepens people's capacities to think, act, and enjoy and thereby increases their productivity in an economic sense. In many cases employers of college graduates are just as interested in hiring students with broad liberal arts degrees as they are those trained in specific vocational majors. What they want are bright young people who know how to think and how to accept responsibility.

Direct consumption

Some part of the educational services produced by colleges and universities consists of direct consumption benefits. Participation in the activities of the institution and interaction with other students in university life yield direct satisfaction to many. Students who have no intention of making their education pay off through increased earning power are prime examples of direct consumers of educational services.

By way of contrast, there are students whose sole purpose in attending college is to enhance their capacities for earning income. Sometimes these are part-time students who are employed by business enterprises. Sometimes they are commuters who attend classes only and do not participate in other aspects of university life. Direct consumption benefits may be zero for them.

For most students the consumption benefits are inextricably mixed with the human investment elements of educational services. Classes, discussions, and social life combine to provide personal satisfaction as well as to increase the capacities of the human resource to produce goods and services.

Social spillovers

Sometimes the production or the consumption of a product yields benefits to people who neither produce nor consume it. Suppose my wealthy neighbor hires an orchestra to play at her garden party and I am not invited. She pays for the pleasure of her guests. But who is to stop me, a lover of beautiful music, from listening to its strains from my own side of the property line? The production and consumption of the music yield *social spillover benefits*.

Production or consumption of a product can yield *social spillover costs*, too. These are costs imposed on people not involved in the production or consumption of the good. If one of my neighbors opens a beauty shop at home, there will be a noticeable increase in traffic on our street. It will be necessary to supervise the kids more closely to keep them from being run over. This nuisance is a social spillover cost.

The widespread provision of educational services is generally thought to have social spillover benefits. It is believed by many that over and above the direct benefits to the individuals who receive them—greater productivity, earning power, and direct consumption benefits—there are additional benefits to the society as a whole. Some of the spillovers commonly cited are reduced fire hazards, reduced crime rates, improved community sanitation techniques and facilities, better governmental services to the community, more enlightened citizens who make the society a more pleasant place in which to live, and a better functioning democratic process stemming from greater voter literacy.

The incidence of the benefits

When individuals obtain college or university educations, to whom do the foregoing benefits accrue? Suppose we look again at the nature of the "product." The direct consumption benefits are easiest to assign. They very clearly add to the level of well-being of the individual student. There are no obvious widespread spillovers of these to others as students work their way through the usual four years of undergraduate study.

The development of human capital also provides first-order benefits to individuals and their families. Individuals who develop engineering skills, or medical skills, or legal skills, or specialized knowledge and teaching skills increase their capacities to contribute to gross national product; however, they at the same time increase their abilities to earn income. The extra income that they can earn will be approximately equal to the value of their additional on-the-job productivity. Society as a whole benefits from this additional productivity—it makes greater supplies of certain goods and services available for consumption, or it may make some available that were previously not available, penicillin, for example. But these are not really social spillover benefits. They represent the same kind of increase in the productivity of the economy's resources that occurs when someone invests in a new, more productive machine. The resource owner is paid for the first-order increases in personal productivity. Then society receives a second-order benefit in the form of a greater gross national product.

To the extent that true social spillover benefits occur from higher education, the society, apart from individuals and their families, must receive them. It is very difficult to identify, quantify, and measure such benefits. Consequently, there is much debate and conjecture about whether they exist and the extent to which they exist for higher education.

Many people argue that the social spillover benefits associated with each additional year of education tend to decrease as an individual moves up through the educational system. They believe that the greatest spillovers come from the achievement of literacy—learning to read, write, and do arithmetic. These are associated with primary education. They expect secondary education to develop skills of interacting with others in the society and to provide some measure of sophistication in the administration of the joint affairs of those comprising the society. They do not believe that higher education provides much more in social spillovers. They believe that it benefits society mostly through the benefits it provides to those who obtain its services.

In summary, then, most of the benefits of higher educational services seem to accrue to the individuals who obtain those services. Society may receive some social spillover benefits, but the magnitude of these is debatable.

ECONOMIC CONCEPT OF COSTS

One of the most important principles of economics is summed up in the statement, "There ain't no such thing as a free lunch." We speak glibly of such things as free medical care, free housing, free food, and free education. What we mean is that those who use the "free" goods and services do not have to pay money for them. All too often our chain of reasoning stops right there. But if we really think that these are free to the society as a whole, we delude ourselves. The production of the "free goods" is costly to someone—perhaps even to their users.

The economic costs of a product may or may not be reflected in the direct money outlays that must be made in producing it. The basic concept underlying economic costs is the *alternative-cost principle.* In considering the costs of producing any given product, it is useful to classify its cost into two categories: (1) *explicit costs* and (2) *implicit costs.*

The alternative-cost principle

According to the alternative-cost principle, the cost of producing a unit of any good or service is the value to the economy of the alternative goods or services that must be forgone in order to produce it. This notion is not really new in our discussion—it was suggested in Chapter 1 in the discussion of the nature of economic activity. We must develop and clarify it at this point, however.

We can start with the production possibilities curve or transformation curve of Figure 3–1, which measures units of educational services along the horizontal axis and composite units of all other goods and services along the vertical axis—all of these in terms of dollar's worths. The curve TT_1 shows all alternative combinations of other goods and services and education that the economy's given resources can produce per year. Suppose that initially combination B, made up of e_2 dollar's worth of education and g_2 dollar's worth of other goods and services, is being produced and the economy's resources are fully employed.

What is the cost to the society of a unit of education when B represents the economy's output mix? *It is the value of the alternative goods and services that must be forgone to produce it.* Let the distance e_1e_2 represent one dollar's worth of education. If this unit had not been produced, the society could have had more of other goods and services, equal to the amount g_2g_1. Thus the society had to sacrifice g_2g_1 dollar's worth of other goods and services to produce the one unit of education. The sacrifice of the other goods and services releases just enough resources to produce the additional unit of education. We call the physical amounts of other goods and services sacrificed the *real cost* of producing the unit of education. The value that consumers attach to the goods and services given up is the true *economic money cost.*

Stated in a slightly different way, *the cost of producing a unit of any one good or service is the value of the resources used in producing it in their best alternative use.* A little reflection will show that this statement of the alternative-cost principle is identical to the one developed in the preceding paragraph.

The alternative-cost principle is capable of general application. In an economy in which resources are fully employed, an increase in the amount of medical services provided draws resources from the production of other goods and services. The value of the goods and services forgone (that is,

FIGURE 3–1
The costs of education

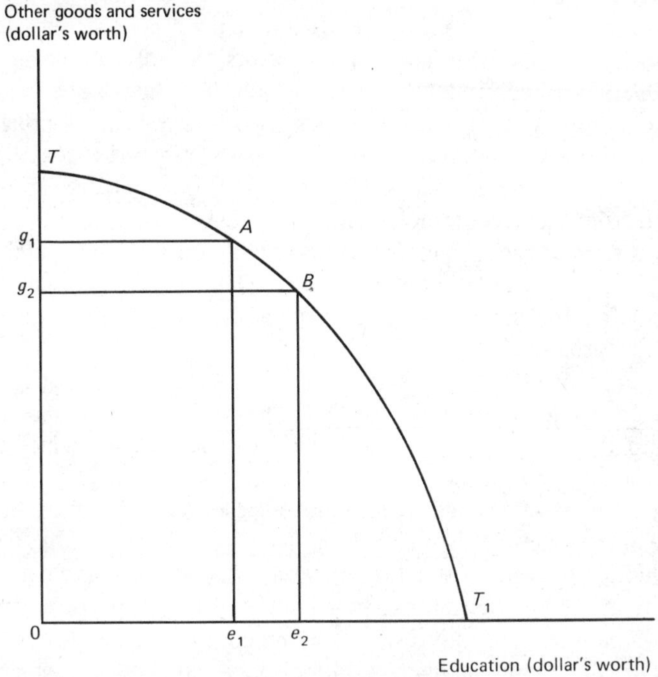

Other goods and services
(dollar's worth)

Education (dollar's worth)

In Figure 3–1, production possibilities curve TT_1 shows all alternative combinations of other goods and services and education that the economy's resources and technology can produce per year. Two possible alternative combinations are represented by A and B. If the economy is initially producing combination B, it is obtaining g_2 units of other goods and services and e_2 units of education. If e_1e_2 represents one unit of education per year, it becomes apparent that g_2g_1 units of other goods and services must have been sacrificed to obtain it. The value of the g_2g_1 units thus measures the cost of a unit of education at the e_2 level of production.

the value of resources that would be used in their production) is the cost of the increase in medical services. The cost of a bushel of wheat is the value of the corn that must be forgone in order to produce it, if corn production is the best alternative use to which the resources used in wheat production could be put. The cost of a soldier in the society's army is the value of what one could have produced as a civilian. Thousands of such examples could be cited.

Explicit and implicit costs

The economic costs to a society of producing a good or service do not necessarily coincide with its accounting costs. As an example, consider a small family-owned grocery store for which the labor is provided by the owning family. A large part of the costs of resources used by the store to put groceries in the hands of consumers—costs of grocery stocks, utilities, and the like—are indeed accounting costs, but some resource costs will be omitted from the accounting records. The costs of labor are not likely to be listed. Amortization and depreciation costs on the land, building, furniture, and fixtures also may be omitted. The family may simply "take what is left" after the out-of-pocket expenses are paid, calling this remainder their "profits."

The costs of resources bought and hired for carrying on the business are called *explicit costs of production.* These are the economic costs that are most likely to be taken into account by the business, since they are usually actual cost outlays.

The costs of self-owned, self-employed resources (like the labor of the family in the example) are called *implicit costs of production.* They tend to be hidden or ignored as costs. Implicit costs of a resource can be identified by using the alternative-cost principle. What the resource would be worth in its best alternative use is determined; this is its cost to the owner-user. Had the family members used their labor working for someone else, this labor would have produced other goods and services and would have earned income about equal to the value of those other goods and services. So the cost of self-employed labor is what it could have earned in its best alternative employment.

THE COSTS OF HIGHER EDUCATIONAL SERVICES

From the point of view of the society as a whole, the services of higher education are not free. Resources used in their production could have been used to produce other goods and services, and the value of those forgone goods and services is the economic cost of higher education. In this section we shall try to pin down the nature of those costs and identify who pays them.

The explicit costs

The explicit costs of the services provided by a college or university are the costs of the resources that it buys and hires to provide those services. These may be costs of capital resources or of labor resources. The university uses land, buildings, equipment, and supplies. It also uses professors, maintenance personnel, administrators, secretaries, and clerks.

The institution's annual budget provides a first approximation of the annual explicit costs of its services. The budget should include amortization costs of major capital outlays, depreciation costs, small-equipment costs, maintenance costs, and the costs of hundreds of kinds of supplies. It should also include the wages and salaries of labor resources used.

The true explicit costs are the values of the resources used by the institution in their best alternative uses. This should be interpreted with some degree of caution. The economic cost of a university's buildings is not what the value of the building would be if the university were to close its doors. Rather it is the value of the goods and services that were foregone in order to build and maintain the building. Whether or not the institution's explicit economic costs are reflected accurately by its accounting records depends upon the accounting procedures it uses.

The implicit costs

The costs to a society of producing educational services greatly exceed the explicit costs discussed above. To obtain educational services most students withdraw their labor wholly or partly from the labor force, thus reducing the amounts of other goods and services available to the society. In order to be students, they sacrifice some of what they could have earned as workers, and society sacrifices the value of the goods and services they would have produced had they been working. These forgone earnings, or the equivalent forgone GNP, are implicit costs to the student and to society of the educational services obtained by the student. They do not show up in the institution's budget or books of account.

Another category of implicit costs of educational services consists of the costs of books and various other miscellaneous items incidental to attending a college or university. The test of whether or not units of some specific good belong to this category of costs is whether they would have been purchased if the users were not in school. Units of textbooks, pencils, paper, some items of clothing, and some forms of recreation or entertainment will pass this test and will be considered implicit costs. Ordinarily these are not a part of the institution's budget or expense accounts.

Sources of support

One of the unique economic features in the production and sale of higher educational services in the United States is the diversity of the sources tapped to pay the costs. Those who have taken on the responsibility of providing higher educational services have traditionally not been willing—or able—to leave them subject to market forces. Neither public nor private universities charge their customers the full explicit costs of the educational services provided, but the extent to which they approach full costing of those services is a key difference between the two types of institutions.

Public institutions. State colleges and universities depend heavily on *state appropriations* to meet their explicit costs. In addition, they receive substantial funds from the federal government. Some community colleges are heavily subsidized by local governments. Governmental units also provide loan funds, work-study funds, scholarships, and other kinds of support for students of public institutions. For 1970–71 the Carnegie Commission staff estimated that governmental sources provided about 80 percent of the funds available to meet the explicit costs of public institutions.[1]

Tuition and fees as a means of meeting explicit costs are relatively low at most public educational institutions. In some—those of the state of California, for example—they approach zero. Usually state colleges and universities charge higher tuition rates for out-of-state than for in-state students, indicating that state appropriations are a substitute for tuition to which they believe only the citizens of the state are entitled. About 17 percent of public institution funds came from this source in 1970–71.[2]

To a relatively small extent, public institutions depend on *donors* to help meet their explicit costs. Funds are received from donors as endowment funds, unrestricted cash grants, scholarship funds, and the like. The donors include foundations, corporations, philanthropists, and alumni who can be convinced that they are contributing to a worthwhile cause. To the public institution, funds from donors, rather than being a primary source of support, tend to be the frosting on the cake that enables it to engage in some activities that no-nonsense legislative appropriations will not permit. These amounted to about 4 percent in 1970–71.[3]

Even at public colleges and universities, students and their families must pay the implicit costs of educational services. If a student does not work at all, the forgone earnings or forgone goods and services for the society as a whole are implicit costs. If the student works part time, the implicit costs are the difference between what could have been earned and what is actually earned. If the husband or wife of a student is forced to accept unemployment or less remunerative employment at the college or university site than could have been obtained elsewhere, forgone earnings will be larger than those for the student alone. In addition to forgone earn-

---

[1] Carnegie Commission on Higher Education, *Higher Education: Who Pays? Who Benefits? Who Should Pay?* (New York: McGraw-Hill Book Co., 1973), p. 24.
[2] Ibid.
[3] Ibid.

ings, implicit costs at the public institution include the costs of books and miscellaneous expenses incidental to the generation of educational services.

Private institutions. Private colleges and universities, since they do not receive state appropriations, must meet the bulk of their explicit costs from the payment of *tuition* and *fees*. About 60 percent came from this source in 1970–71.[4] Contributions from *donors* is also an important source of support—the more they can secure from this source, the less pressure there is to rely on tuition and the better able they are to compete with the low tuition rates of public institutions. Seeking funds from donors is always a major activity of private institutions. They obtained about 25 percent of their explicit costs from donors in 1970–71.[5]

Federal grants to private educational institutions vary widely from school to school. Those that are research oriented have secured sizable research grants. Many schools receive very little from federal sources. For private schools in total, about 15 percent of their funds were obtained from government in 1970–71.[6]

The implicit costs of educational services are the same for private as for public institutions. They amount to forgone earnings, plus the cost of books and other miscellaneous items.

The incidence of the costs

Where do the costs of producing the services of higher education finally rest? Table 3–1 is a rough estimate of the incidence of costs for a typical public institution and a typical private institution. We assume that the kinds and qualities of services provided are the same for each institution and that each is equally efficient in providing them. Three features of the incidence of costs are significant.

First, the implicit costs are a very large part of the total costs of the educational services provided a student. They amount to a little over 70 percent of the total costs. Note that they are the same whether the student attends a public or a private institution. They are borne by students and their families.

Second, the major source of support for the explicit costs of public institutions is state appropriations, while that for private institutions is tuition and fees. Except for a few scholarship holders, tuition and fees in private institutions rest on students and their families. State appropriations are made from general revenue funds in any given state and consist of money collected from taxpayers of the state; consequently, the incidence

---

[4] Ibid.
[5] Ibid.
[6] Ibid.

TABLE 3–1

Typical annual per student cost of higher education by type of institution and source of support

Source of support	Amount of support by type of institution	
	Private	Public
For explicit costs		
Donors	$ 750	$ 130
Federal grants	350	420
State appropriations	—	2,850
Tuition and fees (student and family)	3,000	700
Total explicit costs	$ 4,100	$ 4,100
For implicit costs (student and family)		
Books and miscellaneous expenses	$ 1,200	$ 1,200
Forgone earnings	8,000	8,000
Total implicit costs	$ 9,200	$ 9,200
Total costs	$13,300	$13,300

This table is an approximation of components for a "typical" public university and a "typical" private university. Size of the institutions and quality of educational services provided are assumed to be the same.

of this large part (a little over two thirds) of the explicit costs of public institutions rests on taxpayers rather than on students and their families. Public institutions, then, bring about a shift in the incidence of some two thirds of the explicit costs of higher educational services from students and their families to taxpayers.

Third, private institutions rely more heavily on donors as a source of support than do public institutions. To the extent that funds can be obtained from donors and substituted for tuition, the incidence of explicit costs is shifted from students and their families to donors. About one fourth of the incidence of explicit costs of private institutions is shifted from students and their families to donors.

ECONOMIC EVALUATION OF THE PROBLEMS

While the economic framework established in the preceding sections permits the problems of higher education to be approached in a systematic and logical way, it does not always provide clear-cut, correct solutions. Economic analysis helps determine what causes what, and why. It helps determine, once goals have been set, the most efficient way of reaching those goals. However, economic analysis cannot always provide answers as to what the goals or objectives in higher education or any other activity should be. Equally intelligent people often disagree on the goals that should be sought by a particular society.

What kinds of services?

Are our expectations with respect to the kinds of services higher education should produce realistic? Of course they are! The industry can produce whatever mix of services we as a society want it to produce. The important economic problem is concerned with how well institutions respond to the society's desires or demands for those services. The "relevancy" issue in education during the late 1960s and early 1970s is a manifestation of this problem.

Economic analysis leads to questions as to how responsive the current structure of higher educational institutions permits them to be in meeting societal demands. By and large, throughout the economic system consumers register their demands for goods and services by the ways in which they dispose of or spend their purchasing power. Suppliers respond to the array of prices that results. Is this the way in which the mix of programs that are offered by colleges and universities is determined? Obviously not.

Colleges and universities make little or no use of the price system in determining what programs they will offer. Their officials usually try to offer what they think the society wants. During the onset of the space age in the 1960s, there was much emphasis on engineering programs. Of course, the desires of students and their families must be taken into consideration; otherwise, the enrollments will not be forthcoming. In addition, in public institutions that depend heavily on legislative appropriations, the desires of the legislature are of great importance. The legislature can threaten to withhold appropriations that might be used to expand programs of which the majority of its members may disapprove. In private institutions major donors may be able to influence programs offered; however, the interests of students and their families are likely to receive prime consideration since they represent the main source of revenue to the schools.

One wonders why the price system is so roundly ignored or snubbed in determining program priorities. Most colleges and universities charge the same price (tuition) to all students, regardless of the program of study pursued. College and university administrators and faculties, legislators, and students themselves seem to believe that this is the equitable way to operate the system. Yet, a little reflection will reveal its inefficiency.

Consider two possible undergraduate programs of a university—say, business administration and agriculture. Suppose that initially, student demand for the agriculture program is represented by $D_{a_1}D_{a_1}$ in Figure 3–2. The price per person per year is a composite of all costs except implicit costs to the student of a year of the program. The demand curve for the agricultural program would be expected to slope downward to the right as do most demand curves—the smaller the price of the program,

FIGURE 3-2

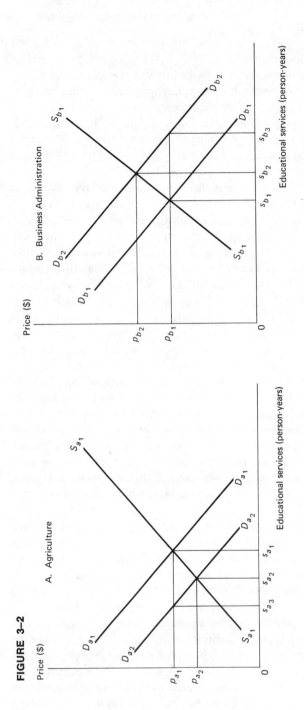

A. Agriculture

Price ($)

B. Business Administration

Price ($)

Educational services (person-years)

Educational services (person-years)

Suppose that in a university $D_{a_1}D_{a_1}$ and $S_{a_1}S_{a_1}$ are the initial demand and supply curves for person-years of agricultural education, while in business administration they are $D_{b_1}D_{b_1}$ and $S_{b_1}S_{b_1}$. Suppose, further, they are such that the explicit costs of each kind of education are the same; that is, $p_{a_1} = p_{b_1}$. Now, suppose that demand for business administration increases to $D_{b_2}D_{b_2}$ and that for agriculture falls to $D_{a_2}D_{a_2}$. Maintaining explicit costs (tuition and fees) at $p_{a_1} = p_{b_1}$ results in a surplus of agricultural educational capacity and a shortage of business administration capacity. Letting the tuition and fees for business administration rise to p_{b_2} and those for agriculture fall to p_{a_2} will result in an increase in business administration capacity and a decrease in agricultural capacity, thereby increasing the efficiency with which both are utilized.

the more person-years of it students will demand. The supply curve, $S_{a_1}S_{a_1}$, of the agricultural program would be expected to slope upward to the right. The more money per person-year the university can obtain from sale of the program, the more resources it can attract and use to expand the program. The demand curve, $D_{b_1}D_{b_1}$, and the supply curve, $S_{b_1}S_{b_1}$, for the business administration program are conceptually the same as those for the agricultural program. Ignore $D_{b_2}D_{b_2}$ for the time being. Suppose that, by some great coincidental accident, the initial supply and demand curves for both programs are such that the person-year prices are the same for each; that is, p_{a_1}, equals p_{b_1}. The program sizes are s_{a_1} and s_{b_1}, respectively.

Now, let student demand for the business administration program increase relative to that for the agricultural program—the business administration demand shifts to $D_{b_2}D_{b_2}$ and the agricultural demand curve shifts to $D_{a_2}D_{a_2}$. What are the effects of maintaining equal prices for the two programs as colleges and universities now tend to do? At price p_{b_1}, the university cannot expand its business administration program and cover the costs of doing so. A shortage of business administration faculty and facilities will result. Classes will be larger and rooms will be more crowded. The quality of instruction will deteriorate. In the agriculture program, keeping the price at p_{a_1} induces the university to continue with its initial faculty and facilities. Class sizes will fall and facilities will be less fully utilized. There is a relative surplus of faculty and facilities. Shortages and surpluses of these types are common in colleges and universities today. They represent inefficiency in the production of educational services.

If the university were to use a differential pricing scheme for different programs, it could increase both its efficiency and its responsiveness to its customers. Let tuition and fees in business administration rise to p_{b_2}. Additional revenue is obtained to expand the program to s_{b_2}, taking care of the increased demand. The price increase also serves to reduce the pressure on facilities by reducing enrollment from s_{b_3} to s_{b_2}. Let tuition and fees in agriculture fall to p_{a_2}. The university has an incentive to cut the program back to s_{a_2} at which it is once more just covering costs. Incidentally, the decrease in the price of a person year of agriculture from p_{a_1} to p_{a_2} will increase the enrollment after the decrease in demand has occurred from s_{a_3} to s_{a_2}.

To make the preceding economic analysis a little more general, suppose that in a university a demand arises for a program that has previously not existed—say, for ecology studies. Costs of supplying different numbers of person years of the program can be determined and the supply curve can then be matched up with the demand curve. The resulting equilibrium price will reflect the cost of the program to the university and the values of the program to students. The corresponding equilibrium quantity reflects neither a shortage nor a surplus.

Experience suggests that public colleges and universities will be more inclined to maintain the status quo than will private ones. Legislatures move slowly, and many functions other than education occupy their time and attention. Yet they are not inclined to give the regents, administrations, and faculties of colleges and universities under their control a free hand, since the legislatures remain "accountable" to the general public for how appropriations are spent. The programs of private colleges and universities are likely to be more flexible over time and to be more responsive to student desires.

How much service?

Economic analysis provides a conceptual answer to how much educational service the economy should produce relative to other goods and services. The resources used in producing educational services can be used to produce other goods and services, and, from the alternative-cost principle, the costs of educational services are the values of those resources in their alternative uses. Consequently, if the value to society of a unit of educational services is greater than its costs—the resources used in producing it are more valuable in the production of education than in alternative ones —then the output of educational services should be expanded. On the other hand, if the value of a unit of educational services is worth less to the society than it costs to produce it, the output should be reduced.

In terms of demand-supply analysis, let DD represent the demand curve for higher educational services and SS be the supply curve for them in Figure 3–3. If the economy is presently providing a quantity of s_1 person-years, the value of a unit to demanders (students) is v_1 but the cost of a unit to the society is c_1. The excess of the value of a year's education over its cost indicates that resources needed to produce a year of education are more valuable if they are so used than they would be in their best alternative uses. Educational services should be expanded relative to the production of other goods and services in the economy. The correct amount of educational services for the society is s_2 priced at p_2 per person-year. What can you say about quantity s_3?

The value of higher educational services in relation to their costs is obscured by the way they are provided. Higher educational services are not priced in the marketplace in a way that will cause the quantity supplied to be adjusted to the quantity demanded. On the demand side it is difficult, if not impossible, for students in the present system to make known how they value alternative quantities of educational services. The combination

FIGURE 3-3

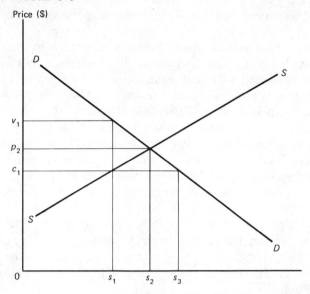

If s_1 person-years of educational services are provided in the society, the value of a person-year exceeds its cost indicating that an expansion of services is in order. At the s_2 level of services, the value of a person-year is equal to the costs of providing it. The correct amount for the society is s_2.

of public and private sources of support on the supply side compounds the difficulties of valuing educational services and of determining how much should be produced.

On the demand side, consider potential students who want educational services in some specific field—say medical training. In medical schools throughout the country, the annual number of openings for students is limited. At current levels of costs to students, many more want training than can be accepted—that is, there is a shortage of medical training services. This is the same thing as saying that potential medical students would be willing to pay more for the services of medical schools than they are now required to pay. However, students are not permitted to bid up the price at which these educational services are offered, and hence the price system cannot express their valuations of them. The same kind of analysis holds true for a great many other fields of specialization.

The supply of educational services made available by public higher education institutions is not a direct response to student demands. The amounts supplied are determined primarily by the appropriations public institutions receive from the stage legislatures rather than by what students are willing to pay. Colleges and universities compete with a number of other state-supported activities for the dollars that legislatures have available to appropriate and, since state revenues are limited, they will never receive as much as educational administrators think they ought to have. At the same time, such public institutions are reluctant to supplement the funds received from the state with tuition receipts. Tuition is supposed to be kept low because of state appropriations—this is the purpose of the state-allocated funds. The higher the tuition rates set by the public institutions, the less will be their bargaining power for state-appropriated funds.

State colleges and universities can be expected to encounter a continuous financial crisis. The services they can supply are limited by the always inadequate appropriations received from the state while the demands for their services are augmented as they succumb to the pressure to keep their tuition rates low.

At the same time, the relatively lower tuition rates of the public institutions enable them to draw students away from private institutions. The competition of public institutions limits the services that can be provided by private institutions. It also sets upper limits on the tuition rates that private institutions can charge and still remain in business. Pressure on private institutions to obtain gifts, grants, and the like is increased. Competition from public institutions makes it very difficult for private colleges and universities to stay solvent.

Who should pay?

The controversy over who should pay for higher educational services is undoubtedly the key problem faced by higher education. If this problem could be resolved, answers to "what kind" and "how much" would be much easier to determine. At one extreme of the controversy are those who maintain that educational services should be "above" market forces. Education is seen as the great equalizer, providing opportunities for self-development and self-realization. Everyone is entitled to as much education as one is able to absorb, and consequently, educational services should be free. At the other extreme are those who believe that each student and family should bear the full costs of that student's education.

"Free" education. What is meant by "free" education? The economic aspects of higher education discussed in this chapter make it clear that there is no such thing from society's point of view. Neither is education free from the individual student's point of view—unless, of course, both explicit and implicit costs are covered by scholarships. Ordinarily education is said to be free if state appropriations to state colleges and universities are large enough so that no tuition is charged. This has been the case in the California system of higher education. In most states public colleges and universities are not tuition-free; state appropriations simply permit them to charge substantially lower tuitions than do private institutions.

The differences in costs between what is generally called a free education in a state college or university and what is called a full-cost education in a private college or university is nowhere near as great as tuition differentials would lead us to believe. In the example in Table 3–1, the annual costs borne by the student and family in a public institution would be about $8,750, while in the private institution they would be about $10,600.

State support of higher education. In terms of economic analysis, state support of higher education means that some part of the costs of obtaining educational services is shifted from the student who receives the services to taxpayers. State appropriations to the college or university decrease the tuition that students are required to pay. Funds appropriated to the institution by the state are obtained from taxpayers. Thus state support constitutes a *transfer* of purchasing power from taxpayers to college and university students.

Under what circumstances do such transfers seem to be in order? It appears that they are defensible: (1) to the extent that social spillover benefits are generated by higher education and (2) as a means of enabling children of the poor to develop their human resources.

When the consumption or utilization of some good or service by one or more people results in spillover benefits to others, those who receive the spillover benefits are in a good position to be *free riders*. Direct consumers of an item pay for the direct benefits they receive; otherwise, they will not be able to obtain whatever it is they want to consume. Those who receive the spillover benefits receive them whether they pay anything or not; their tendency is to be free riders and pay nothing. Direct consumers are in no position to force the free riders to pay, but what they cannot do as individual private citizens they may be able to accomplish collectively through their government. The government can levy taxes on the free riders, thus coercing them to pay for the spillover benefits they receive. The government is a unique and logical agency for this purpose.

If social spillover benefits from higher educational services exist, the use of state taxing powers and state support of higher education sufficient to pay for those benefits would seem to be reasonable. Several questions arise. The most important one is whether or not significant social spillover benefits are generated in the provision of higher educational services. If they are, they have never been unambiguously identified, much less measured in value terms. Further, if they do exist, they are generated by private colleges and universities as well as by public institutions. On these grounds, should not the higher education provided by private universities be subsidized to about the same extent as that provided by state universities?

The other major argument for state support of higher education is that it enables capable but poor students to obtain a college or university education. Education serves to increase the capacities of human resources to produce and to earn income. Since poor families do not have the means of paying for higher education for their children, and this is not the fault of the children, the state can do much to enable them to escape from poverty by providing them with the same kind of educational opportunities that are still available to the children of middle and higher income families.

The case has much merit. One of the generally recognized functions of government in the modern world is that of mitigating poverty. In the United States a very substantial part of both state and federal budgets is for this purpose. Welfare programs, farm programs, and income taxes that are intended to take larger proportions of the incomes of the rich than of the poor provide examples. It seems reasonable that state support of higher education for the poor should be an integral and important part of any antipoverty program.

However, though state support looms large in meeting the explicit costs of educational services, the implicit costs that still must be met by the student and the student's family are a very substantial part of the total costs. The inability of a poor family to meet the implicit costs—the need for children to go to work and earn income—discourages the children of the poor from attending *any* college or university, public or private. *State support of public institutions does not really transfer purchasing power from taxpayers to the children of the poor.* It transfers purchasing power from taxpayers to students already able to meet the implicit costs of higher education, and most of such students are from the middle and upper income groups.

The foregoing statement is substantiated by 1972 data on entering freshmen in the United States as a whole. For public and private institutions combined, about 80 percent of the entering freshmen came from families earning over $10,000 per year. Only 3.4 percent came from families with income levels below $4,000 per year. At a typical state-supported land-grant university in a state with per capita income substantially below the average for the United States, about 75 percent of the entering freshmen came from families with income levels above $10,000 per year, and about 5.1 percent came from families with income less than $4,000 per year.[7]

Student self-support. Many people believe that students and their families rather than the state should bear the costs of higher education. This does not necessarily mean that there should be no such institutions owned and operated by the state. A state-owned college or university can recover the full costs of education through tuition and fees levied on students as easily as a private one can. There are two main arguments why students should pay for their own education. These are that (1) those who benefit are the ones who should pay, and (2) economic resources would be used more efficiently, that is, some waste would be avoided.

The argument that those who benefit should pay is rooted in equity grounds. It asks why one group of persons—taxpayers—should be forced to pay a part of the educational costs of another group—students and their families. To be sure, there will be overlapping of the two groups; students and their families are taxpayers. However, a much larger proportion of taxpayers are not college and university students, and neither are their children. Many of these are poor families; as indicated above, three fourths of the freshmen entering a typical state-supported institution in 1972 came from families with incomes above $10,000 per year. Is it equitable for the state to levy taxes that rest partly on poor nonstudent families to help pay for the education of children from middle-income and wealthy families?

The argument maintains further that investment in human capital is essentially comparable to investment in material capital. Suppose a high school graduate has a choice of investing in an education or investing in a business. One considers the payoff of each in terms of future well-being and makes the choice that one (and one's family) thinks will yield the highest return on the investment. This is the way that intelligent economic decision making should be accomplished. Ordinarily we do not expect taxpayers to bear a part of the investments of high school graduates in businesses. Why should we expect them to bear a part of such investments in higher education?

Another argument for student self-support is that people tend to waste whatever is free to them and to economize or conserve whatever they have to pay for. The greater the cost of a purchase relative to one's income, the more incentive one has to use the item carefully in order to increase the possible returns from it. This is said to be the premise underlying high charges made by psychiatrists for their services. The argument is used extensively by those who think students should pay for their own education.

---

[7] American Council on Education, Office of Research, *Summary of Data on Entering Freshmen, Fall 1972.*

If higher educational services are provided at reduced or free tuition costs to students, the incentive to economize on or make the best possible use of the resources providing those services is weakened—so the argument runs. Low tuition induces students who have no interest in learning to attend the university, whereas higher tuition charges would make them or their parents think more carefully about whether or not they should do so. Further, those who do attend would be inclined to make more of their opportunities if they cost more. There would be less inclination to waste professors' time or to destroy property.

Which way?   Which of the arguments is correct? If the student and family reap the benefits of higher education—that is, if the benefits of higher education are primarily private human capital development—then a strong case can be made that the student and family should pay its full costs. If substantial social spillover benefits result from putting some part on the population through the processes of higher education, or if higher education is used effectively as a campaign against poverty, a strong case can be made for shifting a part of its costs to taxpayers.

An alternative institutional structure

When an activity such as higher education has been pursued over a long period of time, a set of institutions is developed to carry on the activity. The structure of the set that evolves becomes very difficult to change. First, people think in terms of the structure to which they have become accustomed and find it hard to think in terms of alternatives. Second, the present structure is the known here and now; the alternative might not work. Third, many people build up vested interests in the existing structure and can be expected to resist changes that would affect them.

It appears that higher education may be saddled with just such an outmoded institutional structure. Some 65 percent of college and university students in the United States are enrolled in public institutions that receive the bulk of their support from legislative appropriations. The rationale for the state supported system is that (1) it makes higher education available to the children of poor families and (2) it encourages large enrollments, to increase the social spillover benefits of higher education. As we have seen, it does not appear to serve either of these purposes very well. The implicit costs of higher education are so great that even with the low tuition rates of public institutions, few children of the poor find it possible to attend. It appears that the most important effect of the low tuition rates of public institutions is to divert students from private to public institutions rather than to bring about any substantial increase in enrollment in all institutions. In addition, the present system does not enable the society to place accurate demand values on the services being provided, nor does it provide the mechanism for colleges and universities to be responsive to the demands of the society.

The alternative to the present higher education institutional structure is one that would make greater use of the price system in the production of higher educational services. The key feature of the alternative is that students obtaining educational services would pay tuition to the colleges and universities they attend sufficient to cover the full explicit costs of the services obtained. There would be no differentiation between private and public institutions in this respect. If public institutions were to remain public, they would be required to pay their own way without obtaining direct appropriations from legislatures.

If the society desires to help the children of the poor to obtain educational services, it can do so easily and directly. Instead of allocating money to public colleges and universities, legislatures can make grants directly to the children of the poor, letting them choose for themselves which institution they will attend. Presumably each will attend the institution that best meets his or her needs. Thus, the antipoverty aspects of state support will be realized directly and efficiently. The state will not be supporting those who are not in need; with the present system, most of those it supports are not in need.

If, because of spillover benefits, the state desires to encourage larger enrollments than would occur if all students were required to pay the full costs of the services they obtain, this also can be done easily and directly. By raising the minimum income standards used to define what constitutes a poor family, the state can increase the number of students eligible for state support. In addition to tuition scholarships to meet explicit costs, various devices now in use can continue to assist students from low-income families in meeting their implicit costs. These include access to loan funds, part-time employment, and the like.

Such an institutional structure should go far toward solving the problems that confront higher education. It would attack the problem of who should pay, moving toward a structure in which those who receive the benefits are the ones who pay the costs. But note that this *does not* preclude using the system of higher education as a part of an antipoverty program, nor does it preclude government (taxpayer) support of higher education. Government support would contribute more directly and more efficiently to making higher education available to the children of the poor.

Such a structure would also move toward a solution of the perpetual financial crisis of higher education. Government support of higher educational services—whatever the amount of such support the society desires —would be provided to students and not to institutions. This would eliminate the primary cause of the crisis—the support of public institutions by the state, which, though usually thought to be inadequate, entails low-tuition competition and attendant financial problems for private institutions.

Further, it would tend to induce the education industry to supply the quantity of educational services the society wants relative to the quantities of other goods and services produced in the economy. Tuition would be the main source of revenue for institutions; it would cover the full explicit costs of services supplied. Colleges and universities would supply services to as many persons as are willing to pay that tuition. Persons not willing to pay the full tuition are saying in effect that alternative ways of spending that amount of money yield greater satisfaction to them.

Finally, the proposed institutional structure should be responsive to its clientele—students and their families. Institutions not responsive to the wants of students and their families would lose students to those that are. Competition among institutions for students' tuition should generate greater efficiency and a variety of innovations in programs and in the techniques of providing educational services.

SUMMARY

Colleges and universities face many problems, most of them stemming from four fundamental issues: (1) what kinds of services they should provide, (2) how much service should be provided, (3) what is the appropriate institutional structure and (4) who should pay for it. These are issues about which economic analysis has much to say.

Institutions of higher education use resources to produce educational services. These services provide (1) investment in human capital, (2) direct consumption benefits, and (3) social spillover benefits. By far, the greater part of educational services appears to be composed of investment in human capital. There is controversy over the extent to which social spillover benefits exist, but these are not likely to be a large part of the total. The first-order benefits of educational services accrue mainly to the student who obtains them, although society gains from secondary benefits just as it does from investment in material capital.

Higher educational services, like other goods and services, have economic costs. All economic costs are measured by the alternative-cost principle. Some costs are explicit in nature, while others are implicit. The explicit costs of higher education services are the costs of the capital and labor resources used by colleges and universities. Most people view these as the total costs. However, to students and their families there are implicit costs that are greater in amount than the explicit costs. Most important of these are the forgone earnings of students and their families.

Sources of support (payment of explicit costs) for higher educational institutions in the United States are different for public than for private institutions. Structurally, the system of institutions consists of public institutions, which receive the bulk of their revenues in the form of state legislative appropriations, and private institutions, which receive the bulk of their revenues from tuition. The implicit costs to students do not enter into college and university budgets and are the same whether they attend public or private institutions. The incidence of the costs of higher educational services rests most heavily on the student and family, even in public institutions, with their relatively low tuition levels.

An economic evaluation of the fundamental problems involved in the provision of higher educational services highlights several shortcomings of the present institutional structure of higher educational facilities. Public institutions, supported primarily by legislative appropriations, are likely to be more responsive to the demands of legislators than to the demands of students in the determination of what kinds of services should be provided. The amounts of services provided also are determined by legislative appropriations rather than by the economic factors of demand and costs. As a device for making educational opportunities available to the children of the poor, public institutions leave much to be desired.

An alternative structure for higher educational institutions that appears worthy of serious consideration is one in which the tuition rates charged are sufficient to cover all of the explicit costs of providing educational services. This would tend to make institutions more responsive to the demands of students and their families. It would tend toward the production of the "correct" amounts of higher educational services, as compared with other goods and services. It would also provide a structure in which state (taxpayer) support of the educational costs of the children of the poor could be met directly and efficiently.

SUPPLEMENTARY READINGS

Alchian, Armen A. "The Economic and Social Impact of Free Tuition." *New Individualist Review,* Winter 1968, pp. 42–52.

Discusses the economic and social impacts of a low or zero-tuition method of providing higher educational opportunities. It is asserted that a system of full tuition will yield a greater variety of educational opportunities and a higher quality of education.

Bowen, Howard R. "Who Pays the Higher Education Bill?" In *Financing Higher Education: Alternatives for the Federal Government,* edited by M. D. Orwig. Iowa City: The American College Testing Program, 1971, pp. 281–98.

Discusses the incidence of higher education costs and concludes that the student and family now bear the major costs. Bowen proposes a grant-loan plan to students combined with grants to educational institutions. The grant-loan plan is designed to help students from low-income families, while grants to institutions are intended to help institutions meet rising costs of education.

Buchanan, James M., and Devletoglou, Nicos E.   *Academia in Anarchy,* part 1, pp. 3–62. New York: Basic Books, 1970.

A good, provocative summary of the characteristics of public higher education. Points out that to a large extent the students who consume it are not the ones who pay for it; the faculties that produce it do not sell it; and the taxpayers who own it do not control it.

Carnegie Commission on Higher Education.   *Higher Education: Who Pays? Who Benefits? Who should Pay?* New York: McGraw–Hill Book Company, 1973.

The most thorough study available on the questions raised in the title, together with a set of recommendations for financing colleges and universities.

Carnegie Commission on Higher Education.   *Tuition.* New York: McGraw–Hill Book Company, 1974.

A supplement to the 1973 study.

Hansen, W. Lee, and Weisbrod, Burton A.   *Benefits, Costs, and Finance of Public Higher Education,* chaps. 1–4, pp. 7–77. Chicago: Markham Publishing Co., 1969.

Adopts a benefit-cost approach to higher education, with particular reference to the state of California. Study identifies the forms of benefits and costs associated with higher education and attempts to assess the incidence of each.

Windham, Douglas M.   "The Economics of Education: A Survey." In *Contemporary Economic Issues,* rev. ed., edited by Neil W. Chamberlain, pp. 159–217. Homewood, Ill.: Richard D. Irwin, 1973.

A good general reference. The nature of education as an economic good is elaborated on, and the present means of financing higher education and some possible alternatives are presented.

Chapter 4

THE ENERGY PROBLEM

CHECKLIST OF ECONOMIC CONCEPTS

Demand [
Changes in demand
Supply
Changes in supply
Ceiling prices
Shortages
Imports
Inflation
Subsidies and their effects
Allocations and rationing
Efficiency
Profits
Monopoly and competition

4

The energy problem

Must simple things be made complex?

Ellen and Eli Higgenbottem were a little bit angry and more than a little bit puzzled. As good citizens, they tried hard to observe the voluntary energy conservation measures urged on the general public by the government. They maintained their thermostat at 68° in the winter and at 78° in the summer. But most of their friends did not. On their summer vacation trip from Pennsylvania to California, they had carefully observed the national 55 mile-per-hour speed limit. But on the long drive cars whizzed around them continuously. The failure of their fellow citizens to abide by the rules was annoying to say the least.

The Higgenbottems were uneasy about the Carter administration's plan to bring domestic crude oil prices up to the level of the world crude oil prices set by the Organization of Petroleum Exporting Countries (OPEC). Surely such a move would raise the prices of gasoline and fuel oil above their already exorbitant levels, cutting further into the couple's monthly paychecks. On the other hand they applauded the administration for assuring that oil companies would not receive windfall profits in the process. They were pleased to see that prices received by oil companies would continue to be subjected to ceilings and that a tax equal to the differences between controlled prices and the world prices would be the device used to bring the domestic price of oil up to the world price level. They saw no need for oil companies to reap the rewards of the domestic price increase.

The energy problem provided Eli with an unexpected bonus. It made feasible the realization of his long-standing desire to learn to fly. His job called for frequent trips to Catskill City about 200 miles away. With a speed limit of 55 miles per hour, making the round trip in one day by automobile simply did not leave enough working time to accomplish his objectives. With no such limitations on a small airplane and with costs per mile not much different from those of an automobile, both his boss and his wife had readily acquiesced to his suggestion that he obtain a private pilot's certificate.

THE PROBLEM

In April of 1977 President Carter called on the people of the United States to fight the "moral equivalent of war." In the years since 1971— and especially since the Arab oil embargo of 1973–74—many have believed that our energy-hungry economy would become increasingly hard pressed to satisfy its appetite. Acute shortages of gasoline and fuel oil occurred during the embargo. Since 1974 gasoline and fuel oil prices have risen considerably but the actual shortages appear to have abated. However, we continue to be informed by Congress, the administration, the news media, and others that we face an energy problem that President Carter characterizes as "the greatest challenge our nation will face during our lifetime."

The crisis in the United States centers primarily on petroleum which provides some 46 percent of the total energy requirements of the economy. Another 28.4 percent is filled by natural gas. Coal takes care of 18.8 percent of the total requirements and the remaining 6.8 percent comes from hydro and nuclear sources.[1]

The average citizen in the United States finds the energy picture confusing. The main thrust of the Carter administration's energy policy is conservation. Threats of running out of oil—of freezing to death in the dark—are continually dangled before us. Our proven reserves of crude oil and natural gas are reported to be dwindling. Yet, except for isolated incidents like the gasoline shortage of the winter of 1974–75 and the natural gas shortage of January–March of 1977, we can purchase about as much energy as we desire.

We are told, also, that we must cut down our imports of foreign oil— particularly that produced in the Middle East. In 1974 and 1975 complete independence of foreign oil sources was said to be a goal of the Ford administration's energy policies but its achievement was doomed to failure. As a matter of fact our imports of foreign oil have been increasing consistently in the 1970s. In addition, since 1973 the Organization of Pe-

---

[1] U.S. Department of Commerce, Bureau of the Census, *Statistical Abstract of the United States, 1976* (Washington, D.C.: U.S. Government Printing Office, 1977), p. 549.

troleum Exporting Countries (OPEC) from whom we buy about half our imported crude oil has quadrupled the price that they charge us.[2]

Rising energy prices receive a part of the blame for inflation. Much rhetoric has been directed toward the contribution of rising energy prices to the rising consumer price level. Consequently, many people believe that price controls on energy in its various forms are needed.

ECONOMIC BACKGROUND OF THE PROBLEM

Basic economic analysis is useful in sorting out and evaluating the various facets of the energy problem. The crux of the problem in the United States is that the demand for energy has been increasing faster than the supply. Further, from 1971 through 1973 the U.S. government pursued a set of policies that insured the development of shortages. Since that time its policies have contributed to declining levels of domestic production and increasing levels of imports.

Demand

For nonhuman energy in all forms about one half of the total direct demand originates with *industrial* users. *Transportation* users create an additional one fourth, while *residential* and *commercial* users generate about one fourth of the total demand. For the petroleum component of energy, transportation users demand the largest amounts. Next in line are residential and commercial users, followed by industrial users. Electricity-generating plants, which are classified as industrial users, provide a converted source of energy for users of all types. They obtain about half of their primary energy from coal, with the rest coming from natural gas, petroleum, hydropower, and nuclear power, in that order.

In the transportation area, automobiles, trucks, buses, and airplanes are the important petroleum energy users. The number of automobiles, trucks and buses on the road has almost tripled since World War II, and, in contrast to Europeans, our tastes have been strong for large, powerful cars that consume prodigious amounts of fuel. Our concern with environmental quality in recent years has led to mandatory antipollution devices on our motorized vehicles that have in turn reduced the miles per gallon obtained and increased their total fuel consumption. In commercial aviation, piston engine airplanes have been replaced by the fuel-hungry blowtorches that we call jets. Even the number of piston engine general avi-

---

[2] OPEC countries are the Arab countries of Abu Dhabi, Algeria, Iraq, Kuwait, Libya, Qatar, and Saudi Arabia, and the non-Arab countries of Ecuador, Gabin, Indonesia, Iran, Nigeria, and Venezuela.

ation airplanes has been increasing rapidly, although quantitatively these are not yet a significant factor in the total demand for petroleum products.

Increasing residential and commercial demand for petroleum products reflects general economic expansion and rising affluence. The population is growing; greater numbers of houses are being built; and houses are larger in size. Central heating and air conditioning induce us to heat more rooms in our homes than we did with the space heaters and floor furnaces of years ago. Numbers of commercial establishments and the average size of the areas enclosed by them have been increasing commensurately.

Industrial demand for petroleum products has been rising over time for two reasons. The first and most obvious reason is the expanding industrial activity associated with economic growth. The second is the shift that has been occurring away from coal and toward petroleum as an energy source. To be sure, the industrial demand for coal continues to increase, but industrial demand for petroleum products—fuel oil—has been increasing faster. The important factors causing the relative shift are (1) environmental considerations—coal is a dirtier fuel—and (2) the historically relatively lower costs of petroleum energy.

It should come as no surprise that the demand for petroleum by electricity-generating plants is growing rapidly. Again, economic growth and rising affluence create rising needs for electricity for lighting, heating, and cooling and for running the ever-growing masses of appliances that come on the market. Power-generating plants have relied heavily on coal as a fuel, but the same factors that tend to shift other industrial plants toward petroleum has affected power plants, too.

Supply

Energy supplies in the United States have been increasing over time but have not kept pace with the increasing demands for them. The production of bituminous coal has been increasing steadily over the past ten years, but the output of the cleaner-burning Pennsylvania anthracite has been decreasing. Natural gas production has been increasing slowly, largely because relatively low price ceilings have been set by the Federal Power Commission, making it unprofitable to increase production significantly. Nuclear power has not yet been tapped in any sizable quantities, but its use is growing rapidly as the costs of more conventional energy sources rise. Thus, petroleum, which accounts for half of our energy supplies, has been the crucial element in the supply picture over the past decade and will continue to be for several years to come.

The production of crude oil in the United States rose steadily until 1970. Most people believed that the annual increases in output could go on forever. However, U.S. production of crude oil peaked in 1970 and declined somewhat in 1971. A slight increase over 1971 was registered in 1972, but since that time domestic production has declined back to its 1965 level. These trends through 1976 are shown in Table 4–1 (page 100) and Figure 4–1 (page 101).

Imports of crude oil largely complete the supply picture. Over the years the percentage of crude oil supplies imported to total crude oil supplies available (including imports) rose from 12.6 percent in 1960 to 40.5 percent in 1976. In 1977 we depended even more heavily on imports. For the first two months of the year 45.6 percent of total supplies were imported. The trends are shown in Table 4–1 and Figure 4–2 (page 102). Total supply trends for the same period are shown in Figure 4–3 (page 103).

Not quite half of the U.S. imports of crude oil come from the Middle East. Canada has supplied large amounts, but our large suppliers outside the Arab world are Algeria, Nigeria, Venezuela, and Indonesia. Not shown in our tables and diagrams are the large amounts imported of finished and partly finished petroleum products—mostly residual fuel oil, but also motor gasoline, jet fuel, and distillate fuel oil. In 1976, total imports of these items were 748,736 barrels, as compared with crude oil imports of 935,142,000 barrels. These finished products come mostly from Central America, the Caribbean, and South America.[3]

Nevertheless, it was the embargo that the Arab countries placed on shipments of crude oil to the United States that triggered the energy crisis of 1973, and looming large in current official thinking in Washington, D.C., is the possibility of Arab manipulation of current and future supplies from the Middle East. As Table 4–1 shows, from 1965 through 1970, U.S. imports from the Middle East countries fluctuated up and down, with a predominantly downward trend. Since 1970, they have increased sharply as U.S. production dropped off. As Table 4–1 shows, in 1971 Middle East oil comprised 3.7 percent of the total crude available to the United States. In 1972 it made up 4.6 percent of the total and, as Table 4–1 indicates, for the first three quarters of 1976 it averaged over 16 percent of the total U.S. supply.

As we indicated earlier, much is made in official Washington of dwindling oil and gas reserves. The Carter administration continually raises the spectre of exhausting finite supplies in the next one or two decades. But *proven reserves* are notoriously poor indicators of what will be available in the future. *Proven reserves* represent known pools of oil and gas that are recoverable with present technology at present cost levels. As such they are much the same thing as business inventories. They tend to expand when the industry is profitable and to contract when profits in the

---

[3] U.S. Department of the Interior, Bureau of Mines, *Mineral Industry Surveys, Crude Petroleum, Petroleum Products, and Natural Gas Liquids,* December 1976.

TABLE 4–1
Total supplies of crude oil in the United States, 1960 and 1965–1976 (000 barrels)

Year	Domestic production	Imports Middle East countries*	Percent of total U.S. supply	Total	Percent of total U.S. supply	Total U.S. supply
1960	2,574,933	114,342	3.9%	371,575	12.6%	2,946,508
1965	2,848,514	137,941	4.2	452,040	13.7	3,300,554
1966	3,027,763	133,608	3.8	447,120	12.9	3,474,883
1967	3,215,742	84,588	2.3	411,649	11.4	3,627,391
1968	3,329,042	124,716	3.3	472,323	12.4	3,801,365
1969	3,371,751	125,256	3.2	514,114	13.2	3,885,865
1970	3,517,450	86,674	2.2	483,293	12.1	4,000,743
1971	3,453,914	150,505	3.7	613,417	15.1	4,067,331
1972	3,459,052	197,879	4.6	811,135	19.0	4,270,187
1973	3,206,012	343,897	7.8	1,183,996	27.0	4,390,008
1974	3,056,936	360,483	8.3	1,269,155	29.3	4,326,091
1975	2,918,924	485,437	11.0	1,498,181	33.9	4,417,105
1976	2,838,466	828,326	17.4	1,935,142	40.5	4,773,608
1977 (Jan.–Feb.)	445,047	162,276	19.8	372,997	45.6	818,044

* Egypt, Iran, Iraq, Kuwait, Libya, Saudi Arabia, United Arab Emirates.

Sources: U.S. Department of the Interior, Bureau of Mines, Mineral Industry Surveys, *Crude Petroleum, Petroleum Products, and Natural Gas Liquids,* 1960, 1965–77 issues.

FIGURE 4–1
U.S. production of crude oil, 1965–1975

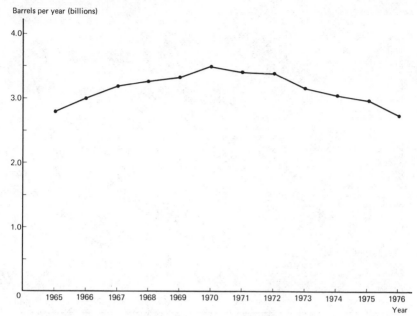

Sources: U.S. Department of the Interior, Bureau of Mines, Mineral Industry Surveys, *Crude Petroleum, Petroleum Products, and Natural Gas Liquids,* 1965–77 issues.

industry are pinched. Improvements in the technology of finding and re-covering oil and gas together with higher prices received by firms engaged in the business could alter the proven reserve picture considerably.

On the supply side, then, it appears that fears of running out of oil in the near future are unduly exaggerated. Isn't there a missing link some-where in the chain of events that have led us into a serious energy problem?

Governmental policies

There is indeed such a missing link, and it is called policies of the fed-eral government. It does not appear that the government has *failed* to do enough to avert a problem, as many seem to believe. Rather, it seems that the government has done too much; its actions appear to have brought on and accentuated the problem.

Prior to 1970, there was no real hint of an energy crisis. We heard, of course, from geologists, oil companies, and others concerned with energy supplies that on down the road there would be a day of reckoning when energy supplies would fail to meet rapidly expanding energy demands.

FIGURE 4–2
U.S. imports of crude oil, 1965–1975

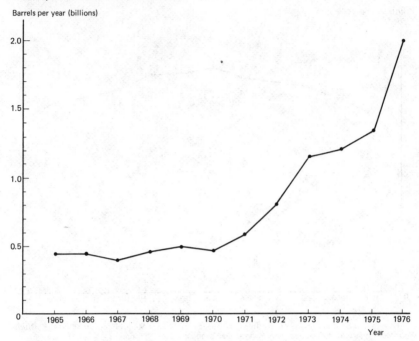

Sources: U.S. Department of the Interior, Bureau of Mines, Mineral Industry Surveys, *Crude Petroleum, Petroleum Products, and Natural Gas Liquids,* 1965–75 issues.

But vocalizations of these sorts are commonly heard from producers' special-interest groups seeking governmental subsidization and/or protection. There were no economic indications that we would be unable to buy as much gasoline and fuel oil as we desired. To put it in familiar economic terms, equilibrium prices prevailed in these markets until late 1971. Markets for crude oil and its products were in equilibrium. Using gasoline as an example, Figure 4–4 (page 104) shows an equilibrium price of p_1 prevailing; buyers want quantity q_1 at that price, and suppliers are willing to place quantity q_1 on the market.

Now take inflation and economic expansion into account. Inflation occurs whenever aggregate demand is increasing faster than aggregate supply. The demands for petroleum products and other energy sources in an expanding inflationary economy tend to increase even more rapidly than the aggregate demand of which they are component parts. The results are illustrated for gasoline in Figure 4–5 (page 105). An increase in demand from D_1D_1 to D_2D_2, which outstrips an increase in supply from S_1S_1 to S_2S_2, brings about a price increase in gasoline from p_1 to p_2. This is the

FIGURE 4–3

Total supply of crude oil in the United States, 1965–1975

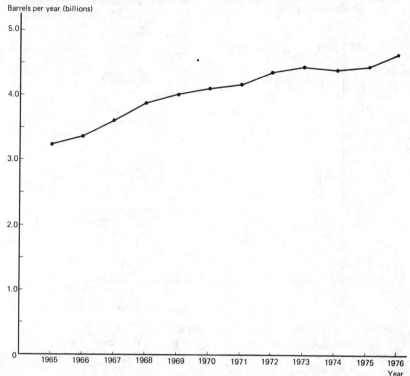

Sources: U.S. Department of the Interior, Bureau of Mines, Mineral Industry Surveys, *Crude Petroleum, Petroleum Products, and Natural Gas Liquids,* 1965–75 issues.

nature of the inflationary process. As such, it is a part of the inflation problem, but it generates no energy crisis.

The energy shortages began to make themselves felt following the wage-price freeze of August 17, 1971. They became more and more intense through the various phases of price controls in 1972 and 1973. Then with the cutoff in Arab oil in October 1973, they suddenly began to appear catastrophic.

As we noted in Chapter 2, wherever price controls are effective in holding prices *below* their equilibrium levels, shortages occur. This is precisely what has happened in the petroleum case. Petroleum product prices were held below equilibrium levels by the government, creating shortages of gasoline, jet fuel, and fuel oils. Consider Figure 4–5 (page 105) again. When demand increases to D_2D_2 and supply increases to S_2S_2, suppose that price controls hold the price of gasoline at p_1. At that price level con-

FIGURE 4–4

Equilibrium price and quantity of gasoline

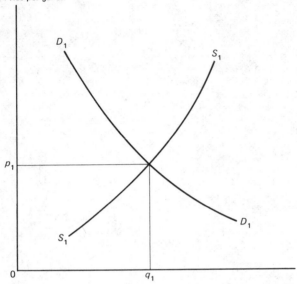

Price per gallon

Gasoline (gallons per month)

Given the demand D_1D_1 and the supply S_1S_1 of gasoline, the equilibrium price will be p_1 and the equilibrium quantity will be q_1. At the equilibrium price there is neither a surplus nor a shortage.

sumers now want q_3 gallons, but suppliers are willing to place only q_4 on the market, leaving a shortage of q_4q_3 gallons. Now, if on top of this an Arab embargo occurs, the supply curve for gasoline shifts to the left, to S_3S_3. If a price ceiling of p_1 is maintained, the shortage increases to q_5q_3. Shortages would be expected to continue as long as petroleum product prices are held by the government below their equilibrium levels. Effective price controls on gasoline ended when the Arab embargo was lifted in 1974 and the gasoline shortages no longer occurred.

Crude oil markets were a different story. In accordance with the Emergency Petroleum Allocations Act of 1973 and the Energy Policy and Conservation Act of 1975 the Federal Energy Agency maintained and extended a complicated set of price controls on crude oil produced domestically. Oil was classified into three groups: (1) old oil, (2) new oil, and (3) oil from stripper wells. Old oil was defined as that produced by wells in existence in November 1975, up to the amounts they were producing monthly at that time. Its controlled price was about $5.25 per bar-

FIGURE 4–5

Effects of changes in demand for and supply of gasoline with and without price controls

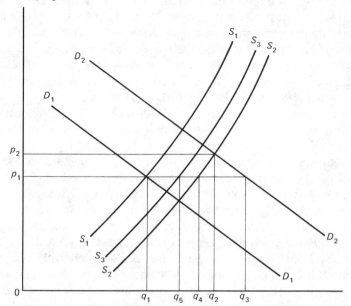

Price per gallon

Gasoline (gallons per month)

An increase in demand from D_1D_1 to D_2D_2, accompanied by an increase in supply from S_1S_1 to S_2S_2, causes the price of gasoline to rise from p_1 to p_2, and there is no shortage. If the price is controlled at p_1, a shortage of q_4q_3 will occur. If supply then decreases to S_3S_3 and the price is held at p_1, the shortage will increase to q_5q_3.

rel. New oil was from wells put in production after that time plus output from old wells that exceeded the base period output levels. The controlled price was about $11 per barrel. Oil from stripper wells was sold at free market prices, that is, what it costs to import crude oil from abroad. Import prices were around $14.50 per barrel.

Obviously refiners want to purchase crude oil at the lowest possible price. Quantities supplied of old oil at controlled prices were insufficient to meet their demands. At controlled prices shortages of new oil existed, too. To alleviate the shortages refiners bought stripper oil and imported oil from abroad.

The shortages of both old oil and new oil opened up possibilities of great inequities in the cost of crude oil to different refiners. Those able to get old oil were in a favored position over those which were not. Similarly those unable to get either new or old oil and which were required to pay the import price were the most unfavorably situated.

To reduce the inequities the Federal Energy Agency established an elaborate program of entitlements and allocations among crude oil refiners. In essence each refiner was issued "entitlement" tickets giving it the right to purchase certain amounts of domestic oil on which the price was controlled. The number of entitlement tickets that a refiner could obtain depended upon the refiner's total crude oil use—both price controlled oil and that which was not price controlled. The right to purchase crude oil at the lower controlled prices was thus tied to the refiner's purchases of stripper well and imported oil at uncontrolled prices. The effective price per barrel paid by the refiner was thus an average of the controlled and uncontrolled prices.

The entitlements program in effect places a tax on domestic production of crude oil and at the same time subsidizes refinery purchases of imports of oil and stripper-well production. In Figure 4–6 suppose initially that all crude oil is produced domestically. The demand and supply curves are D_dD_d and S_dS_d, respectively. The price is p_d per barrel and the quantity exchanged is q_4 barrels per month. Now suppose that we can import oil at p_f per barrel (the OPEC price). Domestic producers will place q_3 on the market at that price and imports will amount to q_3q_5. Note that we are getting more oil at a lower price than we would if we depend on domestic production only. Now consider the effect of the entitlements program. For simplicity we assume that the controlled price of both old and new domestic oil is the same and is p_c. But refiners are entitled to buy it only in proportion to the quantity of oil that they buy at the world price of p_f. The price of oil to refiners, p_a, is an average of the world price p_f and the domestic controlled price p_c. Refiners purchase q_6 barrels per month at the average price p_a. Since domestic producers get only p_c per barrel they will place only q_1 barrels on the market. The difference between the average price p_a that the refiners pay and the controlled price p_c is like a tax on domestic producers that is used to pay a subsidy of the difference between p_f and p_a to refiners for each barrel of oil that they import. Total imports are q_1q_6 barrels per month. Refiners import more and domestic producers produce less crude oil than would be the case if there were no price controls on domestically produced crude oil and no entitlements program.

President Carter presented the Congress and the U.S. public with his administration's proposed energy program in April 1977. It contained four major points. First, he proposed to center all energy-related activities of the federal government in a cabinet-level Department of Energy. Second, the core of the program was to be conservation. Third, emphasis was placed on the development of alternative (to petroleum) energy sources. Fourth, domestically produced oil would be subjected to price controls

FIGURE 4–6

Effects of the FEA entitlements program

Price per barrel

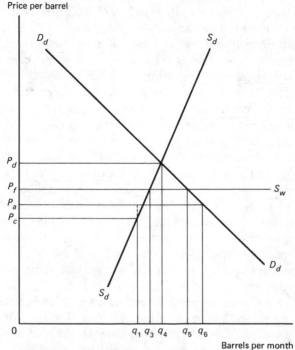

Barrels per month

If D_dD_d and S_dS_d represent the domestic demand and supply curve for crude oil the equilibrium price and quantity would be p_d and q_4, respectively. In the absence of price controls and a world crude oil price of p_f at which refiners can purchase as much as they want the effective supply curve to domestic refiners becomes S_d up to quantity q_3 and S_w for larger quantities. The price of oil would be p_f and the quantity q_3q_5 would be imported. The entitlements program in effect makes imported (and stripper-well) oil available at p_a inducing refiners to take quantity q_6. Domestic crude oil producers receive a controlled price of p_c and will place only q_1 on the market. The entitlements program increases imports to q_1q_3 whereas in the absence of entitlements imports would be q_3q_5 barrels.

until 1981 with the level of the controlled price to be raised in equal annual steps until, in 1981, the controls are completely removed.

The first point is a matter of administrative efficiency. Policies relating to energy have been diffused among several government agencies, the most important ones being the Federal Energy Agency, the Energy Research and Development Agency, and the Federal Power Commission. Others include the Department of Defense, the Department of Transportation, and the Wage and Price Council. Activities of these diverse agencies have frequently been conflicting and counterproductive.

The Carter administration has chosen to concentrate on conservation of petroleum products—to coerce the general public into consuming less. Proposed conservation measures include a tax of say an additional five cents per gallon on gasoline and if the consequent higher price to consumers does not reduce quantity demand enough, the tax would be further increased in amount. Another measure is a tax or penalty on so-called gas-guzzling automobiles sold after a certain date, say 1981. Still another is continuation of a mandatory 55-mile-per-hour national speed limit. There is some talk of rationing gasoline if tax measures do not reduce gasoline consumption as much as government officials believe it should be reduced.

The third point of emphasis in the Carter proposals, development of alternative energy sources, centers on forcing industry—public utilities, particularly—to switch from fuel oil and natural gas to coal as an energy source. In addition, business use taxes on oil and gas would be levied to encourage those exempt from mandatory changes to turn away from oil and gas energy sources.

Finally, the Carter proposals intend to keep price controls on both crude oil and natural gas in place for a number of years. With regard to crude oil a tax equal to the difference between the controlled domestic price and the world price would be levied on each barrel of oil. The result would be that refiners would face the world price of crude oil regardless of whether they import it or buy it from domestic producers. However, domestic producers would receive only the controlled price. The difference —the tax—would go to the federal government. The purpose of an arrangement of this sort is to prevent "windfall profits" from accruing to crude oil producers from the sale of domestic crude oil at the world price level.

In summary, the Carter program emphasizes control of consumption of oil products. Production of oil is discouraged. Some energy users are forced and others are encouraged to shift to alternative energy sources.

ECONOMIC ANALYSIS OF THE PROBLEM

The adequacy of future petroleum supplies

The question in most of our minds is that of whether future petroleum supplies will be adequate for our needs. There is a great temptation—and something to be learned from it—to project future demands and future supplies forward by 20 or 30 years. But we are unlikely to come up with definitive numerical answers. Our study of economic principles tells us why this is so.

On the demand side, we can expect that in an expanding economy demand curves for petroleum (and for other energy resources) will continue shifting to the right. But we should not forget that demand curves also slope downward to the right. For any given petroleum demand curve, the higher the relative price the smaller will be the quantity taken. Quantities demanded in the future, then, are determined by two sets of forces: (1) the nature and the extent to which the demand curve shifts and (2) the price at which the product is sold. The greater the projected expansion of the economy, the more will be demanded. The higher the relative price, the less will be demanded.

Supply forecasts have in the past been notoriously misleading. Doomsday prophets look at U.S. proven reserves of crude oil and pronounce an early death sentence on this form of energy. But what they overlook is that proven reserves are the result of investment in exploration and that it does not pay producers to invest in exploration and the establishment of proven resources beyond some level. We do not really know the extent of the *unproven* oil reserves of the United States—on private lands, on federal land, in Alaska, and offshore. The ultimate capability of the world to produce oil is completely unknown.[4]

In the United States, we are not really confronted with a problem of "running out of oil." Our real problem is that of how best to cope with an energy situation that has been generated by the government. Rapid economic expansion from 1962 through 1973, inflation, a set of price controls, and the realization by the OPEC countries that they can gain much by acting in concert have created rapidly rising prices and fears of shortages. Have we let a short-run situation unduly color our long-run vision?

The era of cheap energy may indeed be over, but there is nothing catastrophic in higher and relatively rising energy costs. The using up of easily available oil pools means that the supply curve is shifting to the left as in Figure 4–7 (or, what amounts to the same thing, upward). But if prices are not controlled the price of oil will rise to equilibrium levels such as from p_1 to p_2 and there will be no shortages in evidence. Rising prices will in turn generate three types of economic adjustments to the diminishing quantities of the now relatively inexpensive petroleum. First, they will induce greater recovery than would occur if the price were controlled at p_1. Such a controlled price brings forth quantity q_3, but if the price is allowed to rise to p_2, recovery from existing wells and from less accessible oil pools will increase the quantity to q_2. Second, the higher prices induce users

---

[4] See Edward J. Mitchell, *U.S. Energy Policy: A Primer* (Washington, D.C.: American Enterprise Institute for Public Policy Research), pp. 4–11.

FIGURE 4–7
The effects of declining crude oil supplies

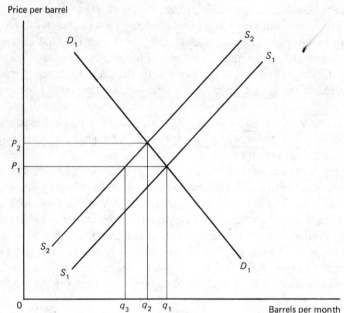

Price per barrel

Barrels per month

The depletion of easily available crude oil pools shifts the sup-
ply curve to the left from S_1S_1 to S_2S_2, causing the price to rise to p_2.
If the price were controlled at p_1 there would be a shortage of q_3q_1
barrels. If the price is allowed to rise producers will increase output
from quantity q_3 to q_2 and consumers will reduce consumption from
q_1 to q_2, eliminating the shortage.

voluntarily to reduce their use of oil from q_1 to q_2. As the price rises, users
have an incentive to conserve, putting oil to its most valuable uses and
cutting back on the amount consumed in lower value uses. Third, and most
important of all, users of oil will have incentives to *voluntarily* turn to and
develop alternative energy sources.

Alternative energy sources

Petroleum is by no means the only source of energy. Natural gas, coal,
nuclear processes, hydroelectric processes, wind, and the sun are among
the alternative sources of power available to us. Of these sources, natural
gas has been the most prominent because of its clean-burning characteristics and, more important, because it has been relatively cheap.

Natural gas, like petroleum, has been in short supply over the last few years; however, the shortage results from government pricing policies of the resource rather than from low potential reserves. Since 1960 the Federal Power Commission has imposed strict controls on the price of natural gas at the wellhead. The controlled price has discouraged exploration and expansion of supplies while, at the same time, it has encouraged expanding consumption. Like any other effective price ceiling, this one, too, has resulted in shortages. It is generally believed by those in the industry and by academic observers that higher relative prices of natural gas would bring forth significantly greater quantities.[5]

The United States has no shortage of coal. Vast reserves occur both in the older coal fields of the East and in the newer areas of Wyoming and Montana. Coal has fallen into disfavor in recent years for several reasons, the most important one being the relatively low prices of clean-burning natural gas and of fuel oil. Coal has been the target of environmentalists on two counts: (1) the relatively high sulphur content of its emissions as it burns and (2) damage to the landscape from strip mining activities. Neither of these are insurmountable obstacles to a significant expansion in the use of coal as an energy source. At a price, both can be successfully counteracted. In addition, a whole new technique of coal gasification is in the process of development.

Nuclear processes hold promise as an energy source, although their success to this point in time has been something less than spectacular. There has been considerable fear by the public that wastes from nuclear power plants constitute a danger to the community; however, there is little hard evidence that this is so. For technological reasons relatively low-cost generating plants have not been forthcoming. In addition, the federal government has put formidable obstacles in the way of using plutonium, the most promising of nuclear fuels.

Still other potential energy sources hold promise for the future as new techniques are developed to exploit them. These include large quantities of shale oil, hydroelectric potential, the wind, and the sun. A major problem in harnessing the almost unlimited supplies of wind and solar energy is that of low-cost storage. But, if past experience in technological development tells us anything, we can expect that this, too, will eventually be solved.

The use of legislation and government coercion to turn energy users away from petroleum toward alternative energy sources is highly questionable from the point of view of economics. Energy users do not continue to use the petroleum source because they are addicted to it. They use it because it is still plentiful enough to be *less expensive* than equivalent energy obtained from other sources. If the price of crude oil is not controlled,

[5] Ibid., pp. 72–73.

diminishing supplies over time will cause the price of petroleum-based energy to rise. As it becomes more expensive relative to equivalent energy from alternative sources the shift to alternative sources will be made voluntarily and gradually. As a matter of fact, the *prospects* of relatively rising petroleum prices in the future will *induce* energy-supplying businesses to engage in research and development in alternative energy sources. Government mandated shifts to alternative fuels or energy sources are necessary only if price controls are kept in effect, preventing the price system from doing its job.

The consequences of price controls

It is unfortunate that we are forced to grapple with an energy problem at the same time that the economy is so beset with other problems. On the other hand, if the problems of inflation and recession had not arisen, it is entirely possible—even probable—that there would be no energy problem either. In any case, the energy problem has become inextricably entangled with inflation, recession, and unemployment, making it extremely difficult to put it in its proper economic perspective.

The wage-price freezes of 1971–74, the Arab embargo of October 1973, and the inevitable shortage of petroleum products made allocations and rationing necessary in 1973 and 1974. Domestic oil-producing states had no difficulty in meeting their own needs. However, a number of states, particularly those in the Northeast, not only had the imports upon which they depended heavily cut off, but because of price controls they could not bid the prices of petroleum products up enough to induct the producing states to ship to them. Consequently, the Federal Energy Office, set up by President Nixon at the beginning of the embargo, was charged with the task of allocating petroleum products among geographic areas. Although no formal consumer rationing scheme was enacted by the government, rationing to dealers was accomplished by an allocations program.

The allocations program of the Federal Energy Office was far from satisfactory.[6] Shortages and long lines of consumers at gasoline stations plagued the Northeastern states throughout the embargo. Certain rapidly expanding regions were hurt because allocations were based on past consumption rates. Many gasoline stations went out of business, and their allocations were lost to the regions in which they were located. Special-interest groups—for example, farmers and truckers—fought with each other over the available short supplies. In general, the program was a divisive, frustrating experience.

---

[6] See Richard B. Manche, *Performance of the Federal Energy Office* (Washington, D.C.: American Enterprise Institute for Public Policy, February 1975).

Although the general wage-price freeze expired in 1974, price controls for crude oil were continued as we noted previously. The price control program insured that the energy problem of the early 1970s would continue and become progressively worse. It has held domestic production below the levels that would be forthcoming if there were no price controls. It has encouraged ever-increasing oil imports. It has done nothing to hold down the prices of petroleum products to consumers. And it has caused a grotesque bureaucracy to become established in the Federal Energy Agency to police price controls, allocate old and new oil among refiners, and in general to do at the cost of several billion dollars per year what the price system would do more efficiently for nothing.

The efficiency of the price mechanism

Basic economic principles—demand and supply analyses—suggest, and experience tends to bear out, that there is a rather simple solution to our energy problems. It is that the government withdraw from, rather than enter more extensively into, the markets for energy resources. When prices are permitted to rise to their equilibrium levels, shortages disappear. Government pricing, allocation, and rationing decisions become unnecessary.

The evidence with respect to gasoline and fuel oil since the wage-price freeze ended in early 1974 demonstrates what the market can do. To be sure, prices have risen but we have no difficulty in filling our gas tanks or our fuel tanks to whatever extent we desire. The three-level price system for crude oil creates serious allocation problems among users of crude oil and inefficiencies in its use, but these will disappear when the system is scrapped and like grades of oil are priced uniformly.

The end of the era of cheap petroleum energy that prevailed in the 20th century through the 1960s may have arrived, but it is not necessary that it have doomsday implications. If demand for energy resources is increasing faster than supply, energy prices in the absence of controls will rise relative to other prices because units of energy are becoming relatively more valuable to the economy. This will induce each of us to examine our uses of energy, to eliminate the less important uses, and to utilize available supplies for the more important uses.

Households vary a great deal in what they consider to be the most important uses for an item such as gasoline. One family likes large automobiles while another prefers minicars. Another household places a high value on travel. Some families prefer not to travel at all. Shortages, caused by government-imposed price ceilings below equilibrium levels, open the door for government officials to specify the uses to which gasoline should be put. The automobile industry can be ordered by the government to produce only minicars—a move that will be applauded by minicar fans but not by tall people or those who like luxury cars. Travel can be curtailed. Various foolish (?) uses of gasoline can be banned. But, are government officials uniquely qualified to determine what are and what are not the most important uses for gasoline? In a shortage situation, the price system, if allowed to operate, moves the price in an upward direction; and, as the price rises, each household curtails those uses of the item that are least important to it. Thus, all households together adjust to the available supply, each in the manner best suited to its own preferences.

As energy becomes relatively more scarce and as its relative price rises, there is an inducement for producers to seek out and develop additional and alternative forms of energy supplies. Removing the $5.25 price ceiling for old oil increases the rate and extent of recovery from old wells. Rising relative prices of oil encourage exploration and drilling activity. Removal of price controls on natural gas make it economical to open up vast new reserves of this important fuel. Higher prices of petroleum energy encourage the development of shale oil recovery techniques and stimulate the development of nuclear technology. They also encourage research and development in the conversion of coal to clean-burning forms and in the development of wind and solar energy sources.

The free-market equilibrium price solution of the energy shortage problem has much to commend it. The primary argument in its favor is simply the argument for a private enterprise economic system *vis-à-vis* a socialistic economic system. The price system induces consumers to voluntarily limit their consumption of each good or service to the available supply. It also induces producers of each good and service to increase the quantity available, up to the point at which consumers value a unit of it at approximately what it costs to place it on the market. The price system induces buyers of goods and services and resources to put the supplies available to them to their most efficient uses. Relative prices, relative costs, and relative profits continually induce transfers of resources and goods from less valuable to more valuable uses. All of this is done automatically and impersonally. No coercion is necessary. We avoid putting our economic fate in the hands of government bureaucrats who may or may not be knowledgeable of the consequences of their actions, regardless of how good their intentions may be. Watergate and its aftermath have left many of us wary of both the intentions and the actions of politicians and bureaucrats!

There are three primary arguments against the free-market price solution. First, people argue that it would enable oil companies to make large windfall profits. Second, they maintain that it would discriminate against the poor. Third, they fear that it would contribute to inflation. All of these are probably correct conclusions, but are they valid arguments against the free-market solution?

With regard to windfall profits, several observations can be made. In the first place, when oil company annual profits since 1970 are averaged they are certainly less than spectacularly large. In the second place, it is profit possibilities that encourage exploration and discovery in a risky industry such as oil. If the government can be counted on to confiscate profits when they do occur smaller supplies will become a certainty.

Increases in the prices of petroleum products may or may not affect the poor in greater proportion than the more well-to-do. Only to the extent that the poor spend larger proportions of their total incomes on petroleum products than do wealthier people will an increase in the prices of those products reduce their real incomes in greater proportion. In any case, to the extent that we have poverty problems, those problems can be attacked most efficiently by direct means, as we note in Chapter 10. Poverty problems result from low incomes, not from relatively high prices of specific products. Have rationing schemes as we have known them in the past ordinarily operated in ways that favor the poor?

To attribute inflation to rising energy prices is to confuse cause and effect. The primary and continuing causes of inflation are contained in the fiscal and monetary policies of the federal government. Energy prices are *components* of the general price level. In any economy without inflation, the prices of some products rise and the prices of other products fall over time as conditions of demand for and supply of them change. Inflation is a phenomenon of aggregate demand changes or aggregate supply changes, and its causes are forces that change aggregate demand or aggregate supply. The impact of those changes on prices of specific items and on the general price level is an effect rather than a cause; although rapidly rising oil prices and restrictions on the use of oil may have some adverse effects on aggregate supply. We are not likely to stop—or even slow—inflation with ceiling prices on petroleum or other forms of energy.

The price mechanism operates most efficiently in competitive situations —and the oil industry is accused by many of being monopolistic. The major oil companies are indeed among the largest firms in the United States, but size alone does not necessarily imply monopoly power. Some 10,000 firms, for example, are engaged in the production of crude oil; however, the largest 20 firms account for about 75 percent of total domestic production. In gasoline refining, there are over 100 companies operating with the largest twenty accounting for about 80 percent of total domestic production.[7] These data tell us little about the actual competitive situation. They let us know, however, that the *potential* for competition exists if the government will refrain from policies that restrain it and will insure that the antitrust laws are applied to the industry.

---

[7] U.S. House of Representatives, Committee on Banking and Currency, *Oil Imports and Energy Security: An Analysis of the Current Situation and Future Prospects* (Washington, D.C.: U.S. Government Printing Office, 1974), pp. 54–55.

The role of the government

Energy problems have absorbed a tremendous amount of time for Congress and the Administration since 1973. There is little evidence that the debate, the furor, and the consequent actions will solve the problems; in fact, it appears that governmental intervention in energy markets has tended to reduce energy supplies and efficiency in energy production rather than to increase them. Is there any positive role that the government can take in planning for the future in this area? There are several ways in which the government can contribute toward the efficient use of energy and the development of future supplies, but past experience suggests that direct intervention in the market place is not one of them.

The government can act to make energy producers more competitive. The oil industry and other energy industries can be scrutinized carefully to identify and to eliminate monopolistic practices and/or monopolistic agreements that may occur. Toward this end, the government can also stop its *market-demand prorationing activities.*[8] Prorationing serves as a government-supported monopolizing device and has been used in the states of Texas, Louisiana, New Mexico, Kansas, and Oklahoma, which collectively account for about two thirds of the crude oil production in the United States. It is accomplished by state commissions such as the Texas Railroad Commission in Texas and the Oklahoma Corporation Commission in Oklahoma for two stated purposes: (1) to conserve crude oil reserves and (2) to divide the market equitably among producers.

In practice, prorationing serves as a government-supported monopolizing device that enables producers to act jointly to reduce supplies of crude oil placed on the market and to receive higher prices for their product than would be the case in competitive markets. The commission in a given state determines how much crude oil is to be produced and allocates quotas to the producers of the state. Ordinarily low-volume, high-cost wells are permitted to produce as much as they are capable of, while production from high-volume, low-cost wells is restricted. The results are restricted production and higher costs of recovery from wells that are operating currently, as well as reduced incentives for exploration and development of new oil fields. In the interests of efficiency and of expanding domestic production of crude oil, prorationing, as well as other monopolizing or restrictive devices, must be eliminated.

The government can also support or subsidize research and development in the energy field. It can help finance pilot projects and experimentation with alternative energy sources. But by and large the government's effective role in this respect is relatively small. If the expected benefits exceed

---

[8] James C. Burrows and Thomas A. Domencich, *An Analysis of the United States Oil Import Quota* (Lexington, Mass.: D. C. Heath & Co., 1970), pp. 62–68.

the expected costs of research and development, private concerns will have incentives to accomplish it and government effort will not be needed.[9]

SUMMARY

The U.S. public was confronted with an energy crisis in the winter of 1973–74 and has since been persuaded that a long-range energy problem exists. The problem centers on petroleum, which provides over 40 percent of U.S. energy supplies.

Since 1970 demand for petroleum products has been increasing faster than supply. The wage-price controls of 1971–74, together with the 1973–74 Arab oil embargo, turned these demand-supply relationships into acute shortages. The shortages, even after they ceased to exist, triggered fears of impending and future shortages as well as rising energy prices.

Although we appear to be in no immediate danger of running out of oil, its growing relative scarcity would be expected to cause the prices of petroleum products to rise over time relative to other prices in the economy. Rising petroleum prices will in turn encourage additional search and exploration for petroleum reserves. They will also encourage the development of promising alternative energy sources such as coal, synthetic fuels, nuclear power, wind, and solar power.

Direct intervention by the government has undoubtedly increased rather than decreased energy problems. Price controls from 1971 to 1974 brought on shortages. The three-price system for crude oil and government allocations of domestic oil have reduced efficiency in energy production and distribution and have held domestic supplies below what they would otherwise be. They have also encouraged a rising volume of imports. Free market prices for energy supplies appear to provide the best answer to efficient use of energy and to the avoidance of shortages.

The government can play a limited positive role in the energy field. It can act to increase competition among energy suppliers. It can help support research and development activities. It should probably avoid direct intervention in energy markets.

SUPPLEMENTARY READINGS

Cogan, John; Johnsen, M. Bruce; and Ward, Michael P. *Energy and Jobs: A Long Run Analysis.* Los Angeles: International Institute for Economic Research, 1976.

---

[9] See Murray L. Weidenbaum and Reno Harnish, *Government Credit Subsidies for Energy Development* (Washington, D.C.: American Enterprise Institute for Public Policy Research, 1976).

An excellent economic analysis in terms of demand and supply of the nature and the effects of federal energy policies.

Friedman, Milton. "The Inequity of Gas Rationing." *Newsweek,* December 10, 1973, p. 113.

In assessing the equity of a rationing system, Friedman compares it with a subsidy system.

Friedman, Milton. "Why Some Prices Should Rise." *Newsweek,* November 19, 1973, p. 130.

Presents a case for using the price system rather than governmental allocations and rationing to meet the energy crisis.

Gramm, W. Philip. "The Energy Crisis in Perspective." *Wall Street Journal,* November 30, 1973.

Points out that the energy problem is nothing new and that if the price system were allowed to operate, forces would be set in motion that would solve the problem.

Hall, Robert E. and Pindyck, Robert S. "The Conflicting Goals of National Energy Policy." *The Public Interest,* no. 47, Spring 1977, pp. 3–15.

Points out inconsistencies in federal energy policies, analyzes the effects of the "entitlements" program, and draws conclusions with regard to what energy policies should and should not do.

Mitchell, Edward J. *U.S. Energy Policy: A Primer.* Washington, D.C.: American Enterprise Institute for Public Policy Research, June 1974.

An excellent survey of the economics of U.S. policies with respect to petroleum and natural gas. The argument is predominantly for a free market in the industry.

"What Price Energy." *Newsweek,* May 2, 1977, pp. 12–30.

A review of the energy program proposed by the Carter administration, along with comments on the program by Nobel prize winners Milton Friedman and Paul Samuelson.

"What U.S. Can Do to Tap Energy Sources Closer Home." *U.S. News and World Report,* December 3, 1973, pp. 25–26.

Catalogs the energy sources available to the United States in the face of the cutoff of oil shipments from Arab countries. These include crude oil reserves, shale oil reserves, natural gas, and nuclear energy in the United States, Canada, and Latin America.

Chapter 5

ECONOMICS OF CRIME AND ITS PREVENTION

CHECKLIST OF ECONOMIC CONCEPTS

Individually consumed goods and services beneficial to consumer
Collectively consumed goods and services '' to all
Semicollectively consumed goods and services benefits 1 but more
Social spillover benefits bene. to others fr. 1's consumption
Social spillover costs imposing on others bec. of 1's consumption
Economic costs Value of prev. as opposed to other goods+services
Marginal benefits Bene. gained from increasing 1 unit
Marginal costs Cost of increasing 1 unit
Equimarginal principle Correct level MC=MB
Alternative-cost principle
"Free rider" problem

5

Economics of crime and its prevention

How much is too much?

It seemed to Linda that somehow, somewhere, things were all mixed up. The police had swarmed in on the students in her apartment last night, and three of her friends were in jail on pot possession charges. Fortunately, Linda was clean. Sure, the three who were arrested were smoking the stuff, but whom were they hurting? It was a relatively quiet, peaceful gathering. They listened to a few records that may have been a little loud for the neighbors, but mostly there was just talk. A little pot never hurt anyone—why do people get all uptight about it? Everyone knows that smoking pot, if it leads to any problems at all, has much less serious consequences than the use of alcohol, and in most places it is no crime to drink.

Why don't the police go after the real criminals and leave the young people alone? Why don't they spend their time fruitfully, tracking down and apprehending murderers, rapists, muggers, thieves, and the like? Just last week two men had followed her friend, Jim, into his apartment house and pulled a gun on him, taking his watch and the little bit of money he had in his billfold. Why don't law enforcement officials do something about such serious crime problems as the Mafia and other organized crime? It seemed to Linda that the police spend their time picking on young people and let the real criminals get by with—murder.

Criminal activities create an important set of social problems in the United States. They affect our general well-being by threatening the loss of money and property and generating concern for physical safety. Yet, for most of us, crime is something we read about in the papers—something which usually affects other people but always has the potential of affecting us. We seldom look at crime from a systematic analytical point of view, but if we are to do anything about the problem this is what we must do.

WHAT IS CRIME?

It seems almost silly to raise such a question as "What is crime?" However, if we are to look at crime analytically, we must have a solid base from which to work. The concept of what constitutes criminal activity is often not clear in the mind of any one person and may be ambiguous from one person to another. Some people think of crime in terms of that which is immoral; others think of it in terms of that which is illegal.

Immorality?

Are immoral acts criminal? The answer to this question is not easy. In the first place, many acts do not fall clearly into a moral-immoral classification. In modern societies some acts are generally considered to be immoral—murder, and most kinds of theft, for example. But there are many other acts, the morality of which depends upon what group in the society is evaluating them. Examples include pot smoking, driking alcoholic beverages, betting on horse races, homosexual activities, and many more. It appears that morality versus immorality does not provide a clear basis for defining whether or not specific acts are criminal.

Illegality?

A definition that seems to be meaningful and useful analytically is that a criminal act is one the society (or one of its subdivisions) has decided it is better off without and which it has therefore made illegal through laws, ordinances, and the like. It may or may not be immoral. For example, is it immoral to inadvertently drive 30 miles an hour along a deserted street that is posted for 20 miles an hour, or to accidentally run a stop sign at an intersection where there are no other cars, or to catch a fish in a mountain stream before you have obtained a fishing license? As you quickly discover when you are caught, these acts may very well be criminal in nature. On the other hand, if gambling, drinking, and prostitution are immoral, there are many places where they are not illegal and are, therefore, not criminal.

Acts that are illegal or criminal are designated as such by legislative bodies, such as city councils, state legislatures, and Congress. There are a number of reasons for making certain acts illegal. Some acts may indeed be offensive to the moral standards of a majority of legislators and their constituents. Murder, rape, and theft are cases in point. Others may lead to consequences (in the minds of legislators, at least) of which the doer is ignorant. The consumption of alcohol, or pot, or heroin thus may be made illegal because legislators fear that those who try them may become addicted, with disastrous consequences to themselves. Still other acts are designated illegal in order to prevent chaos or to promote order—violation of established traffic rules, for example. Further, some acts may carry no taint of immorality but may be made illegal because they are considered contrary to the general welfare of the society. Acts of pollution like burning your trash within the city limits illustrate the point.

Classification of criminal acts

Criminal acts are usually classified as (1) violent crimes, (2) crimes against property, (3) traffic in illegal goods and services, and (4) other crimes. Violent crimes are crimes against persons. They include murder, rape, aggravated assault, and armed robbery. Crimes against property include such things as fraud, burglary, theft, embezzlement, forgery, arson, vandalism, and the like. Traffic in illegal goods and services is made up of dealings in such things as gambling, narcotics, loansharking, prostitution, and alcohol. The "other crimes" classification is, of course, a catchall for everything from nonpayment of alimony to speeding.

Crime is generally thought to be a very serious problem in the United States. In every large city and in many small ones people are reluctant to go out at night for fear of being robbed, raped, beaten, or even murdered. And there is no evidence of improvement in the situation. From 1960 to 1970 the overall crime rate—the number of reported offenses per 100,000 persons—*increased* at an average annual rate of 8 percent. From 1970 to 1974 the average annual rate of increase was 5 percent. From 1974 to 1975 the rate of increase was 9 percent. Violent crime alone rose at an annual rate of 9 percent from 1960 to 1970, at an annual rate of 6 percent from 1970 to 1974; and at an annual rate of 4 percent from 1974 to 1975.[1]

Causes of crime

Criminal activity stems from many sources. Some are economic in nature and others are not. Different kinds of crime may have their roots in different sources. The problem of the causes of crime is a hard one to attack—like asking what causes a society to be what it is. We can, however, identify some of the broad factors that tend to result in criminal activities.

[1] U.S. Department of Commerce, Bureau of the Census, *Statistical Abstract of the United States, 1976,* p. 153.

Unrestrained passions or emotions are an important factor in many violent crimes. Most murders, for example, result from deep-seated, intense feelings of some sort between the murderer and the victim. The victim may be a wife, a husband, a girlfriend, or the guy who cheats in a poker game. The level of the murderer's emotion pushes aside the constraints of conscience and law that the society has established. Murders in which the victim is unknown to the murderer are the least common type.

When poverty is coupled with *high levels of economic and social aspirations,* the stage is set for criminal activities—particularly robbery and dealing in illegal goods and services. People who are thwarted in obtaining desired social and economic goals legally may seek to obtain them illegally. In addition, the costs of being apprehended and convicted of a crime are less for those living in poverty than for persons from middle and upper income groups. The latter certainly have more to lose in terms of income —if not in terms of social status. Thus we find that ghettos of large cities produce a disproportionate share of criminals. The incidence of robbery and traffic in illegal goods tends to be high among minority groups who feel the burden of both economic and social discrimination.

The standards of social values of a society are an important determinant of criminal activities. Society's attitudes toward cheating on one's income tax, stealing from one's employer, embezzlement, wiretapping and other interferences with the right to privacy help set the stage for acts which may be considered criminal. The real tragedy of Watergate was not so much what the bugging did to the Democrats, but the low level of social values shown to be held by people in positions of public trust.

THE COSTS OF CRIME

That crime has economic costs is certain. The measurement of those costs, however, is at the present time very inaccurate. In the first place, many criminal activities go unreported. In the second place, an accurate dollar value cannot be attached to the cost of those crimes that do occur. Nevertheless, estimates of the costs of crime are necessary if decision making regarding the level of crime prevention activities is to have any degree of economic soundness. The better the estimates, the better the decisions that can be made.

The basis of measuring the cost of crime is the alternative-cost principle. The net economic cost of crime to the society is thus the difference between what gross national product would be if there were neither criminal nor crime prevention activities and what GNP currently is, given present criminal and crime prevention activities.

Current reports on crime are concerned solely with the number of crimes committed and not with dollar estimates of their costs. To estimate correctly the cost of violent crime we would start with the loss of earnings (or value of production services rendered) of the victims and of those close to the victims. Obvious costs of crimes against property are the values of property destroyed or damaged. It is not at all clear that there is a comparable direct cost to the society of traffic in illegal goods and services— the production and sale of these *adds to* the well being of their consumers and may at the same time impose offsetting spillover costs on the society as a whole. Additional costs of the whole range of criminal activities consist of the costs of prevention, apprehension, and correction, since resources used for these purposes could have been used to produce alternative goods and services valuable to consumers. Many items thought to be costs are really transfers of purchasing power to the perpetrators of the crimes from their victims. In the case of theft, the thief is made better off at the same time that the person from whom the item is stolen is made worse off. Reprehensible as theft may be, it is difficult to conclude that it represents a large net economic cost to society. It may, however, represent sizable costs to the individual victims.

Criminal activities in the aggregate lower GNP below what it would be without them. *Crime prevention activities* should, if effective, raise GNP above the level that would occur in their absence. Crime prevention activities can thus be considered an economic good or service, since GNP is higher with them than it would be without them. We can think of crime prevention activities as using productive resources—labor and capital— going into the production process. The costs of these services are measured by applying the alternative-cost principle: the costs of resources used in crime prevention are equal to the value these resources would have had in their best alternative uses. Present data on the expenditures of federal, state, and local governments for law enforcement and justice show an estimated figure of $14,954 million for 1974.[2]

In summary, satisfactory measures of the costs of crime in terms of GNP lost because of it have not yet been devised. The costs of crime prevention activities can be estimated with a fair degree of accuracy; however, these leave out of account a substantial part of the total costs of crime.

INDIVIDUALLY AND COLLECTIVELY CONSUMED GOODS

Would a 5 percent increase in the police force of your city be worth anything to you personally? Would an increase or a decrease in the number of patrol cars on the city's streets affect you directly? Would it benefit

---

[2] Ibid., p. 164.

you if there were an increase or decrease in the number of courts and judges in the system of justice? Your answers to these questions will be either "No," "I don't know," or "Possibly."

Such questions lead us logically to a useful threefold classification of the economy's goods and services. The first includes those that are *individually consumed*. The second includes those that are *collectively consumed*. The third is made up of *semicollectively consumed* goods and services.

Individually consumed goods

The concept of individually consumed goods and services is straightforward. It includes those that directly benefit the person who consumes them. Much of what we consume is of this nature—hamburgers, suntan lotion, pencils, and the like. The person doing the consuming is able to identify the benefits received. For example, eating a hamburger gives pleasure to the eater and reduces hunger pangs.

Collectively consumed goods

Collectively consumed goods and services lie at the opposite pole from those that are individually consumed; in this case, the individual is not able to isolate or identify a specific personal benefit. Consider national defense services. What part of the total defense services provided by the economy can you identify as being consumed by you, and what is your estimate of the resulting increase in your well-being? Services like this contribute to the welfare of the group to which we belong, but it is not possible to pick out the part of the benefit that accrues specifically to any one person. An additional characteristic of a collectively consumed good is that once it is provided no individual can be excluded from its benefits. Can the government exclude you from the benefits of national defense?

Many kinds of services produced and consumed by a society are collectively consumed. They include national defense, crime prevention, space exploration, some aspects of public health, and most antipollution measures.

Semicollectively consumed goods

Semicollectively consumed goods and services yield identifiable benefits to the one who consumes them, but their consumption by one person yields spillover benefits to other persons. My neighbors' consumption of the various items that lead to beautiful landscaping on their property benefits me as well as them. When other people in a democratic society consume the services of primary education—learn to read, write, and do arithmetic—they benefit directly and I benefit, too, because a literate population improves the functioning of the democratic processes. When other people purchase sufficient medical care to avoid epidemics, I benefit from their purchase of health care.

A great many items that people consume and which yield direct benefits to them also yield benefits to others as the consumption occurs. These benefits to persons other than the direct consumers were identified in the last chapter as *social spillover benefits*. We also noted that the consumption of some semicollectively consumed goods may yield *spillover costs* to persons other than the direct consumers. Cigarette smoking in a classroom in which there are nonsmokers may be a case in point. So may onion or garlic eating.

The "free rider" problem

A society may have difficulty in getting collectively consumed goods produced because of a tendency for some of the benefactors of the goods to be "*free riders*." The nature of the free rider problem can be illustrated by an example from the Old West. On the plains of Oklahoma, Texas, Kansas, and other frontier cattle-raising states, cattle rustling posed a serious problem. In order to deal effectively with the problem in one area (say, the Dodge City environs), it was advantageous for the cattle raisers of the area to band together. They organized a vigilante group of sufficient size to make rustling in the area an exceedingly dangerous business—as a few who were caught and hanged would have testified, if they had been able. All the cattle raisers of the area contributed to the cost of organizing and maintaining the vigilante group.

As the problem was brought under control, however, it became difficult to meet the costs of holding the vigilante group together. Any one rancher was inclined to think that if the others maintained the group they could not keep the one from benefiting from its activities. If rustlers were afraid to operate in the area *everyone* benefited, even those who did not help pay the costs. Each rancher therefore had an incentive to withdraw support from the group and to become a "free rider," since no producer, even one who did not pay a part of the costs of protection it provided, could be excluded from its benefits.

Government production of collectively consumed items

Historically, groups of people have found that in banding together they can do things collectively that they are not able to do as individuals. One of the first things discovered was that the group provides better protection from outsiders than individuals can provide on their own. They also found that group action is well suited to protecting the members of the group from predators in their midst.

Group action on a voluntary basis is technically possible, of course. The vigilante group of the Old West provides an excellent example. But voluntary associations to provide collectively consumed goods have a tendency to fall apart because of the incentives that induce some people to become free riders and because free riders cannot be excluded from the benefits of the good. Thus the voluntary association is a tenuous mechanism for this purpose.

Supplanting the voluntary association with the coercive association that we call *government* can effectively remedy the free rider problem. A coercive governmental unit (and the power of coercion is an essential feature of government) simply requires that all who receive the benefits of a collectively consumed good or the service it provides should pay appropriate taxes for it. Thus the provision of national defense, crime prevention, pollution prevention, and other collectively consumed goods and services become a government function. These items are often referred to as *public goods*.

Most modern governments do not confine their production of goods and services to collectively consumed or public goods. Name any good or service, and there will probably be a government somewhere that produces it. A major difference between a private enterprise economic system and a socialistic economic system is that the government of the latter is responsible for the production of individually consumed as well as collectively consumed and semicollectively consumed items. The government of the former will leave the bulk of individually consumed goods to private business, although it may play a relatively important role in the provision of such semicollectively consumed goods as education.

THE ECONOMICS OF CRIME PREVENTION ACTIVITIES

The "correct" level

What is the appropriate level of expenditures on crime prevention activities by any governmental unit? Is a $15- to $16-billion level more or less "correct" for the United States as a whole? The same question can be asked appropriately about any category of government activity and expenditure. To find the answer, *cost-benefit analysis* is used. In this type of analysis, estimates are made of the benefits of the activity, its costs are determined, and we look for the level at which the costs of an increase in the activity begin to exceed the benefits of that increase.

The framework for such a problem is set up in Table 5–1. Suppose the

TABLE 5-1
Estimated benefits and costs of crime prevention, typical U.S. community

(1) Units of crime prevention per year	(2) Total benefits	(3) Marginal benefits	(4) Total costs	(5) Marginal costs	(6) Total net benefits
1	$ 200,000	$200,000	$ 60,000	$60,000	$140,000
2	380,000	180,000	120,000	60,000	260,000
3	540,000	160,000	180,000	60,000	360,000
4	680,000	140,000	240,000	60,000	440,000
5	800,000	120,000	300,000	60,000	500,000
6	900,000	100,000	360,000	60,000	540,000
7	980,000	80,000	420,000	60,000	560,000
8	1,040,000	60,000	480,000	60,000	560,000
9	1,080,000	40,000	540,000	60,000	540,000
10	1,100,000	20,000	600,000	60,000	500,000

annual benefits and costs of crime prevention at various levels have been investigated thoroughly and the estimates have been recorded in columns 1, 2, and 4. A "unit" of crime prevention is a nebulous concept, a composite of police personnel, patrol cars, courthouses, judges' services, prison costs, and the like. The definition of physical units is avoided by using arbitrary $60,000 units of crime prevention, and it is assumed that each $60,000 chunk is spent in the best possible way.

The money expense of crime prevention to the community is met by levying taxes. The *economic cost* is the value of the goods and services that resources used in crime prevention activities could have produced if they had not been drawn into crime prevention. The *benefits* of crime prevention are the community's best estimates of how much better off the suppression of crime will make them—the value of the extra days they can work as a result of *not* being raped, maimed, or murdered, plus the value of property *not* destroyed or stolen, plus the value of the greater personal security they feel, and so on. Obviously, the benefits will be much more difficult to estimate than the costs. In fact, the most difficult and vexing part of the problem is the estimation of the benefits that ensue from various kinds of crime prevention activities.

If the benefits and costs are known, and we assume in Table 5-1 that they are, determination of the correct level of crime prevention is relatively simple. Consider first whether there should be no crime prevention at all or whether one unit would be worthwhile. One unit of prevention yields benefits to the community of $200,000—keeps $200,000 worth of GNP from being destroyed by criminal activities—and it would cost them only $60,000 to obtain it. Obviously, this is better than no prevention; the net benefits (total benefits minus total costs) are $140,000.

Now consider two units of prevention versus one unit. The total benefits yielded are $380,000. But note that the increase in total benefits yielded in moving from one to two units is $180,000, somewhat less than the increase in total benefits resulting from a movement from zero to one unit. The increase in total benefits resulting from a one-unit increase in the amount of crime prevention is called the *marginal benefit* of crime prevention. As the number of units of prevention is increased, the marginal benefits would be expected to decline, because each one-unit increase would be used to suppress the most serious crimes outstanding. The more units of prevention used, the less serious the crimes to which they are applied, and, therefore, the less the increase in the benefits from each one-unit increase in prevention.

It pays the community to move from the one-unit level to the two-unit level of prevention because the marginal benefits yielded by the second unit exceed the marginal costs of the increase. *Marginal costs* of crime prevention are defined in much the same way as marginal benefits—they are the increase in total costs resulting from a one-unit increase in prevention. Marginal costs of prevention are constant in the example because we are measuring units of prevention in terms of $60,000 chunks. Therefore, the total net benefits will be increased by $120,000 ($180,000 − $60,000) if the community increases the prevention level from one to two units. (Make sure you understand this before you go any further.)

Using the same kind of logic, it can be determined that it is worthwhile for the community to use a third, fourth, fifth, sixth, and seventh unit of crime prevention. For each of these increases, the marginal benefits are greater than the marginal costs—that is, each adds more to total benefits than it adds to total costs. Therefore, each brings about an increase in total net benefits. Total net benefits reach a maximum of $560,000 at the seven-unit level. If the level of prevention is raised to eight units, no harm is done. Marginal benefits equal marginal costs, and there is no change in total net benefits. But if the level is raised to nine units, total net benefits will fall to $540,000.

As citizens we *must* understand the logic underlying determination of the correct amount of government activity in crime prevention—or in anything else. It is very simple, very important, and usually overlooked. If a small increase in the level of an activity yields additional benefits worth more than the additional costs of providing it, it should be expanded. On the other hand, if its marginal benefits are less than its marginal costs, it should be contracted. It follows that the correct level is that at which marginal benefits are equal to marginal costs. (Study Table 5–1 until you understand this thoroughly.)

The foregoing economic analysis suggests something about dealing with increasing crime rates. If, when crime prevention activities are stepped up, the cost of an increase in prevention is less than the benefits it realizes, we ought to be engaged in more crime prevention activities. We are irrational if we do not. However, if a unit of prevention is not worth to us what it costs, then it is irrational to attempt to suppress crime at present levels of crime prevention activities. Complete suppression of crime is never logical from the point of view of economics. There will be some level of crime prevention at which the benefits of an additional unit of prevention are simply not worth what they cost. (What about ten units of prevention in Table 5–1?)

The *economic* analysis developed above, as important as it is, fails to touch on a very large part of the problems of crime. It does not consider, for example, such questions as: What gives rise to crime in the first place? What causes children to become delinquent and to grow up as criminals? What causes adults to turn to criminal activities? Can criminals be rehabilitated, or should they simply be punished? These and many other questions are *psychological, social,* and even *political* in nature. Given the social milieu in which crime takes place, however, economic analysis is valuable in determining the level at which prevention activities should be pursued.

Allocation of the crime prevention budget

Economic analysis also has something to contribute in determining the efficiency of crime prevention activities. There are several facets to a well-balanced governmental crime prevention program. Ideally, it should deter people from engaging in criminal activities. Failing in this—as it surely will—it must first *detect and apprehend* those engaging in criminal activities. This is primarily a police function. To *determine the guilt or innocence* of those charged with criminal acts, the legal system utilizes courts, attorneys, judges, and juries. Those convicted are fined and/or put in prison to *rehabilitate and/or punish* them. Reference to the prison system as a corrections system indicates hope that those incarcerated will somehow be rehabilitated and deterred from engaging in further criminal activities. In practice, the sentences of those convicted of crimes usually take on at least some aspects of punishment.

How much of a governmental unit's crime prevention budget should be allocated to police departments? How much for courts, judges, and prosecutors? How much for corrections, rehabilitation, and punishment? Detection and apprehension of persons thought to be committing criminal acts is of little value unless there are adequate court facilities for trying them. Trying persons apprehended and sentencing those convicted presupposes an adequate system of corrections or punishment. No one facet of crime prevention can contribute efficiently unless the others are there to back it up.

The correct or most efficient mix of the different facets of crime prevention is determined logically by what economists call the *equimarginal principle*. The crime budget should be allocated among police, courts, and corrections so that the last dollar spent on any one facet yields the same addition to the benefits of crime prevention as the last dollar spent on the others. Another way of saying this is that the budget should be allocated so that the marginal benefits from a dollar's worth of police efforts will equal the marginal benefits of a dollar's worth of judicial effort and a dollar's worth of corrective effort in the overall suppression of crime.

As an example, suppose that the crime prevention system is overloaded in the area of detection and apprehension. The courts cannot handle all those who are being arrested, so many of them must be set free without trial or in the case of plea bargaining, sentenced for a lesser crime than that committed. The mere fact of arrest will have some crime-deterring effects, but they will be much less than would be the case if there were adequate court facilities to try the persons apprehended.

The contribution to crime prevention of an additional dollar's worth of police activity at this point is low. On the other hand, an expansion of court facilities would increase the likelihood of trial and conviction of those apprehended. We would expect the crime-deterring effect of a dollar's worth of such an expansion to be greater than that of a dollar spent on detection, apprehension, and subsequent freeing of those apprehended. Suppose that taking a dollar away from police work brings about enough of a crime increase to cause a 75-cent loss to the community. Now suppose that if court activity were increased by one dollar's worth, this increased activity will deter criminal activity enough to make the community better off by $3. Under these circumstances, the community will experience a net gain of $2.25 by a transfer of a dollar from police activities to court activities. Such net gains are possible for any $1 transfer among police activities, court activities, and corrections activities when the marginal benefits of a dollar spent on one are less than the marginal benefits of a dollar spent on either of the others. No further gains are possible when the crime prevention budget is so allocated that the marginal benefits of a dollar spent on any one activity equal the marginal benefits of a dollar spent on any of the other activities.

THE ECONOMICS OF LEGALIZING ILLEGAL ACTIVITIES

Economic analysis also provides information that is useful in the determination of whether or not certain activities should be considered illegal. There has been much controversy historically over legalization of the purchase, sale, and consumption of alcohol. More recently, drugs have come into the picture—especially marijuana. So has abortion. Although prostitution is illegal in most parts of the United States, legalization of the practice comes up for discussion periodically. Various forms of gambling also figure in arguments as to what should and what should not be illegal.

The purchase and sale of abortions provide an excellent example of the contributions that economic analysis can make in a controversy over whether or not an activity should be legal. Most of the states of the United States have had laws making abortions illegal, many of which were struck down by a Supreme Court decision. The underlying basis of these laws is morality. Antiabortionists contend that abortion destroys a human life. Proabortionists argue that a woman should be free to make the choice of whether she wants to have a baby, and the passing of an unborn fetus is not equivalent to destroying a human life. The central disagreement is over the point at which a fertilized egg becomes a human being. It must be recognized at the outset that economics can tell us nothing about the moral issues involved. It can, however, provide important information regarding the conditions of purchase and sale when the activity is illegal, as compared with when it is legal.

In Figure 5–1, suppose that D_1D_1 and S_1S_1 represent the demand curve and the supply curve for abortions when this type of medical service is illegal. The fact that abortions are illegal does not drive all potential customers out of the market, but it does suppress the number who would buy abortions at each possible price. Neither does it completely eliminate the supply, but it does affect the segment of the medical profession from which the supply comes. Part of it is rendered by poorly trained personnel of the midwife or unscrupulous druggist variety. Part of it comes from medical doctors who are in difficulty with their profession for one reason or another and who are more or less barred from practicing medicine legally. Almost all of the illegal abortions must be performed with inferior medical facilities —for example, the home "office" of the illegal practitioner—under circumstances that are likely to be unsanitary.

Prices are likely to be very high as compared with other comparable medical services for two reasons: (1) because of the limited quantities of facilities and abortionists available, and (2) in order to compensate the abortionist for the risk of being caught and prosecuted. An interesting side effect is that abortions will be much more readily available to the rich, for whom the high price is less important, than for the poor, who are priced out of the market. The price of an illegal abortion in Figure 5–1 is p_1, and the quantity performed is A_1.

Now suppose that abortions become legal. There will be some increase in demand, say to D_2D_2, since the taint of illegality is removed. There will, of course, still be moral constraints that prevent some women from aborting unwanted babies. The effects on supply are likely to be more dramatic. Abortions can now be performed in hospitals under controlled sanitary conditions, and in medical terms they are no big deal. They will be performed by doctors whose competency for this operation is as great as for

FIGURE 5–1
Economic effects of legalizing abortions

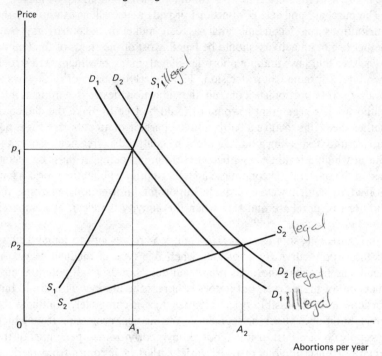

Abortions per year

When abortions are illegal, the demand and supply curves are D_1D_1 and S_1S_1, respectively. Legalization will increase demand to some extent, shifting the demand curve to some position such as D_2D_2. Supply is likely to be greatly increased, as shown by the shift of the curve from S_1S_1 to S_2S_2. The quantity exchanged rises from A_1 to A_2 and the price falls from p_1 to p_2.

any other. The risk of being caught and prosecuted has been removed and no longer enters into the cost picture.

The costs of supplying abortions now are the alternative amounts that physicians could earn from operations of similar difficulty and duration. The cost spread for different quantities supplied will not be great—that is, quantity supplied will be very responsive to changes in the price. The price of legal abortions will be p_2, and the quantity purchased will be A_2.

To summarize the economic effects of legalizing abortions, first, the supply of the product increases. Second, there is also an increase in demand, but it is not as great as the supply increase. Third, the quantity exchanged is greater, and the price is lower. Fourth, the service becomes as accessible to the poor as any comparable operation. Fifth, there is an improvement in the quality of the product.

The economic analysis of legal versus illegal traffic in other goods and services is virtually the same as it is for abortions. When the purchase, sale, and consumption of an item—be it alcohol, prostitution, or marijuana—are made illegal, it can be expected that there will be a decrease in quantity exchanged, a rise in price, and a deterioration in the quality of the product.

SUMMARY

Criminal activities are defined as activities that are illegal. They may or may not be immoral. They are usually classified as (1) crimes against persons, (2) crimes against property, (3) traffic in illegal goods and services, and (4) other crimes.

Crime constitutes a serious problem in the United States; crime rates generally have been increasing over the years. Some of the underlying causes of crime are (1) unrestrained passions or emotions, (2) poverty coupled with high levels of economic and social aspirations, and (3) low standards of social values.

Good information on the costs of crime are not available because many criminal activities go unreported and because it is difficult to place dollar values on the results of some kinds of these activities. Some reported "costs" of crime are not really economic costs to the society as a whole but are transfers of income from the victim of the crime to its perpetrator.

In an economic analysis of crime it is useful to classify goods and services into three categories: (1) individually consumed, (2) collectively consumed, and (3) semicollectively consumed items. Governments, with their coercive powers, are in a unique position to produce such collectively consumed items as crime prevention. Consequently, collectively consumed services of this type are usually provided by governments.

Cost-benefit analysis can be used to advantage in determining the level of crime prevention activities in a society. The costs of crime prevention can be easily determined, but the benefits—many of which are intangible—are hard to estimate. Conceptually, they are the difference between what GNP would be *with* crime prevention and what it would be *without* such activities. On the basis of the best estimates that can be made, the society should seek that level of crime prevention at which the total net benefits are greatest. This will be the level at which the marginal benefits of crime prevention are equal to its marginal costs.

Once the level of the government's crime prevention budget is determined, it should be efficiently allocated among the different facets of crime prevention activities. These include detection and apprehension of violators, determination of their guilt or innocence, and corrections. The equimarginal principle is appropriate to use for this purpose. The budget should be allocated so that the marginal benefits from a dollar's worth of any one of the foregoing facets are equal to the marginal benefits from a dollar's worth of each of the others.

From time to time certain kinds of activities—usually purchase and sale of items—that have been illegal are made legal. The economic result usually is that greater quantities of the legalized item will be exchanged at a lower price, the item becomes generally more available to the poor, and there will be an improvement in the quality of the product.

Economic analysis alone will not solve crime problems, but it can be very useful in making logical attacks on them.

SUPPLEMENTARY READINGS

Federal Bureau of Investigation. *Uniform Crime Reports for the United States.* Washington, D.C.: Government Printing Office.

> Sums up all reported crimes in the United States on an annual basis, providing the most complete statistical data available on kinds of crime and who commits them. It also provides trend data for key types of crime statistics. There is very little analysis of the data.

McKenzie, Richard B., and Tullock, Gordon. "Crime and Dishonesty." *The New World of Economics.* Homewood, Ill.: Richard D. Irwin, Inc., 1975, pp. 129–80.

> An analysis of the costs and benefits of crime to the criminal, and of costs to the victims of crime and to the society. The sociology of crime is compared with the economics of crime. Traffic violations, tax evasion, lying, and cheating are also discussed.

North, Douglass C., and Miller, Roger L. "The Economics of Crime Prevention." *The Economics of Public Issues.* 2d ed., chap. 22. New York: Harper & Row, 1973.

> Discusses the "correct" allocation of a governmental unit's crime prevention budget among the various facets of a balanced crime prevention program.

President's Commission on Law Enforcement and Administration of Justice. *Crime and Its Impact—An Assessment.* Washington, D.C.: Government Printing Office, 1967.

> This Task Force Report pulls together and analyzes existing data on the extent of and trends in criminal activities. Of particular interest for our purposes is chapter 3, "The Economic Impact of Crime." While the report does much with the data available, the need for more complete data reporting and for additional systematic analysis of the economic impact of crime becomes abundantly clear.

Rogers, A. J., III. *The Economics of Crime.* Hinsdale, Ill.: Dryden Press, 1973.

> A good elementary exposition of the economic motivations for criminal activities and the economic consequences of those activities. Contains very little on the economics of crime prevention.

Chapter 6

POLLUTION PROBLEMS

CHECKLIST OF ECONOMIC CONCEPTS

Collectively consumed goods and services *Causes pollution*
Demand
Supply
Alternative-cost principle *what resources cld. earn in other empl.*
Production possibilities curve
Cost-benefit analysis
Marginal cost
Marginal benefit
Externalities
Spillover costs
Private cost
Economic efficiency

6

Pollution problems

Must we foul our own nests?

The high-pitched whistle of departing jets was deafening as John Q. Smith stepped outside the terminal building and walked toward the parking lot. He located his three-year-old car, got it started, paid the parking fee, and wheeled out onto the congested freeway, adding his own small carbon monoxide and hydrocarbon contributions to the pall that hung over the city. On his left the Contaminated Steel Company was belching noxious streams of dense smoke into the heavy air, ably assisted by the nearby coal-burning power and light plant. Where the freeway joined the river's edge, a pulp and paper mill could be seen spewing its wastes into the river. He held his breath as long as he could along the two-mile stretch of road adjoining the stockyards. Then with a sigh of relief he swerved off the freeway and turned down the country road that would take him home. Once out of sight of human habitat, he stopped the car and relieved himself at the side of the road, noting as he did so the accumulating litter of beer cans, paper, and cellophane bags on the shoulder of the road and in the ditch.

John Q.'s house was located on a lake. Since a group of industrial plants had been built along the lakeshore several miles away, it was not as pleasant to swim and water-ski in the lake as it had been previously. The fishing didn't seem to be as good, either. Recently he had been having problems with a backed-up sewer, and he wondered as he turned in the driveway if the plumber had been there to clean out the sewer line that reached from the house to the lake. John Q. had grown up in the great outdoors (this is

139

why he had built the house on the lake), and he was much concerned about its deterioration.

Most of us, like John Q. Smith, are concerned about environmental problems, but we are not quite sure what we can do about them. As individuals, we seem to believe that we can do little. In fact, we are likely to add to the problems by thinking that our own bit of pollution is just a drop in the bucket.

Public reaction to pollution varies a great deal. At one extreme are the amateur environmentalists, or nature-lovers, who object to everything that decreases the purity of the air and water, or that mars the natural beauty of the landscape. At the other extreme are those who seem not to value at all clean air, water, and natural beauty. Most of us are scattered along the line between these two extremes.

A sensible attack on pollution problems requires the use of economic analysis along with inputs from other disciplines—especially the natural sciences. In particular, economic analysis may help us (1) determine why and under what circumstances economic units pollute; (2) determine the extent to which pollution control should be exercised; and (3) evaluate alternative antipollution activities of the government.

WHAT IS POLLUTION?

We will not make much progress in an economic analysis of pollution until we are familiar with both the nature of the environment in which we live and what it is that constitutes pollution of that environment. We shall consider these two concepts in turn.

The environment and its services

The environment is easily defined. It consists of the air, water, and land around us. These provide us with a variety of important services.

First, the environment provides a *habitat* or surroundings in which both plant and animal life can survive. Temperature ranges on the planet are neither too hot nor too cold for survival. The air, the water, and the land contain the elements needed to sustain living matter as we know it.

Second, the environment contains *resources* that are usable in the production of goods and services. These include minerals such as petroleum, coal, and a wide assortment of ores that can be processed into metals and metal alloys. They include soil properties and plant life supported by the soil. Resources include the plant and animal life yielded by water as well as the inherent properties of water used directly in production processes. They also include oxygen and nitrogen, along with other elements and properties found in the atmosphere.

Third, the environment furnishes many *amenities* that make life more enjoyable. It opens up possibilities of a walk along a river, through an alfalfa field, or in a rose garden. It provides an area in which you can fly kites or have picnics, a place to take your girlfriend or your boyfriend—or even your husband or your wife. You can sit in it and enjoy the sunset. Or, if you so desire, you can paint it or photograph it.

The services of the environment are used by production units and household units as they engage in activities of various kinds. Production units lay heavy claims on the environment's resources, but they may also make use of its habitat and amenity characteristics.

As production units engage in the process of transforming raw and semifinished materials into goods and services that will satisfy human wants, there are at least three ways in which the environment can be affected. First, some of the environment's stocks of exhaustible resources may be diminished. These include coal, petroleum, and many mineral deposits. Second, it is called upon for replaceable resources like timber, grassland, oxygen, and nitrogen. Third, it is used as a place to dispose of the wastes of the production and consumption processes—as a gigantic garbage disposal.

Recycling of wastes and the concept of pollution

The pollution problem arises primarily from the use of the environment by producers and consumers as a dumping ground for wastes. We litter the countryside with cans, paper, and the other residues of consumption and production. We dump the emissions from our automobiles and factories into the atmosphere. We empty sewage and residue from production directly and indirectly into streams, rivers, and lakes.

As wastes from production and consumption are dumped into the environment, nature sets recycling processes in motion. Animal life uses oxygen, giving off carbon dioxide wastes. But plants use carbon dioxide, giving off oxygen wastes. Dead plants and animal life are attacked by chemical elements that decompose them, restoring to the soil elements that the living organisms had withdrawn from it. Living organisms frequently contribute to the decomposition process. Iron and steel objects rust and disintegrate over time. So does wood and other matter. Wastes that can be decomposed in air, water, and soil are said to be *biodegradable*. But there are some wastes that are not biodegradable. Aluminum containers like beer cans are a case in point.

Recycling—the transformation of wastes into raw materials that are again usable—require variable lengths of time, depending on what it is that is being recycled. It takes many years for a steel pipe to rust away. Wood varies a great deal in the time it takes for its complete disintegration. But many plant and animal products require only a very short time to decompose.

Pollution consists of loading the environment with wastes that are either not completely recycled, are not recycled fast enough, or are not recycled at all. It involves a diminution of the capacity of the environment to yield environmental services. Pollution occurs when recycling processes fail to prevent wastes from accumulating in the environment.

Common forms of pollution

Pollution is as old as civilization itself. Wherever people have congregated, their wastes have tended to pile up more rapidly than the forces of nature can digest them. As long as the world was sparsely populated and no permanent cities existed, no great problems were created. When the extent of pollution in one locale imposed costs on the people living there that outweighed the costs associated with moving, they simply moved away from it. Then, given time, natural recycling processes could in many cases take over and restore the excess wastes to usable form.

When towns and cities came into existence, pollution raised more serious problems. How could body wastes from humans and animals, as well as refuse from the daily round of living, be disposed of? Until fairly recent times it was not disposed of in many instances—levels of sanitation were unbelievably low, and levels of stench were unbelievably high. As the density of the world's population has increased and as it has become more difficult to move away from pollution problems, the human race has turned its attention more and more toward the development of control measures. But in order to control pollution, it must be identified as accurately as possible in its various forms.

Air pollution. In the processes of production and consumption, five major kinds of wastes are dumped into the atmosphere. Most are a result of combustion and have caused local problems for a long time. Since there are millions of cubic miles of atmosphere to absorb these wastes, however, air pollution has not caused great concern until the past few decades. These wastes are carbon monoxide, sulfur oxides, nitrogen oxides, hydrocarbons, and particulates.

Carbon monoxide, an odorless, colorless gas, makes the atmosphere a less hospitable habitat for animal life. In concentrated amounts, it causes dizziness, headaches, and nausea in humans. Exposure to a sufficiently high concentration—about 100 parts per 1 million parts of atmosphere—for a few hours can be fatal. About 64 percent of the carbon monoxide emissions into the atmosphere in the United States comes from automobiles, and another 12 percent comes from industrial sources of one kind or another.[1] The greatest concentrations of carbon monoxide occur in large cities. On New York City streets concentration levels as high as 13 parts per 1 million parts of atmosphere have been recorded.

Sulfur oxides constitute a second major source of atmospheric pollution. Where they are heavily concentrated, they cause damage to both plant and animal life. Oxides result largely from the combustion of fuel oils and coal. Consequently, high levels of concentration are most likely to occur where these are used for the generation of electricity and for residential heating.

A third atmospheric pollutant is *nitrogen oxides.* These can cause lung damage in human beings and may also retard plant growth. The main sources of the pollutant are automobiles and stationary combustion processes such as those used in generating electric power.

Hydrocarbons constitute a fourth kind of waste emitted into the air. At their present concentration levels no direct harmful effects have been attributed to them. However, they combine with nitrogen oxides and ultraviolet rays of the sun to form photochemical smog. The smog may produce breathing difficulties and eye irritation for human beings. In addition, it speeds up the oxidation processes to which paints and metals are subject, resulting in substantial damages to industrial plants and equipment. Over 50 percent of hydrocarbon emissions in the United States comes from automobiles, and the rest from other combustion processes.

A fifth air pollutant consists of a heterogeneous mixture of suspended solids and liquids called *particulates.* These are largely dust and ash, along with lead from automobile exhausts. The major source of particulates, however, is fuel combustion in stationary sources and in industrial processes. Open fires used to burn trash and garbage also make their contributions. Particulates serve to lower visibilities. Some, such as lead from automobile exhausts, may be directly harmful to human beings.

Water pollution. Water pollution is ordinarily measured in terms of the capacity of water to support aquatic life. This capacity depends upon (1) the level of dissolved oxygen in the water and (2) the presence of matters or materials injurious to plant and animal life.

The level of dissolved oxygen is built up through aeration of water and through the photosynthetic processes of plant life living in the water. It is destroyed by its use to decompose organic matter that occurs in or is dumped into the water. The oxygen needed for decomposition purposes is referred to as *biochemical oxygen demand,* or BOD. The level of dissolved oxygen available for supporting aquatic life, then, depends upon the bal-

---

[1] U.S. Department of Health, Education, and Welfare, National Air Pollution Control Administration, *Nationwide Inventory of Air Pollutant Emissions, 1968* (August 1971).

ance between aeration and photosynthesis on the one hand and BOD on the other.

The level of dissolved oxygen is affected by several factors. First, it tends to be higher the greater the amount of a given volume of water exposed to the atmosphere. In nature, fast-running streams, rapids, and waterfalls contribute to aeration. Artificial aeration is frequently accomplished by shooting streams of water through the air. Second, it tends to be higher the greater the amount of photosynthesis that occurs in the water. In some instances the amount of photosynthesis that occurs in aquatic plant life may be reduced by air pollution. In this way, air pollution may be a source of water pollution. Third, it tends to be higher the lower the temperature of the water—use of the water for cooling by firms such as steel mills, oil refineries, and electricity-generating plants raises the temperature of the water and lowers its capacity to hold dissolved oxygen. Fourth, organic wastes that create BOD come from both domestic and industrial sources, so the level of dissolved oxygen varies inversely with the amounts that are dumped. The decomposition of such wastes can be greatly facilitated and BOD can be correspondingly reduced by chemical treatment of such wastes before they are discharged into streams, rivers, lakes, or oceans.

The capacity of water to support aquatic life is reduced when various kinds of materials and matters are dumped into it. Among these are toxins which do not settle out of the water and are not easily broken down by biological means. Mercury is a toxin that has created problems of contamination in tuna and salmon. So are phenols, herbicides, and pesticides. There have been heated discussions in recent years over the propriety of using them in large quantities. Questions have been raised also as to whether the oceans should be used for the dumping of nuclear wastes and for undersea nuclear explosions.

Land pollution. Land pollution results from the dumping of a wide variety of wastes on the terrain and from tearing up the earth's surface through such activities as strip mining. Highways are littered with refuse thrown from passing automobiles. Junkyards grow as we scrap over 7 million automobiles per year, to say nothing of the prodigious amounts of other machinery and appliances that are retired from use. Garbage dumps and landfills grow as towns and cities dispose of the solid wastes they collect and accumulate. All of these reduce the capacity of the terrain to render environmental services.

The growing emphasis on coal as an energy source creates mounting concern over the effects of mining on the landscape. Strip mining has typically left unsightly blemishes on the countryside. Can and should the mined area be restored? In pit mining areas can and should steps be taken to make slag and rock piles more attractive esthetically?

ECONOMICS OF POLLUTION

No one likes pollution. Almost everyone would like to see something done about it. Toward this end we shall consider in this section the fundamental economics of the pollution problem. We shall examine the reasons why pollution occurs, analyze the effects of pollution on resource allocation, look at the costs of pollution control, and identify its benefits. We shall attempt to establish criteria for determining the appropriate level of control.

Why polluters pollute

Why is it that pollution occurs? What is there about environmental services that causes consumers and producers to use the environment as a free dumping ground? Ordinarily, pollution results from one or both of two basic factors: (1) the fact that no one has property rights or enforces them in the environment being polluted, and (2) the collectively consumed characteristics of the environment being polluted.

If no one owns a portion of the environment or if an owner cannot police it or have it policed, then it becomes possible for people to use a river, a lake, the air, or an area of land as a waste basket without being charged for doing so. Because no one owns the air above city streets and highways, automobile owners can dump combustion gases into it without paying for the privilege of doing so. Similarly, a paper mill can dump its wastes into the river without charge because no one owns the river. But even ownership of the environment may not be enough to keep pollution from occurring. How many times have you seen litter accumulate on a vacant lot, or junk dumped in a ditch in a pasture away from town, because the owner was not there to prevent the dumping?

In addition, many environmental services are collectively consumed or used. It is hard to single out and determine the value of the air that one person—or an automobile—uses. Similarly, it is often difficult to attach a value to the water deterioration caused by one industrial plant when thousands dump their wastes into a river. Would any one person be willing to pay someone *not* to take an action that would destroy a beautiful view across the countryside? When values cannot be placed on the amounts of environmental services used by any one person, it is difficult to induce people not to pollute by charging them for the right to do so.

Pollution and resource use

In the process of polluting the environment, polluters impose spillover costs on others. Polluters' costs are thus reduced below what they would be in the absence of pollution. Similarly, costs to others (nonpolluters) of using environmental services are greater than they would be if there were no pollution. Polluters, then, are induced to overuse environmental services at the expense of other users, and other users of the polluted environment are induced to underuse them. Thus, pollution involves inefficient use or misallocation of environmental services among those who use them.

Suppose, for example, that two industries are located along a riverbank. An industry producing paper is located upstream, using the river as a place to discharge its wastes. Downstream is a power-generating industry that requires large amounts of clean water for cooling purposes. If the paper industry were not there, the water from the river would be clean enough for the power industry to use. But since it is there—just upstream —the firms in the power industry must clean the water before using it.

Since the use of the river by one set of parties as a dumping place for wastes may reduce the value of the river's services to other users, a transfer of costs may be incurred by the dumping. If recycling of the dumped wastes occurs fast enough, or if the environment is large enough relative to the wastes dumped into it so that no one is injured by the dumping, no cost or pollution problems occur.

The use of the river for waste disposal by the paper industry decreases the value of the river's services for power production in the example, so cost transfers are involved in that dumping. In effect, the paper industry shifts some of its costs of production to the power industry. It is the power industry that must pay for cleaning the water, but it is the paper industry that makes it dirty.

Consider first the power industry situation if there were no pollution by the paper industry. In Figure 6–1, the demand curve for power is D_eD_e and the supply curve in the absence of pollution is S_eS_e. The equilibrium output is e and the equilibrium price is p_e per kilowatt hour. The cost of producing a kilowatt hour at output level e is also p_e.

Suppose, now, that the power industry must clean the water before using it. Since it must cover its costs, the price that it must receive in order to induce it to produce any specific quantity of electricity will be higher by an amount equal to the costs per kilowatt hour of cleaning the water. The supply curve is thus shifted upward by that amount—c_1f_1 or cf—to some position such as $S_{e_1}S_{e_1}$. If the output of the power industry were e_1 kilowatt hours, the price necessary to bring forth that output in the absence of pollution is e_1c_1. With pollution occurring, the necessary price is e_1f_1 or p_{e_1}, with c_1f_1 being the cost per kilowatt hour of cleaning the water. Similarly, for an output level of e, the required price in the absence of pollution is ec, with pollution it is ef, and the cost per kilowatt hour of cleaning is cf. So the

FIGURE 6–1

Effects of water pollution on water users

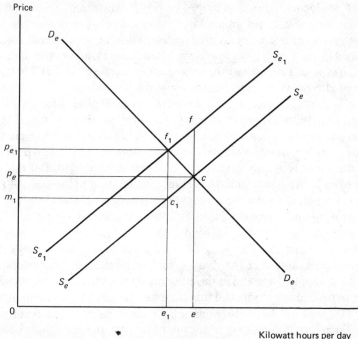

The demand curve for the output of the power industry is D_eD_e. Its supply curve, when it can obtain clean water for its use, is S_eS_e. Consequently, it will produce and sell e kilowatt hours per day. However, if a paper industry located upstream pollutes the water, costs of cleaning the water before using it move the supply curve upward (or to the left). The power industry accordingly reduces its output to e_1 and raises its price to p_{e_1}. The power industry—or its customers—thus pays the costs of cleaning the paper industry's wastes from the water.

supply of electricity is decreased by the pollution of the paper industry from what it would be in absence of pollution.

The effects of the decrease in the supply of electricity are a smaller quantity bought and sold, a higher price paid by consumers, and a lower return to producers than would be the case without the paper industry's pollution of the water. The quantity exchanged is reduced to e_1; the price paid by consumers goes up to p_{e_1}; and the return to producers after paying the cleaning costs for water decrease from p_e to m_1 per kilowatt hour. Thus, we see that the costs of pollution by the paper industry are borne by both the consumers and the producers of electricity.

In addition, the power industry is induced to underproduce. The supply curve $S_e S_e$ shows the alternative costs per kilowatt hour to the economy of producing various quantities of power when unpolluted water is used. For example, at output level e, it shows that ec dollars must be paid for the resources necessary to produce one kilowatt hour at this level of output. This is what those resources could earn in alternative employments; it is what they are worth in those other employments, and it represents the alternative costs to the economy of a kilowatt hour of electricity. Similarly, at output level e_1, the *alternative cost* of producing a kilowatt hour is $e_1 c_1$. With the paper industry polluting the river, however, consumers pay $e_1 f_1$ per kilowatt hour, which is more than the costs of production. Wherever consumers are willing to pay more for an item than it costs to produce it, it is usually desirable that output be expanded. But this will not happen in the power industry because, in addition to the costs of producing electricity, it must incur an additional outlay, $c_1 f_1$, to clean the water; that is, to undo what the paper industry has done.

The supply curve of the paper industry is increased by its access to the river for waste disposal. In Figure 6–2 let $S_r S_r$ be the paper industry's supply curve, assuming that the river is *not* available as a "free" dumping space. The supply curve shows the alternative prices that must be received by the paper industry to induce it to produce and sell various quantities of paper. To induce it to produce and sell r reams, the price per ream must be rg. To induce it to place r_1 reams on the market, the price must be $r_1 g_1$. Suppose now that the river is made available to the paper industry as a "free" dumping ground for wastes. The costs of producing a ream of paper are now reduced, and for an output level of r reams per day the price need not be higher than rh—if the cost saving per ream is hg. Similarly, for r_1 reams and a cost saving of $h_1 g_1$, the necessary price is $r_1 h_1$. The supply curve of paper is thus shifted to the right by the accessibility of the river as a "free" place to dispose of its wastes.

The same type of reasoning that tells us the power industry underproduces because of the paper industry's pollution also tells us the paper industry overproduces. In Figure 6–2, $D_r D_r$ is the demand curve for paper. If the paper industry were to bear the costs of its dumping of wastes by leaving clean water for the power plant, its supply curve would be $S_r S_r$; its price would be p_r; and its output level would be r. However, since it is able to use the river for waste disposal, its supply curve becomes $S_{r_1} S_{r_1}$, and it produces r_1 reams of paper per day selling it at a price of p_{r_1} per ream. The evidence of overproduction is that *alternative costs* per ream of paper exceed what consumers pay to get it. The alternative costs per ream are $r_1 g_1$. Of this amount, $r_1 h_1$ is the cost to the paper industry of resources other than waste disposal used in the production of a ream of paper at output level r_1, and $h_1 g_1$ is the cost of waste disposal that is transferred to the

FIGURE 6–2
Effects of water pollution on the polluter

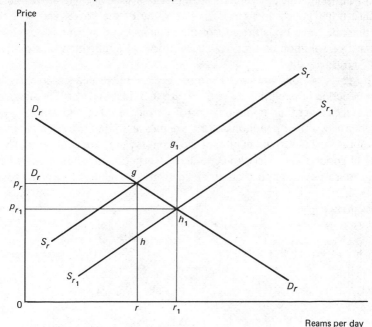

The demand curve for the output of the paper industry is D_rD_r. When it must clean its own wastes, its supply curve is S_rS_r, and its output level will be r reams of paper per day. If it can dump its wastes into the river, cleaning costs are saved, and its supply curve shifts downward (to the right). Its output will increase to r_1. It is able to shift a part of its costs to downstream users of the water.

power industry per ream of paper produced. This latter amount is not taken into account by the paper industry, so the true cost of a ream of paper exceeds what it is worth to consumers.

The costs of controlling pollution

Our reactions to pollution often take the form of, "Let's wipe it out." We maintain that we are entitled to clean air, clean water, and clean land. But how clean is clean? Cleanliness, like goodness, is a relative rather than an absolute quality. To determine the amount of pollution, if any, that should be allowed, the *costs* of keeping the environment clean must first be considered.

Pollution control is not costless. An industrial plant that scrubs or cleans its combustion gases before discharging them into the air must use re-

sources in the process. Labor and capital go into the making and operation of antipollution devices, and resources so used are not available to
produce other goods and services. The value of the goods and services
that must be given up is the cost of the plant's pollution control activities.
The cost of pollution control is a straightforward application of the alternative-cost principle.

The costs of pollution control to society are illustrated graphically by
the production possibilities curve of Figure 6–3. Dollars' worth of all goods
and services other than pollution control are measured on the vertical axis,
and dollars' worth of pollution control are measured on the horizontal axis.
At point A_1 the labor and capital of the economy are producing q_1 dollars'
worth of goods and services and c_1 dollars' worth of antipollution activities.
If still more pollution control—a cleaner environment—is desired, some

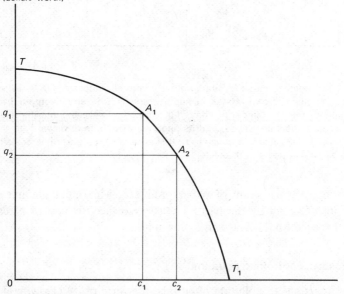

FIGURE 6–3
The costs of pollution control

The combinations of other goods and services and pollution control that the resources of the economy can support are shown by the
production possibilities curve TT_1. By giving up q_1T dollars' worth of
other goods and services, the economy can have c_1 dollars' worth
of pollution control, as shown at point A_1. If c_1c_2 more dollars' worth of
pollution control are to be obtained, the cost will be q_2q_1 additional
dollars' worth of other goods and services.

value of goods and services must be sacrificed. By giving up q_2q_1 dollars' worth of goods and services, pollution control can be increased by c_1c_2 dollars' worth. Thus, q_2q_1 dollars' worth of goods and services is the economic cost of an additional c_1c_2 dollars' worth of control or of a cleaner environment.

The benefits of controlling pollution

The benefits of pollution control consist of the increase in the well-being of the members of the society that results from pollution control activities. To measure the benefits of a pollution control activity, the value of the increase in well-being that it generates must be determined. Suppose, for example, that smog permeates a particular metropolitan area but that pollution control activities can reduce or perhaps even eliminate it. To determine the benefits of, say, a 50 percent reduction in smog, we can ask each individual living in the area how much such a reduction would be worth personally. By totaling all the replies we would arrive at the dollar value of the expected benefits.

The appropriate level of pollution control

Since pollution control—a cleaner environment—has costs, society must make a choice between the level of goods and services its resources will be used to produce and the degree of cleanliness of its environment. If the society experiences a level of pollution that is distasteful to it, it will be willing to sacrifice some quantities of goods and services for some level of pollution control.

The appropriate level of pollution control is determined by weighing its benefits against its costs. If the benefits of additional control—what cleaner air is worth to the citizens of the society—exceed the costs of the additional control, then pollution control should be increased. However, if the benefits of additional control are less than what it costs in terms of sacrificed goods and services, the additional control is unwarranted.

As an illustration, consider a community of 10,000 persons that is pervaded by a nauseating stench from an incinerator used to dispose of the community's garbage. Suppose that the odor can be completely eliminated by an expenditure of $100,000 per year for an alternate method of garbage disposal (carrying it away and burying it in a landfill outside the town) and that it can be partially controlled by using various combinations of burning and burying.

Suppose that the costs of different levels of partial control are those of columns 1, 2, and 3 of Table 6–1. By spending $10,000 on carrying and burying, the community can eliminate 10 percent of the stench; each addi-

TABLE 6–1
Annual costs and benefits of pollution control

(1) Pollution control or eliminated stench	(2) Total cost of control	(3) Marginal cost of control	(4) Per person marginal benefits of control	(5) Community marginal benefits of control	(6) Total benefits of control	(7) Net benefits of control
1st 10%	$ 10,000	$10,000	$10.00 ea.	$100,000	$100,000	$ 90,000
2d 10	20,000	10,000	8.00 ea.	80,000	180,000	160,000
3d 10	30,000	10,000	6.00 ea.	60,000	240,000	210,000
4th 10	40,000	10,000	4.00 ea.	40,000	280,000	240,000
5th 10	50,000	10,000	2.00 ea.	20,000	300,000	250,000
6th 10	60,000	10,000	1.60 ea.	16,000	316,000	256,000
7th 10	70,000	10,000	1.20 ea.	12,000	328,000	258,000
8th 10	80,000	10,000	0.80 ea.	8,000	336,000	256,000
9th 10	90,000	10,000	0.40 ea.	4,000	340,000	250,000
10th 10	100,000	10,000	0.20 ea.	1,000	341,000	241,000

tional $10,000 expenditure eliminates another 10 percent of the original total stench, until with a $100,000 expenditure the pollution is entirely eliminated.

Column 3 of Table 6–1 lists the *marginal costs* of pollution control. The concept is essentially the same as the marginal costs of crime prevention—it shows the change in total costs per unit change in the amount of pollution control. Since each increment in pollution control (an increment is defined as 10 percent of the control needed to eliminate the odor) adds $10,000 to the total cost of pollution control, the marginal cost of pollution control at each control level is $10,000.

The benefits of pollution control to the community are shown in columns 4, 5, and 6. Before any control is undertaken, each person in the community is asked for an opinion of what a 10 percent reduction in the stench is worth. Suppose each person indicates a willingness to pay $10 for it. We conclude that $100,000 measures the total benefits yielded by the first 10 percent reduction. Since the benefits exceed the costs by $90,000, the first 10 percent reduction is clearly warranted.

The question now arises as to whether a second 10 percent reduction in the stench is worthwhile. Since the pollution is not as intense as it was with no control, a second 10 percent reduction is of less value than was the first one. Suppose each person values the move from 10 percent control to 20 percent control at $8, so that the community valuation of the extra control—or the marginal benefits of it—is $80,000. Since the marginal costs of the additional control are only $10,000, putting it into effect adds $70,000 to the total net benefits of control and is, therefore, a good investment for the community.

Column 5 shows the community's *marginal benefit* at different levels of control. Marginal benefits of pollution control, like the marginal benefits of crime prevention, are defined as the *change* in total benefits per unit *change* in whatever it is that yields the benefits. Note that the *total benefits* at any given level of control are obtained by adding up the marginal benefits as the level of control is increased unit by unit up to that level.

Marginal benefits, as shown in Table 6–1, decline as the level of pollution control is increased (the level of the stench is decreased). This is what we would expect to happen in the case at hand. The greater the amount of control, or the lower the level of the stench, the less urgent additional control becomes. This will be the usual situation in controlling pollution.

The level of pollution control yielding the maximum net benefits to the people of the community is that at which the marginal benefits just cease to exceed the marginal costs. The marginal benefits of the first two 10 percent increments in the total amount of control needed to eliminate the stench exceed the marginal costs of making them. Thus, net benefits are increased by increasing control at least to the 20 percent level. The third, fourth, fifth, sixth, and seventh 10 percent increments also yield marginal benefits exceeding their marginal costs, and they increase the net benefits of control to the community. Now consider the eighth 10 percent increment. Marginal benefits are $8,000, and marginal costs are $10,000. Extending pollution control from the 70 percent level to the 80 percent level *reduces* the net benefits by $2,000. The eighth 10 percent increment is not worth to the community what it costs.

The principle is perfectly general. Net benefits will always be increased by increasing control if the marginal benefits of the increase are greater than the marginal costs of making it. Net benefits will decrease from an increase in the control level if the marginal benefits of that increase are less than its marginal costs. The appropriate level of control is the one that approaches as closely as possible the one at which the marginal benefits equal the marginal costs but does not go far enough for marginal costs to exceed marginal benefits.

WHAT CAN BE DONE ABOUT POLLUTION?

Human beings often react to problems with their emotions rather than with the capacity for logic with which they are endowed. Policies recommended to control pollution reflect this human characteristic. Typical recommendations call for direct control of pollution by the state. But this is only one of the possible avenues of reducing pollution problems. Others include indirect control by the state through a system of incentives encouraging potential polluters not to pollute or to limit their pollution, and an examination of the institutions of private property rights and markets to see if they can be modified to provide the desired limitations on polluting activities.

Direct controls

An appealingly simple way to control pollution is to have the government ban polluting activities or agents. If phosphates contaminate water, then ban the use of phosphates in detergents. If DDT pollutes water and land, ban the use of DDT. If the burning of fuel oil and coal increases the sulphur oxide content of the atmosphere, prohibit their use. Require industrial plants to clean the pollutants from whatever it is they discharge into the atmosphere or water. The method is straightforward and, on the face of it, seems eminently fair.

Governmental agencies, notably the Environmental Protection Agency (EPA) at the federal level, use direct controls to reduce many kinds of polluting activities. They set and attempt to enforce emission standards for such polluters as automobiles, power plants, and steel mills. State regulation of polluters, to the extent that it is accomplished, is in general supervised by the EPA.

The case of the city with the terrible stench shows that complete prohibition of pollutants is not likely to be worth its costs. Pollution control uses resources that could have produced goods and services, and the value of the goods and services forgone is the cost to society of controlling the pollution. If the damage done by an additional unit of pollution is less than the costs of preventing it from occurring, community welfare is greater if it is allowed to occur. Consequently, direct controls usually should aim at a less idealistic goal than a pollution-free environment. They may take the form of controlling the level of pollution by such devices as setting emissions standards or limits for industrial plants, automobiles, and the like.

One problem raised by the use of direct controls to limit the amount of pollution is that it presupposes the regulatory body can determine what the economically desirable levels of pollution are. This is not an insurmountable problem. Tolerance limits on the amount of pollution to be allowed can be reasonably well established. Within those limits, overall costs can be weighed continually against benefits to establish an approximation of the desirable levels of pollution.

A second problem is the difficulty facing a regulatory body in achieving an efficient allocation of the permissible pollution among different polluters. For example, it may be more costly for a steel mill to eliminate a unit of sulphur oxide from its emissions than it is for a power plant. In the interests of economic efficiency, it is best to eliminate pollution where it is least costly to do so. Thus the power plant should be required to reduce its sulphur oxide emission before the steel mill is required to do so. This is a difficult kind of decision for a regulatory body to make, since it is responsible to a political body for which economic efficiency is not a primary goal. In addition, it is unrealistic to suppose that the regulatory body has a working knowledge of the nature of costs for every polluter.

A third problem is that of enforcing the standards of emissions once it has been determined what those standards should be. Direct controls fail to provide polluters with an economic incentive not to pollute. In fact, it will pay them to seek ways and means to evade the pollution standards set for them. But we should not overstate the enforcement problem. Almost any prohibition of activities that individuals and business firms want to engage in creates enforcement problems.

Indirect controls

It is possible for the government to control many types of pollution by placing taxes on polluting activities. Where the amounts of polluting discharges can be measured for individual polluters, a tax can be placed directly on each unit of discharge. This will induce the polluter to reduce the amount of pollution that is discharged. In some cases where such measurement is not possible, polluters may be taxed indirectly—for example, automobiles not equipped with pollution control devices can be subjected to a tax on a mileage basis. This would induce their owners either to install pollution control devices or to drive less. At this point in time, not much use has been made of this method of control.

Figure 6–4 illustrates the use of a tax to control the amounts of pollutants discharged into the environment. Consider an industrial concern that discharges its polluting wastes into a river. Processes for cleaning the wastes so that the pollution they cause is eliminated or diminished are available. *Marginal cleaning costs,* defined as the change in total cleaning costs per one unit change in the firm's discharge of wastes, are shown by *MCC.* For example, if the level of discharge is q_0, then q_0A_0 is the *addition* to the firm's total cost of cleaning brought about when the amount of discharge is increased from one unit less than q_0 to the q_0 level. Similarly, the addition to total cleaning costs when the firm moves from one unit less than q_1 units to q_1 units is q_1A_1. We show the *MCC* curve sloping upward to the right, indicating that the larger the firm's rate of waste discharge the greater is the cost to it of cleaning an additional unit. This may or may not be the case—we assume here for illustrative purposes that it is. The level of the tax on polluted discharge is T_1 per unit, regardless of the level of the discharge.

A tax per unit of polluted discharge will induce the firm to reduce its polluting activity if the amount of the tax exceeds the marginal costs of

FIGURE 6–4
Control of pollution by means of a tax on polluted discharges

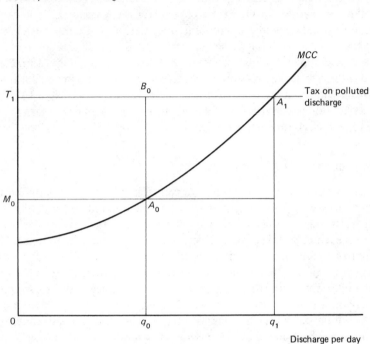

Dollars per unit of discharge

T_1

B_0

MCC

Tax on polluted
discharge

A_1

M_0

A_0

0   q_0 q_1

Discharge per day

If the level of a tax on polluted discharges exceeds the marginal costs of cleaning the discharge, a firm will elect to clean the discharge. This will be the case for all discharge levels up to q_1. If the level of the tax is less than the marginal cleaning costs, the firm will elect to pay the tax rather than clean the discharge. This will occur for all of the discharge in excess of q_1.

cleaning the discharge. If the discharge is less than q_1, say q_0 units per day, it pays the firm not to pollute. It is less costly to clean the discharge than it is to pay the tax. For the q_0 unit of discharge, $q_0 B_0$ would be added to the firm's total costs if it elects to pay the tax and not to clean up the discharge. Only $q_0 A_0$ would be added to its total costs if it elects to clean the discharge and pay no tax. This will be the case for any discharge level up to q_1 units per day. On the other hand, for a discharge level exceeding q_1 per day, the firm will clean q_1 units and pay the tax on the remainder of the discharge. It is cheaper to clean than to pay the tax on each unit up to that level. For units of discharge exceeding q_1, it is cheaper to pay the tax than to clean them.

The tax can be set at any desired level, depending upon the amount of pollution the government decides to allow. Raising the tax will decrease the amount of pollution, and lowering the tax will increase it. Ideally, the tax should be set at a level at which the marginal benefits to society of cleaning a unit of discharge equal the marginal cleaning costs. If the level of polluted discharge permitted is such that the marginal benefits of cleaning the discharge exceed the marginal costs of cleaning it, the tax is too low and should be increased. If the level of polluted discharge permitted is such that marginal benefits of cleaning are less than the marginal costs of cleaning, the tax is too high and should be decreased.

The use of taxes to control pollution has its advantages. A major one is that it provides an incentive to the polluter to seek improved ways and means of cleaning up its discharge. Another advantage is that it prevents the polluter from shifting some of its production costs (pollution costs) to others; it reduces the incentive to overproduce.

There are also disadvantages. First, it usually is difficult to determine the benefits—total and marginal—to society of cleaning the discharge. Second, enforcement of such a tax is not easy. Policing is necessary to determine that the discharge is indeed properly cleaned. Third, taxes are levied by political rather than economic bodies, and politics may well get in the way of the enactment of appropriate tax levels.

The federal government has used subsidies—the opposite of taxes—extensively as a pollution control measure. These consist primarily of grants made to state and local governments for the construction of sewage treatment facilities. For the fiscal year 1976, almost 54 percent of the estimated federal outlays on pollution control and abatement are for construction of this type.[2] Yet, despite relatively large outlays for water pollution control since passage of the water Pollution Control Act of 1956, water quality has continued to decrease. Could it be that subsidized treatment of industrial wastes fails to provide incentives to industries to develop or to seek out low-pollution methods of production?

Private property rights

Since the absence of well-defined property rights provides a primary incentive to polluters to dump their wastes in certain segments of the environment, the assignment of property rights either to firms that pollute or to those that benefit from a clean environment may provide a means of control in some cases. Consider, for example, the upstream paper industry–downstream power industry case described above. Since neither

---

[2] Office of Management and Budget, *Special Analysis, Budget of the United States Government, Fiscal Year 1976* (Washington, D.C.: U.S. Government Printing Office, 1975), p. 270.

owns the river, the paper industry is able to use it for waste disposal, and the costs of the waste disposal fall on the power industry.

Suppose that rights to the river are sold at auction by the government. These rights will be purchased by the industry to which they are most valuable. If the annual value to the paper industry of using the river for waste discharges (the costs of alternative means of disposing of the wastes) exceed the annual cost to the power industry of cleaning the water, the paper industry will buy the rights. The river will be put to its most valuable use—that of being a sink for waste disposal. However, if the value of clean water to the power industry (the costs of cleaning it for power industry use) exceeds the value to the paper industry of using the river to discharge wastes, the power industry will purchase the rights and the river will be put to its most productive (valuable) use—that of furnishing clean cooling water for the generation of electricity.

Regardless of which industry buys the rights, changes in the relative values of the two uses will provide incentives for the river to be put to the use in which it is most valuable. If the paper industry holds the rights to the river but the annual value of clean water to the power industry exceeds the annual value of the river as a waste disposal, the power industry will be willing to pay the paper industry enough to induce it not to pollute—to use alternative means of disposing of its wastes. On the other hand, if the power industry owns the rights and the annual value of the river to the paper industry as a waste disposal exceeds the annual cost to the power industry of cleaning the water, the power industry will sell the paper industry pollution privileges.

SUMMARY

The environment provides environmental services that are used by both household units and producing units of the economy. In the processes of consumption and production wastes are generated. If the ecological system cannot recycle these wastes as fast as they are generated, wastes accumulate. This constitutes pollution.

Economic analysis of pollution provides a perspective on its causes and its effects, along with the costs and benefits of controlling it. Incentives to pollute stem from (1) an absence of property rights in the environment and (2) the collectively consumed nature of whatever is being polluted. Polluters, by polluting, transfer a part of their costs to others. Cost-benefit analysis is useful in determining how much pollution should be allowed. It indicates that it is seldom in the common interest to forbid pollution altogether.

There are three main avenues that governmental pollution control policies can take. First, certain polluting activities may be controlled directly through prohibitions or limitations on polluting activities. Second, they may be controlled indirectly by providing polluters with incentives not to pollute—say through taxation of polluting activities. Third, much pollution can be controlled by selling or assigning individuals property rights to whatever is being polluted, then allowing them to sell pollution rights to would-be polluters.

SUPPLEMENTARY READINGS

Crocker, Thomas D., and Rogers, A. J., III. *Environmental Economics.* Hinsdale, Ill.: Dryden Press, 1971.

Provides a good elementary treatise of the nature of pollution, the economics of pollution, and alternatives available for controlling it. Writing style holds the reader's interest.

Dolan, Edwin G. *Tanstaafl,* chaps. 1, 3, 4, and 6. New York: Holt, Rinehart & Winston, 1971.

A short, interesting book on the broad range of ecological problems— pollution, population, and depletion of natural resources. Elementary economics is used to evaluate the problems and suggest policy alternatives.

Freeman, A. Myrick, III. *The Economics of Pollution Control and Environmental Quality.* New York: General Learning Press, 1971.

This monograph is intended to show how economic analysis can contribute to an understanding of pollution and its control. It is compact and thorough. Although some of the analysis may be beyond the grasp of elementary students, most of it will be readily understandable.

Mills, E. S., and Petersen, F. M. "Environmental Quality: The First Five Years." *The American Economic Review,* vol. 65 (June 1975), pp. 259–68.

An excellent summary and critique of the operation of the President's Council on Environmental Quality and of its annual report, *Environmental Quality.*

North, Douglas C., and Miller, Roger Leroy. *The Economics of Public Issues,* chaps. 13, 14, 19, 20, and 28. New York: Harper & Row, 1972.

Short chapters on several different pollution problems—air pollution, oil spills, hydroelectric projects, and the like. Cost-benefit analysis is introduced, and considerable use is made of the concept of spillovers and the alternative-cost principle.

Ruff, Larry E. "The Economic Common Sense of Pollution." *The Public Interest* (Spring 1970), pp. 69–85.

Provides an elementary economic analysis of pollution. The marginal concept is introduced, along with concepts of social costs, resource allocation, and economic efficiency. The author builds his economic analysis around the problems that must be met and solved by a pollution control board.

Chapter 7

CONSUMERISM

CHECKLIST OF ECONOMIC CONCEPTS

Consumer welfare or well-being
Advertising
Monopoly
Alternative costs
Consumerism
Government regulation
Cost-benefit analysis
Information costs
Spillover costs
Profits

7

Consumerism
The regulators versus the regulatees

Fran Robinson's package was heavy, weighing almost 30 pounds. She staggered out to the car and dumped it on the right front seat. Then she slid under the wheel, buckled her seat belt, put the shift lever in the "P" position, and turned on the ignition. There was no response. What was wrong—the seat belt was buckled, wasn't it? Then she remembered that if the seat is buckled when a heavy object is placed on the right front seat, it must be unbuckled and then rebuckled. With this task accomplished she tried again. No go.

Out came the *Owner's Manual* and the instructions were clear: "Turn the ignition to ON, raise the hood and turn the bypass switch on the fire wall to START." This done she closed the hood, got back in the car and' buckled her seat belt. Fate was on her side and the engine sprang to life. But then it sputtered and died. Fran turned the ignition momentarily to OFF, then tried to restart the engine. But there was only silence, broken by an occasional (deleted).

Once more the hood was raised and the bypass switch was set to START. Rather testily, Fran went through the buckle up and starting procedure and was appropriately rewarded. This time she kept the engine racing until she was moving with the traffic. But she would have given almost anything to get her hands on the diabolical maniac who dreamed up the system!

THE CONSUMER'S PROBLEM

Over the years much concern for the consumer has been evidenced by some segments of the general public and by legislative groups. The individual consumer is a lone voice crying in the wilderness, so the argument runs, since no single consumer is important to a giant business concern. The consumer who does not like what the business firm does is thought to have no recourse. On the other hand the business firm is thought to be very important to the consumer. Thus the business firm presumably has the power to take advantage of the consumer.

Shady business practices

Consumer advocates—those who consider themselves to be speakers for consumers—usually point to four kinds of business practices that they consider adverse to the best interests of consumers. These are: (1) unsafe, impure, and low quality products, (2) deceptive advertising of goods and services, (3) techniques that obscure or hide real prices and (4) poor or inadequate servicing of products.

Unsafe, impure, and low quality products are nothing new to most of us. Automobiles have killed hundreds of persons each year. So have guns and knives. Lawn mowers have sliced off toes. Can openers have been dangerous to fingers. Boats have capsized. The use of the drug thalidomide in Europe and Great Britain a few years ago resulted in a number of hideously deformed children being born. Mercury, found in a batch of canned tuna, caused several deaths. The quality of some brands of wieners has been deteriorated by increasing their fat content. The list can be extended on and on.

Anyone who reads newspapers and magazines or who watches TV knows that deceptive advertising occurs despite the efforts of the Federal Trade Commission to prevent it. One brand of aspirin is said to be more effective than another although both are standard five-grain tablets. Diet supplements are advertised to ward off everything from cancer to the common cold. The sellers of a certain brand of pantyhose tell us they will make even Joe Namath's legs look good! What do the terms "water-resistant," "preshrunk," "sanforized," "moth-resistant," and "shock-resistant" really mean? How can one know that the ride of one automobile is "smoother?" Will *XXX* dental cream really make one's teeth whiter?

Is there anyone lucky enough *not* to have been exposed to misleading or hidden pricing practices? Have you ever observed a firm that advertises a 10 percent discount from list price on its merchandise but that marks the list price of the goods 10 percent higher than it would have been otherwise? Or a sewing machine salesperson who sells a machine at a substantially discounted price, *provided* you purchase the five-year service policy that turns out to cost more than the machine itself? Or a retailer of coffee who sells the two-pound "economy" can at more than twice the price of the one-pound can? Or a firm that advertises a well-known product at a discounted price; that has just sold out when you arrive; but will let you have another lesser-known brand at the same price?

Have you always been happy with the servicing of products that you have purchased? Many have wondered quietly—and some not so quietly —what took place in the auto service department while their automobiles were supposedly undergoing motor tune-ups. How long does it take to obtain the services of a repairperson from the air-conditioning shop that sold you your air-conditioning equipment? If you happen to be an airplane pilot, try finding an avionics shop that you believe does good, reliable repair work on your radios, your transponder, and your autopilot. Replacing the rollers on the sliding glass door that you had installed ten years ago can be a real hassle. Are you sure that your TV set really needed all those parts that the repairperson put in yesterday?

Why the practices occur

Are the many consumer ripoffs that we encounter side effects peculiar to a modern *advanced capitalistic* economic system? Not really. There were hawkers of patent medicines and hundreds of other useless things in frontier days. As far back in history as people have engaged in exchange there have been some who try to take advantage of others, and the ripoff is not confined to capitalistic systems. But rightly or wrongly many believe that in the modern economy the consumer's position has become more precarious than it was in the olden days. They cite several reasons why they think this is so.

In the first place, there is a much wider range of goods and services available now than there was 100 years ago and many of these goods are much more complex in design and operation. The automobile as compared with the buggy is a case in point. The mechanical features of the buggy were well understood by most people and it was not too difficult to detect shoddy workmanship or weak points in its construction. Nevertheless, some buyers found after purchasing a buggy that the wheel spokes were tight only because they had been soaked in water before the sale. The automobile, by way of contrast, is an exceedingly complex machine. Many purchasers know nothing about ignition systems, transmissions, hydraulic systems, and the like. Some of us are inclined to wonder from time to time how much mechanics know! We don't really understand the mechanisms of our refrigerators, freezers, mixers, vacuum cleaners, and hair dryers. There are so many remedies for the common cold on the market that we have trouble choosing among them. Which make and model of single lens reflex camera do you think is the best buy—and why?

In the second place, large-scale factories using mass production techniques have supplanted small home and family-run production units. In the latter craftsmanship was important. The artisan saw the whole production processes through from beginning to end and was proud to attach the family name to the resulting wagon, bicycle, rifle, or bathtub. In a modern factory any one worker accomplishes only one small part of the total production process and is unlikely to feel any great pride of achievement in the individual contribution made to the final product. The modern worker's contribution is impersonal and anonymous. Contact between the producer and the consumer has been lost; consequently, the producer feels little or no responsibility for the consumer.

In the third place, tremendous advances have been made in mass communications. The radio was developed; magazine and newspaper circulation has increased; television has come on the scene. All of these have increased severalfold the opportunities of sellers to advertise their wares to potential buyers. With the growth of the advertising media there has been a corresponding growth in the possibilities available to sellers for shaping consumers' desires and also for misleading consumers.

In the fourth place, it is widely believed that growing monopoly power in the production and sale of products puts consumers in a continuously deteriorating position in the market place. If General Motors places an unsafe automobile on the market, the public presumably not only does not know it but would be unable to do anything about it if it did. In recent years supposed domestic oil monopolies have been accused of making things rough for consumers. The increasing number of industrial giants in the economy leads people to believe that they will be subjected to an ever increasing degree of manipulation in the market place.

Consequences of the practices

The supposed consequences of shady or unfair business practices are, of course, losses in consumers' welfare or well-being. The primary objective of economic activity is to satisfy consumer wants as fully as the economy's resources and techniques will allow. Shady or unfair business practices interfere with the efficiency with which this objective is carried out. They represent slips between cups and lips! There are several ways in which these slips may occur.

Many business practices are thought to shortchange consumers on health and safety grounds. It is often alleged that in a free market producers will take advantage of consumers by selling them items that are harmful to them; that is, that will actually decrease consumer well-being.

Examples include drugs and medicines that may have dangerous side effects and toys that are painted with lead paints. It is also alleged that producers, as well as jeopardizing health and safety by putting things on the market that should not be put there, do the same thing by *not* putting some things on the market that should be put there. Automobiles without seat belts and shoulder harnesses are thought by some to be dangerous. So are electric handsaws without blade guards, and motorcycles without helmets for the rider.

A great many other products, while not actually harmful to consumers are believed to be useless. For example will a Geritol tablet every morning really produce the sweet, loving, understanding, sympathetic helpmate depicted on the TV screen? Will Hai Karate really make it dangerous for a male user to walk near persons of the opposite sex? Will STP in your gasoline really improve the engine performance of your automobile? Will aluminum siding over the present siding on your house really improve its insulating qualities? Consumers buy vast quantities of these and similar products year in and year out.

Further, consumers may waste substantial amounts of time and effort because of shady products and poor service. Even for products under warranty it is usually necessary to box and ship the defective item back to the manufacturer. In any case one must make one or more trips to the retailer to return defective merchandise and to secure the appropriate adjustment for it. How often after having automobile repairs made have you discovered that they were not done properly, necessitating another trip to the repair shop and loss of the automobile's use for another day?

All of the above consequences of shady business practices, to the extent that they occur, waste the resources of the economy. Double harm is done if items on balance are actually harmful to consumers. Their production and sale lowers consumer well-being and in addition the resources to produce them are not available to produce useful items. For items that are useless, but not actually harmful, the society is harmed only by losing the use of the resources needed to make them. Similarly, time and effort spent in getting faulty products repaired, replaced, or re-repaired is not available to spend in either pleasurable pursuits or in the production of useful goods and services.

THE NATURE OF CONSUMERISM

The apparent problems of consumers vis-à-vis business firms have not gone unnoticed historically. They have given rise over time to the movement called *consumerism*. The movement is not new, going back at least to the birth of the consumer cooperative at Rochdale, England, in 1844. It includes the establishment of organizations for consumer education such as the American Home Economics Association in 1908 and the Chicago Housewives League in 1910. It was also given expression in law by the Pure Food and Drug Act of 1906 and by a number of state "truth in advertising" laws in the early 1900s. These were followed by the Federal Trade Commission Act of 1914. Two books published in the decades of the 1920s and 1930s did much to excite the public about consumer problems. These were *Your Money's Worth* by Stuart Chase and Frederick J. Schlink in 1927 and *100,000,000 Guinea Pigs* by Schlink and Arthur Kallet in 1933. Since the Great Depression of the 1930s a spate of state and federal laws have been enacted that ostensibly protect the consumer. But the unprecedented growth of modern consumerism undoubtedly sprang from the publication of Ralph Nader's *Unsafe at Any Speed* in 1965.

Description

What is this "consumerism" that we hear so much about? The concept is somewhat nebulous with different emphases being given to it by different persons. It almost defies definition, but perhaps we can establish a working description that will suffice for our purposes.

Consumerism seems to be a movement shared by a great many people who believe that somehow the consumer is not getting a fair shake in the economic system. They employ several types of activity that they believe bolster the consumer's position with respect to producers and sellers. These include consumer information and educational services performed by organizations such as Consumers' Union, the investigation of practices thought to be adverse to consumer interests and publication of reports by a number of consumer-oriented groups, lobbying by consumer advocates for legislation intended to protect consumers, and the extension of regulatory activities by government agencies for the same purpose. Consumer advocates also initiate activist programs much as the meat boycott of early 1973. Consumerism is at least all of these—and perhaps much more. It is propelled by both private consumer advocates and the government.

Private consumer advocates

There is little doubt that the best known name among modern consumer advocates is Ralph Nader. Nader is a lawyer, educated at Princeton and Harvard. According to reports he lives very modestly devoting most of what he earns from his lectures and books to further investigation of practices that he believes are detrimental to consumers. He is self-employed.

Nader and a group of his followers, known collectively as "Nader's Raiders," engage in extensive and continuing investigations of business and government practices, looking for those that they believe are contrary to the public interest. He buttonholes members of Congress, appears before congressional committees, writes scathing reports, confronts corporation executives, and files suits on behalf of consumers against those alleged to have harmed consumers. Businesses—particularly those in the automobile industry—take him seriously. So do senators and representatives. He is believed to be responsible for the enactment of the National Traffic and Motor Vehicle Safety Act of 1966, the Wholesome Meat Act of 1967, the Natural Gas Pipeline Safety Act of 1968, the Radiation Control for Health and Safety Act of 1968, and the Wholesome Poultry Products Act of 1968. Many other consumer advocates are active but Nader stands head and shoulders above them all.

Much less flamboyant than "Nader's Raiders" are the private consumer information and education organizations. Three of the best known of these are Consumers' Union, Consumers' Research, and Good Housekeeping with its "Seal of Approval." These organizations engage in continual testing and evaluation of different brands of a wide range of products, publishing their results and their recommendations for their subscribers or readers.

The role of the government

Much of consumerism's power and thrust comes from the enlistment of government support to accomplish its purposes. Although private consumer advocacy can be separated conceptually from governmental consumer advocacy, in practice they tend to become inextricably intertwined. The primary avenue used by consumer advocates such as Nader to correct what they conceive to be wrong is the government.

The amount of legislation enacted in recent years and the number of agencies that supposedly protect consumers are rather startling. Some of the legislation attributed to Nader was listed above. In addition, agencies actively engaged in consumer affairs include the Federal Trade Commission, Food and Drug Administration, Interstate Commerce Commission, Federal Aviation Agency, Department of Agriculture Consumer and Marketing Service, Federal Power Commission, Consumer Product Safety Commission, National Transportation Safety Board, Civil Aeronautics Board, Federal Communications Commission, Occupational Safety and Health Administration, Federal Energy Administration, Environmental Protection Agency, Securities and Exchange Commission, and the Cost of Living Council. This list is by no means complete. Certainly one cannot say truthfully that the government ignores the consumer.

THE ECONOMICS OF CONSUMERISM

Do the activities that fall within the domain described as consumerism on balance benefit consumers? There is no unequivocal answer to this question. Some such activities will surely result in net increases in consumer well-being. Others will just as surely bring about net reductions in the level of consumer welfare. Some sort of cost-benefit analysis of each of the activities making up the movement will be of value in determining which should be expanded and which should be curtailed.

The economic benefits

Economic analysis indicates three possible avenues through which consumerism may lead toward higher levels of consumer welfare. First, it may lead toward improvements in the information made available to consumers. Second, it may cut back on the amounts of useless or even deceptive competitive advertising to which consumers are subjected. Third, it may provide increased protection to consumers as they go about their consumption activities.

More accurate and complete information. If consumers are to get the greatest possible amounts of satisfaction from the limited incomes available to them, they must be able to make intelligent choices from the vast array of goods and services available to them. Intelligent choices must be based on, but are not assured by, relatively complete and accurate information. For example, we expect by and large that weights and measures will be correctly represented by sellers, and this information is of inestimable value to us. Similarly, it is helpful to us to know the ingredients comprising a product; what the product can be used for; the way it operates; and how long we can expect it to last under average use conditions.

Information provided by independent testing agencies on comparative qualities and prices of competing product lines often prove useful to consumers. Recommended "best buys" while not infallible guides for all consumers often provide an excellent point of departure for the judicious careful shopper. Two of the best known sources of information of this type are *Consumers' Research* and *Consumer Reports*.

Less deceptive and useless sales promotion. Reductions in deceptive sales promotion activities in and of themselves must increase consumer welfare if we ignore the costs of bringing those reductions about. Misstatements concerning the nature of products and false claims of what those products can do obviously operate to the detriment of consumer well-being. They are the opposite of information improvement—they fog the issues and generate consumer confusion. Deceptive sales promotion activities, together with those that, while not deceptive, provide no useful information to consumers, waste resources. To the extent that they are reduced, the resources that were used to perform them can be used to produce goods and services that increase the welfare of consumers.

Although it is easy to secure agreement in principle that deceptive and useless sales promotion activities should be reduced, it is difficult to draw the line between that which is deceptive or useless and that which is not. What constitutes useless advertising? Those who want it reduced or banned have in mind activities that provide no useful information to consumers—for example, ads stating that automobile X rides smoother, or dentrifice Z makes teeth whiter. However, some sales promotion activities that are useless to some consumers may not be useless to others. One person who frowns on smoking may argue that all cigarette advertising is useless. But a smoker may very well achieve higher welfare levels by discovering from advertisements or other sales promotion sources which brands contain the least amounts of tar and nicotine. Are Saturday morning television cartoons useless? It depends on the values and the tastes of the person making the judgment.

More consumer protection.   The largest part of consumerism activities is directed toward protecting rather than toward educating consumers. They are directed toward protecting consumers from unsafe, impure, and low quality products, and from unfair pricing practices. From the point of view of economic analysis it is useful to classify the goods that are targets of consumerism into two groups: (1) those that generate spillover costs in consumption and (2) those that do not.

Consider first consumerism measures intended to protect persons from the spillover costs of the consumption done by others. Some obvious examples are laws that prevent smoking in elevators, or that require periodic safety checks of automobiles so that drivers will not endanger the lives of others. The reduction of consuming activities that generate spillover costs for others adds to the well-being of those on whom the costs would otherwise be imposed. At the same time it places restrictions on—reducing the welfare of—those whose consuming activities are curtailed. If we believe that those who consume should pay the full costs of consumption we will look with favor on measures that eliminate the spillover costs of consumption or that require the consumer of such goods to fully compensate or make whole those on whom the spillover costs are imposed.

Second, consider consumerism measures that curb or regulate the consumption of goods and services where no spillover costs are generated by the act of consuming. Obvious examples include requirements that seat belts and shoulder harnesses be purchased in automobiles, that motorcycle riders wear helmets, that only Federal Aviation Agency certified parts be used to repair and maintain airplanes, that meat products sold over the counter meet certain quality standards, that only licensed M.D.s be permitted to sell medical services, that only licensed barbers be allowed to sell haircuts. The list can be extended on and on. Most of the controversy over consumerism is centered on this general class of consumer goods and services.

Consumerism measures regulating the sale and consumption of individually consumed goods and services may or may not benefit consumers. Some such measures are intended to protect consumers from their own ignorance. Electrical codes for residential housing are a case in point. So is the licensing of doctors, plumbers, and barbers. Electrical codes specifying minimum wire sizes, fuses, and the like may very well benefit some consumers of residential housing. But at the same time the costs of obtaining minimum quality standards on certain goods and services may price some persons out of markets altogether, precluding their obtaining the benefits of consuming low-cost low-quality versions of those goods and services. Consider, for example the possible impact of requiring that all used cars sold be brought up to new car quality specifications.

Other consumerism measures are intended to protect consumers from unscrupulous sellers—sellers who presumably charge more for goods and services than they are worth to buyers. Price controls on various items fall into this category—price controls on gasoline, maximum rents on housing units, and the like. Those consumers who can get as much at the controlled price as they would purchase at an uncontrolled price clearly gain. Others who would be willing to pay more in order to obtain larger quantities than they currently can purchase just as clearly lose.

The economic costs

Consumerism activities and legislative measures are not a free service to consumers in general—not even those performed gratuitously by Ralph Nader. Two basic sets of economic costs can be readily identified. These are (1) the costs of resources used in effecting consumerism activities or measures, and (2) the costs to some consumers of providing the protection of consumerism to others.

Resource costs. The costs of resources used in effecting any given consumerism activity need not detain us long since they have been alluded to time and again throughout the chapter. The resources used by the Federal Trade Commission in monitoring advertising could have been used to produce other goods and services. The resources used by the Federal Aviation Agency in carrying out its functions of facilitating aircraft movements and enhancing aircraft safety could have been used to produce other goods and services. An interesting fact in this latter case is that the FAA currently employs 2.5 persons for every registered aircraft in the United States.

Costs to consumerism. The direct cost to consumers of consumerism activities consist of the reductions in well-being or forgone well-being experienced by some consumers as the presumed benefits of those activities are extended to others. One of Nader's well-publicized consumerism activities illustrates costs of this type. He was able to force General Motors' Corvair automobile off the market although most of its purchasers had been eminently well-satisfied with the car. The decline in value of Corvairs in existence at the time and the inability of persons who desired to do so to buy new ones after its withdrawal represent the costs of a presumed increase in automobile safety. Other illustrations are easily found. The Consumer Product Safety Commission in its efforts to enhance product safety has imposed substantial costs on consumers. One case cited by Prof. Murray Weidenbaum involved hearings by the Commission to determine whether or not some 4 million electric frying pans were dangerous although no injuries from the pan had ever been reported to the Commission.[1] Hearings and investigations of this type use resources and increase the costs of products, reducing what is available for consumers to buy. It also prevents consumers who desire to do so from trading off some degree of product safety for lower prices—and voluntary tradeoffs of this type would be expected to increase consumer well-being.

EVALUATION

On balance what does economic analysis seem to tell us about consumerism? Above all, the primary economic reason for being of consumerism is to enhance consumer welfare. Each manifestation of it should be subjected to a benefit-cost type of analysis to determine who is helped by it; what the costs of it are; and whether or not the benefits are worth the costs. Again it will be helpful to consider separately those aspects of it that are intended to (1) be informational in nature, (2) prevent the imposition of spillover costs on others and (3) protect consumers from manipulation by business firms.

The provision of information

For any given good or service consumers generally find it useful to know the components or the ingredients that comprise it, what it can do for them, and the terms on which it is available. Against these benefits the costs of obtaining the information must be weighed. There is virtually no economic argument against consumerism measures requiring truth in advertising or a listing of ingredients on labels. The benefits are obvious and

---

[1] Murray L. Weidenbaum, *Government-Mandated Price Increases* (Washington, D.C.: American Enterprise Institute for Public Policy Research, 1975), p. 33.

the costs of providing accurate information is in general no greater than that of providing false or misleading information.

Consumerism activities such as testing agency activities that enhance consumer information on comparative qualities and/or durabilities of different brands of a product are also likely to enhance consumer welfare. The costs of testing must be met by consumer subscriptions to the published results. Consequently, we would expect that the benefits either exceed, or at the very least, are equal to the costs of making the information available. In addition, the extent of consumerism activities of this type will be governed by consumers themselves. They will get the approximate amount that they are willing to pay for—an amount at which the marginal benefits of additional information is approximately equal to the marginal costs of obtaining it.

The prevention of spillover costs

When the consumption of certain items would impose spillover costs on nonconsumers of those items, consumerism activities designed to prevent those spillovers from occurring seem in many cases to be on sound economic ground. If consumers of those items can pass along some of the costs to other persons, they will demand—and receive—disproportionate amounts of the items. The items will tend to be overconsumed and overproduced.

Automobile transportation is a case in point. In the absence of regulation, persons can drive automobiles with defective brakes, occasionally smashing into other cars, properties, and persons. If drivers are allowed to impose such costs on other persons, driving is made less expensive to them inducing them to indulge in more driving than they would if they were required to maintain their autos in a condition such that spillover costs would not be imposed on others. The economically correct amount of driving is that at which the marginal benefits of a mile of driving is equal to the marginal costs of doing it. This is approximately the amount that would occur if drivers are required to pay the full costs of their driving; that is, if they are not allowed to impose spillover costs on others.

There are consumerism measures, banning the use of some products that are thought to generate spillover costs, where the logic is not so clearcut. An example is provided by laws prohibiting the use of DDT and other pesticides. Prohibition of the use of DDT may preserve the purity of water and food for those farther down the watershed from the potential users of DDT. But the cost may be an outbreak of malaria or encephalitis because mosquitos are not kept under control. Weighing and balancing the costs and the benefits of such prohibitions is a very imprecise and difficult business.

Protection from business manipulation

The most questionable set of consumerism activities are those aimed at protecting persons from business manipulation—and a very large part of consumerism activities is for this express purpose. Manipulation of the individual consumer means essentially that a business firm can do with the consumer whatever it desires. It can shape the consumer's tastes and values, sell the consumer unwanted, unsafe, or low quality products, take advantage of the consumer's ignorance, charge exorbitant prices and the like.

When consumer advocates succeed in obtaining legislation that requires products to meet certain quality or safety standards, the advocates—and those who pass the legislation—are supplanting consumer judgments with their own and are coercing some consumers to accept those substitute judgments. The fact that some consumers must be coerced into accepting them means that consumer well-being is decreased. Suppose that I am much less of a risk averter than is a consumer advocate and that I would rather take my chances driving an auto without seat belts and shoulder harness than to pay the extra costs of having them on my car. Yet the advocate is able to sway the legislature and require that all automobiles sold be equipped with these devices. I must buy them even though the benefits they yield to me are less than their costs. My welfare is decreased and no one's welfare is increased.

Similarly, when quality standards for products are legislated some consumers may be made worse off while no one may be made better off. Some consumers prefer a lower-quality product at a lower price than a higher-quality product at a higher price. Legislation that prevents the lower-quality product—say, hamburgers with soybean meal in them—from being sold reduces the welfare of those who would buy it. And there is no offsetting gain in the welfare of others.

What appears to be a fallacy in the reasoning of many consumer advocates is their implicit assumption that business firms profit most from manipulating consumers; that is, from taking advantage of them. To be sure there are unscrupulous and fraudulent sellers. There always have been and probably always will be. But it appears likely that the major part of the business sector of the economy will do better economically by giving the consumer a fair shake for the consumer's money. Who will take a car back a second time to a repair shop that charges for work not performed or for shoddy work? Can Detroit automakers make more money by producing styles and models that consumers do not want, attempting then to alter consumers tastes, or by producing styles and models that meet existing tastes? Are appliance sellers with poor repair services likely to make more profit than those that excell with their repair services?

The final and important question is that of who is the best judge of consumers' interests, consumers themselves or consumer advocates? Some consumers are ignorant and some businesses engage in shady practices. But by and large the advocate is in the position of saying that many people ought not to want what they want—or if they do, they ought not to get it. This is probably correct when applied to other persons. But it is not when applied to me!

SUMMARY

Many people believe that consumers are at a substantial disadvantage vis-à-vis business firms in the U.S. economic system. It is widely believed that businesses take advantage of consumers by selling them unsafe, impure, and low quality products; by engaging in deceptive advertising; by using obscure or deceptive pricing techniques; and by providing inferior servicing of products. These practices are thought to come about because of the wide range of products now being made available to consumers; the supplanting of small family-run production units by large mass-production factories; the great advances that have been made in mass communications; and growing monopoly power. They are alleged to result in restrictions of consumer welfare or well-being because they do not give consumers what they want and they utilize resources that could have been used to produce useful goods and services.

Consumerism is a movement that has developed over time to remedy the supposed inferior position of consumers. It consists of activities and efforts of private consumer advocates and consumer special interest groups as well as governmental activities and efforts.

Consumerism efforts are aimed toward the provision of at least three types of benefits to consumers. These are: (1) to make available more accurate and more complete information to consumers, (2) to reduce the amount of deceptive and useless sales promotion, and (3) to protect consumers from spillover costs of consuming from their own ignorance, and from manipulation by sellers. But activities intended to provide these benefits in turn have their costs. These include the alternative costs of the resources used to provide them and the costs to consumers of not being able to obtain products or product qualities which consumerism activities have succeeded in banning from the market.

Economic analysis seems to indicate that most of the information-providing activities of the consumerism movement will on balance enhance consumer welfare. So will most activities that prevent the imposing of spillover costs by some on others. Activities that protect consumers from their own ignorance and/or from manipulation by business firms are of questionable value to consumers. Some such activities may result in net benefits to consumers while others will involve costs that outweigh the benefits. The primary problem in this area is that consumer advocates and those who pass legislation enforcing advocacy measures are able to substitute their values and their judgments with regard to what consumers in general want and get for the judgments of consumers themselves. This is often costly to consumers and certainly it restricts their freedom in the marketplace.

SUPPLEMENTARY READINGS

Green, Mark J., ed. *The Monopoly Makers*. New York: Grossman Publishers, 1973.

Ralph Nader's study group report on regulation and competition. The activities of several regulatory agencies of the federal government are examined and found wanting in terms of protecting the consumer. Instead, the Nader group finds that the regulatory agencies tend to be used in the interests of the businesses that they are supposed to regulate.

Kelly, William T., ed. *New Consumerism: Selected Readings*. Columbus, Ohio: Grid, Inc., 1973.

A collection of both new and previously published articles intended to present a balanced picture of and evaluation of the consumerism movement. Topics embraced include the history of the movement, why it came into being, what it does, the reactions of business to it, how consumers abuse business, and a look into the future of consumerism.

Nader, Ralph, ed. *The Consumer and Corporate Accountability*. New York: Harcourt Brace Jovanovich, Inc., 1973.

A survey of corporate irresponsibility to consumers as seen by consumer advocates such as Nader, together with a section on what to do about it.

Nader, Ralph. *Unsafe at Any Speed*. 2d ed. New York: Grossman Publishers, 1972.

An extended report on alleged automobile industry disregard for the safety of its product. This is the book which could be said to have launched the modern consumerism movement.

Swagler, Roger M. *Caveat Emptor*. Lexington, Mass.: D. C. Health and Company, 1975.

An excellent elementary survey and analysis of consumer problems and the attacks made on those problems by private consumer advocates and by the government.

Weidenbaum, Murray L. *Government-Mandated Price Increases*. Washington, D.C.: American Institute for Public Policy Research, 1975.

Catalogues and analyzes the impact of federal controls and regulations on the costs and the prices of a wide variety of goods and services. Many cases are cited in which regulations are nullified by other regulations and serve only to increase prices.

Winter, Ralph K., Jr. *The Consumer Advocate versus the Consumer.* Washington, D.C.: American Institute for Public Policy Research, 1972.

A monograph highly critical of consumer advocacy and especially of the government's role in promulgating consumerism.

Chapter 8

HEALTH ISSUES

CHECKLIST OF ECONOMIC CONCEPTS

Elasticity of demand
Changes in demand
Per capita income
Tastes and preferences
Relative prices
Substitution effects
Less than full-cost pricing
Elasticity of supply
Changes in supply
Principle of diminishing returns
Investment
Technological advancements

8

Health issues
Is it worth what it costs?

Even though we are a nation that places a high value on health, we have done very little to insure that quality health care is available to all of us at a price we can afford. We have allowed rural and inner-city areas to be slowly abandoned by doctors. We have allowed hundreds of insurance companies to create thousands of complicated policies that trap Americans in gaps, limitations, and exclusions in coverage, and that offer disastrously low benefits which spell financial disaster for a family when serious illness or injury strikes. We have allowed doctor and hospital charges to skyrocket out of control through wasteful and inefficient practices to the point where more and more Americans are finding it difficult to pay for health care and health insurance. We have also allowed physicians and hospitals to practice with little or no review of the quality of their work, and with few requirements to keep their knowledge up to date or to limit themselves to the areas where they are qualified. In our concern not in infringe on doctors' and hospitals' rights as entrepreneurs, we have allowed them to offer care in ways, at times, in places, and at prices designed more for their convenience and profit than for the good of the American people.

When I say "we have allowed," I mean that the American people have not done anything about it through their government, that the medical societies and hospital associations have done far too little about it, and that the insurance companies have done little or nothing about it.

I believe the time has come in our nation for the people to take action to solve these problems.[1]

---

[1] Edward M. Kennedy, *In Critical Condition: The Crisis in America's Health Care* (New York: Simon & Schuster, 1972), pp. 16–17.

GROWTH AND NATURE OF HEALTH SERVICES

National health expenditures in the United States grew spectacularly in the 1940s, 1950s, and 1960s, at least doubling every decade. The same upward trend looks likely for the 1970s. These expenditures include such health services and supplies as hospital services, physicians' and dentists' services, and drugs and drug supplies, as well as expenditures on research and on construction of medical facilities. In the 36-year span from 1940 to 1976, health expenditures rose from $3.9 billion to $139.3 billion, from $29 per capita to $638 per capita, and from 4.1 percent of the nation's income to 8.6 percent. Figure 8–1 shows these trends and a projec-

FIGURE 8–1

National health expenditures in selected years, 1940 to 1976, and projected to 1980

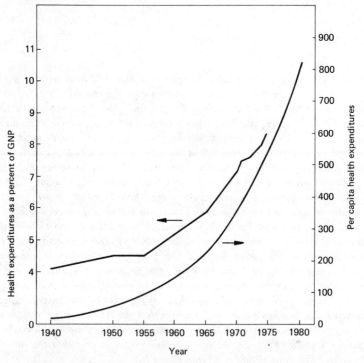

Health expenditures, whether measured as a percent of GNP or per capita, are increasing rapidly.

Source: U.S. Department of Health, Education, and Welfare, Social Security Administration, Office of Research and Statistics, *Medical Care Costs and Prices: Background Book* (January 1972), pp. 79, 90; Barbara S. Cooper and Nancy L. Worthington, "National Health Expenditures, 1929–1972," *Social Security Bulletin*, January 1973, p. 5.; April 1977, p. 4.

tion to 1980 which indicates that per capita health expenditures may reach $814 by the beginning of that decade.

Factors explaining the rise in personal health costs

A number of factors can explain the rise in personal health costs, that is, money spent for health services for the direct benefit of the individual.[2] These factors are the rise in prices for medical services, population growth, and changes in the health care system. Figure 8–2 shows the relative importance of these factors in the rising costs of medical care between 1965 and 1976.

FIGURE 8–2
Factors explaining increase in costs of medical care between fiscal years 1965 and 1976

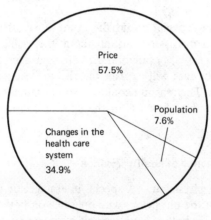

Price
57.5%

Population
7.6%

Changes in the
health care
system
34.9%

Most of the increase in expenditures for medical care is due to an increase in the price of the service.

Source: Robert M. Gibson and Marjorie Smith Mueller, "National Health Expenditures, Fiscal Year 1976," *Social Security Bulletin*, April 1977, p. 16.

Price increases. Between 1965 and 1976, price increases accounted for 57.5 percent of the increase in the costs of medical care. Thus most of the increase in the total costs for health services such as hospital and physicians' services is not attributable to a larger quantity or better quality but to higher prices for given quantities of health services (see Figure 8–2).

---

[2] Personal health expenditures do not include outlays which are spent for the community, such as in construction, research, or disease control.

Population growth.   Population growth accounted for 7.6 percent of the rise in the cost of medical care between 1965 and 1976. In general, the larger the number of people, the more health care is needed and the more resources are channelled into health care. The current slowdown in population growth can be expected to reduce the growth in the costs of medical care. However, the average age of population will increase with a slower population growth rate; as a consequence, a larger proportion of the population may need medical care.

Changes in the system.   People are buying a greater amount and receiving better health services today than in the past. People visit their physicians more often and request the services of hospitals more frequently. Improvements have been made in physician, hospital, and other medical care services. People expect to pay more when they demand greater quantities and qualities of services. These factors and other changes in the health care system explain about one third of the rise in medical care costs during the period 1965 to 1976.

Is there anything special about the rising costs of medical services? There is nothing special or unusual about the rising cost of medical services. Price increases, population growth, and a greater quantity and better quality of services will explain the rise in costs of most, if not all, goods and services. The reason people are so uptight about the rising costs of medical services lies, in part, in the special characteristics of health services.

Special characteristics of health services

The role of the physician.   A special characteristic of health services involves the role of the physician, who operates on both sides of the market. The physician is both a supplier and a demander of health services. It is the physician who provides the consumer directly with services and determines the service she or he needs from other suppliers—hospitals and suppliers of drugs and medicines. Decisions about medications, getting well at home or in the hospital, number of days spent in the hospital, and special medical services required are all made by the physician. Consumers usually do not even determine where they will receive hospital care. The selection of a hospital depends largely on where the physician happens to hold staff positions and which hospital the physician prefers.

Consumer ignorance.   Consumers are probably less informed about medical services than about anything else they buy. They usually can shop around, look, try, and compare goods and services they wish to buy. *Consumer Reports* publishes the results of testing certain products and provides valuable information that can serve as a guide to rational decision making by the customer. Almost no objective information is available concerning the quality of health services, however. Physicians are reluctant to give evaluations of the work of other physicians. Hospital and physicians' services generally are not subject to quality controls. Human errors, mistakes, and incompetencies in the supply of medical services may go undetected until it is too late for the individual buyer.

It is not a usual practice in the health field to disclose a list of prices for units of services. In many instances, consumers do not inquire about and do not know the prices of medical services until they receive their bills—at which time their choices are narrowed down to paying the bills or going to jail. The prices, quantities, and qualities of medical services are well-kept secrets to most consumers. The suppliers of health services have done little to change this situation.

Spillover benefits. In Chapter 3, on education, it was noted that benefits which flow to the specific users of goods and services are called direct benefits. As they use the goods and services, there may be indirect or social *spillover benefits* to other individuals.

The best illustration of social spillover benefits in health services involves communicable diseases. The use of medical services to get well from a disease that may spread to others directly benefits the user of the service and indirectly benefits others. Immunization shots benefit not only the person receiving the immunity from a disease, but the benefit extends beyond the individual user to others in society.

However, benefits from many medical services flow only to the individual users of these services. A heart or kidney transplant benefits primarily the individual receiving the transplant. The increased quantity and quality of medical services from the use of new equipment and intensive-care hospital rooms increases the chances of survival to the individual buyers of these services.

A "right" to good health. Most people regard good health as a "right." They believe that a sick person should have access to medical services regardless of income. This is why people are appalled when they hear on the radio, see on TV, or read in the newspaper that a person in a serious accident or with a serious illness was refused admittance to a hospital because one did not have either money or health insurance to pay for the services needed. The basic idea that health services are essential needs and people have a right to receive them runs consistently through American thought.[3]

Unpredictability of illness. Individuals and families, through budgeting, may carefully plan what goods and services they will buy, the quantities of each, and how much they will save. Some medical and health

---

[3] Herbert E. Klarman, "Requirements for Physicians," *American Economic Review,* May 1951, p. 633.

services can be planned for in this way, and others cannot be. A family may plan to fulfill medical and health needs that are predictable, such as physical examinations or immunization shots, but it is difficult to plan for illnesses or accidents. For one thing, people do not usually like to consider the prospects of illness. Second, and more critical from the viewpoint of family planning, the incidence of illness is uneven and unpredictable for a family.

Voluntary health insurance provides a way for individuals and families with the desire and ability to pay for it to plan for and cover the major risks of illness or injury. The incidence of illness is predictable, and therefore insurable, for the population or large numbers of people. Private health insurance companies cannot provide full protection against the exceptional or extremely high-cost illness, however. The consumer remains in general unprotected against prolonged and catastrophic illnesses or injuries.

HEALTH-CARE PROBLEMS

The special characteristics of health services provide a good background for an understanding of the nature of health services. They do not, however, give rise to a unique set of problems. The major economic problems in the health-care industry are those of efficiency in the supply of health services and equity in their distribution.

The public view

The view of the public concerning the problem in health care is reflected in the following quote:

> A decade ago, one medical group in Manhattan charged $35 for a basic physical checkup; today it charges $65. In those same years the going rate for an appendectomy in New York rose from $485 to $1,175 and the cost of an average hospital stay, for the nation as a whole, rose from $265 to $785.[4]

Most people view the rising costs of health care as the problem. Are they in fact the problem, or, perhaps, the symptom?

The economist's view

Economists in general do not look upon the rising costs of any good or service as necessarily a problem. Changes in prices and quantities of individual goods and services bought and sold may reflect changes in demand

---

[4] Richard A. Lyons, "Dilemma in Health Care: Rising Cost and Demand," *New York Times,* September 13, 1971, p. 1.

and supply in the market. The total amount of money spent for individual goods and services increases when demand and supply for these goods or services rise. There is no problem here. This is what is expected in a market economy.

However, the rising costs of health care may indicate or be a symptom of factors economists are concerned about, such as the restrictions on entry into the health-care industry, the response of supply to demand changes, and the impact of government subsidies on the demand for health services. A central economic problem as seen by economists involves the efficient use of scarce resources in the health-care industry. The analysis of demand for and supply of health services that follows provides a framework for an evaluation of the health-care industry in terms of economic efficiency.

ANALYSIS OF DEMAND FOR HEALTH SERVICES

Elasticity of demand

Consumers of certain health services, such as hospital and physicians' services, are not very responsive to price changes. An increase in price will not reduce the quantity demanded very much, and a decrease in price will not increase it much. In other words, the elasticity of demand for health-care services is low, or inelastic.[5] However, the elasticity of demand for specific medical services may vary from one service to another. For example, the demand for a dangerous surgery may be almost totally inelastic (if price were zero, there would be no more takers than if the price were $10,000). On the other hand, the demand for a physical examination is likely to be more elastic.

The inelastic portion of demand is illustrated in Figure 8–3. An increase in price from p_1 to p_2 decreases quantity demanded from q_1 to q_2. When demand is inelastic, the percentage decrease in quantity demanded is less than the percentage increase in price. Suppose p_1 and p_2 are $4 and $5, respectively, for a visit to a doctor's office and that q_1 and q_2 are ten visits and nine visits, respectively, per month. An increase in price of 25 percent $(5 - 4/4)$ causes the number of visits to the doctor's office to be reduced from ten visits to nine visits per month—a percentage decrease in quantity demanded of 10 percent $(10 - 9/10)$.[6] The elasticity coefficients is 10/25, or 0.40, in this illustration. The price elasticity of demand is said to be inelastic when the elasticity coefficient is less than 1.

[5] Herbert E. Klarman, *The Economics of Health* (New York: Columbia University Press, 1965), pp. 24–25.

[6] It should be noted that elasticity more precisely refers to the response of quantity demanded to a small change in price and that the slope of a demand curve is not a reliable indicator of the degree of responsiveness of quantity demanded to price changes.

FIGURE 8–3
An inelastic portion of demand

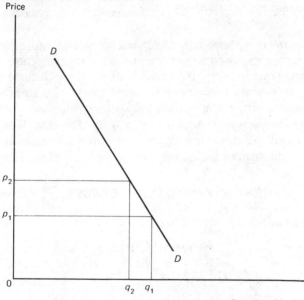

The inelastic portion of a demand curve is that over which
a given percentage change in price results in a smaller percentage change in quantity demanded. For demand to be inelastic between prices p_2 and p_1, the percentage change from
q_2 to q_1 must be smaller than the percentage change from
p_2 to p_1.

Factors changing the demand for health services

Changes in per capita income. Rising per capita incomes in the
United States have caused the demand curve for health services to shift
to the right. This is illustrated in Figure 8–4. Increases in income cause
the increases in demand from D to D_1 to D_2. The increases in price from
p to p_1 to p_2 and the increases in quantity demanded from q to q_1 to $\check{q}_2$ are
due to the rise in demand for health services.

Changes in tastes and preferences. Changes in consumer tastes and
preferences also change demand. An increase in tastes and preferences for
medical services increases demand for these services. This means that consumers are willing to buy larger quantities of medical services at every
possible price. It cannot be said for certain, but an increase in tastes and
preferences for medical care appears to have played at least a small part in
stimulating the demand for health services.

FIGURE 8–4

An increase in demand due to income growth

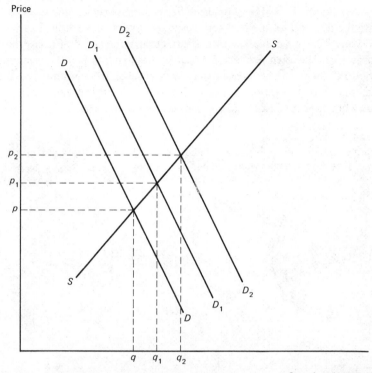

The demand curve is shifting outward because of increasing income and changing tastes and preferences. As a result, both the price and quantity demanded of health services are increasing.

Changes in relative price. Changes in price of goods and services which may be substituted for medical services change the demand for medical services. For example, suppose the price of recreational services declines relative to the price of medical physical examinations. The effect of this will be to encourage consumers to substitute the less costly service for medical services, if this is feasible. The result is a decline in the demand for medical services. Since there are a limited number of substitutes for medical services, however, the demand for medical services is probably not appreciably affected by changes in relative prices.

Less than full-cost pricing. Consumers do not directly pay the full costs of health services. Direct consumer payments represent about 32 cents out of each dollar spent for personal health; the remaining part of each dollar is paid by third parties—health insurance, private gifts, and government. The rise in the relative importance of third-party payments is shown in Figure 8–5. The impact of these third-party payments is to increase the demand for medical services. Consumers view medical care as a "good buy," since a dollar's worth of services may be bought for less than a dollar out of their own pockets. Of course, they have to pay the remainder of the full cost in the form of higher taxes and health insurance premium payments. A higher rate of consumption of goods and services will likely ensue when they are priced at less than full cost to the user.

FIGURE 8–5

Percent distributions of personal health-care expenditures by direct and third-party payments in selected years, 1950–1976

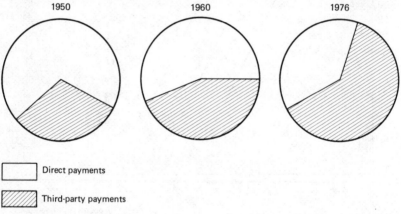

Third-party payments increased from 31.7 percent of health-care expenditures in 1950, to 44.7 percent in 1960, to 68.6 percent in 1976.

Source: Nancy L. Worthington, "National Health Expenditures, 1969–74," *Social Security Bulletin,* February 1975, p. 17.; Robert M. Gibson and Marjorie Smith Mueller, "National Health Expenditures, Fiscal Year 1976," *Social Security Bulletin,* April 1977, p. 8.

Medicare and Medicaid. An important reason for the increase in demand for medical care and the rise in medical-care costs has been the development since 1966 of two large government health programs— Medicare and Medicaid. The Medicare program covers the major costs of hospital and physicians' services provided to the aged under social security, and Medicaid pays for the costs of hospital and physicians' services provided to people who are poor. The combined estimated cost of Medicare and Medicaid in fiscal year 1976 was $33.1 billion. Medicare and Medicaid expenditures account for an important portion of the growth in medical care costs in recent years. Between fiscal years 1974 and 1976, for an example, about three fourths of the growth in personal health costs of $29.1 billion was attributable to the growth in Medicare and Medicaid expenditures.

The growth in the cost of medical care due to Medicare and Medicaid is only one side of the coin. Health benefits are the other side. Many aged persons now can receive adequate medical care because of Medicare, and many poor persons can receive it under Medicaid. Medicare and Medicaid are providing the means of payment for many persons who could not afford health care otherwise. By increasing demand, they have increased prices and the use of health services. In addition, the tradition among doctors of providing free medical care to the poor may be discouraged by the growth of government in the health field. This tradition, however, perhaps was not the best way of assuring that the poor receive adequate health care.

ANALYSIS OF SUPPLY OF HEALTH SERVICES

Supply characteristics: Physicians

Source of supply. The main source of supply of physicians in the United States is, of course, the U.S. medical schools. These schools are graduating more than 10,000 doctors annually. In 1974, they graduated 105 percent more doctors than in 1950.[7] Another supply source of physicians is from abroad. Physicians trained abroad have come into this country to practice medicine at a rapidly rising rate—exceeding 7,000 in 1974. Physicians trained abroad constitute 19.4 percent of all physicians practicing in the United States in 1975.[8]

Elasticity of supply. The supply of physicians is inelastic in the short run. Thus an increase in demand for physicians in the short run will have an impact primarily on prices. However, in the long run the supply curve of physicians is more elastic, and a rise in demand is expected to increase the number of physicians. After remaining approximately the same in the 1950s, the ratio of physicians to the population increased in the 1960s and early 1970s (see Table 8–1).

Estimated supply and requirements. Figure 8–6 shows estimated supply of physicians and requirements for physicians during the period 1970–80. On certain assumptions concerning the number of physicians required to meet the medical needs of the population, the U.S. Public Health Service estimated that there was a shortage of 50,000 physicians

---

[7] Bureau of the Census, *Statistical Abstract of the United States, 1976*, table 115, p. 77.

[8] Office of Management and Budget, *Special Analyses, Budget of the U.S. Government Fiscal Year 1978* (Washington, D.C.: U.S. Government Printing Office, 1977), p. 205.

TABLE 8–1
Physicians, nurses, hospital personnel, and short-term hospital beds per
100,000 population, selected years 1950–1974

Year	Physicians*	Nurses	Hospital personnel	Short-term hospital beds
1950	149	249	697	330
1960	148	282	888	360
1965	153	319	1,009	390
1970	166	345	1,245	420
1972	174	376	1,283	420
1974	186	404	1,381	440

* Doctors of medicine and osteopathy.
  Source: Bureau of Census, *Statistical Abstract of the United States, 1975*, p. 79; *1976*,
pp. 5, 77, 81, 82.

FIGURE 8–6
Estimated supply and requirements for physicians, 1970–1980

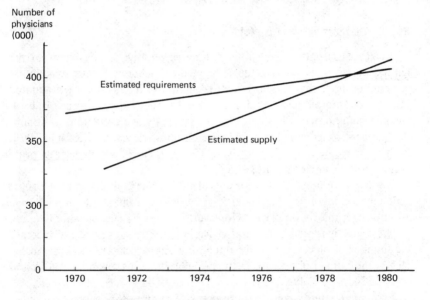

There will continue to be a shortage of physicians through the 1970s. However, by 1980 it is estimated that the shortage will disappear, and a surplus of
physicians may occur.

Source: Charles T. Stewart, Jr., and Corazon M. Siddayao, *Increasing the Supply of Medical
Personnel* (Washington, D.C.: American Enterprise Institute, 1973), p. 25.

in 1969. Beginning with this shortage, and on the same assumptions about
the required ratio of physicians to the population, it is estimated that supply
will catch up and there will be a surplus of 3,000 physicians by 1980.

Physicians' income. The median income of physicians almost doubled between 1959 and 1974, increasing from $22,000 to $44,580.

This growth in income and the relatively high income of physicians attract foreign-trained physicians to this country to practice medicine and encourage more qualified persons in this country to select medicine as a profession. Supply, then, has responded to the rising demand for physicians, but not fast enough to prevent rapidly rising prices for physicians' services. There are two reasons for this. We have mentioned one reason for the slow response of supply, namely the low elasticity of supply in the short run. The second is the restrictions on entry into the field of medicine. The first reason is a technical characteristic associated with the time it takes to train physicians. The second is a market defect attributable to the establishment of barriers to keep human resources out of the medical field.

Supply characteristics: Hospitals

The short-run supply curve of hospital services is the quantity of hospital services that will be supplied at different prices, given or holding constant the number of hospitals and hospital equipment, technology, and the prices of hospital inputs. The long-run supply curve differs from the short-run curve in that hospital investment (hospital facilities and equipment) may vary in the long run. Changes in hospital investment, technology, and the prices of inputs cause shifts in the short-run supply curve.

We expect the short-run supply curve of hospital services to be upward sloping, indicating the greater quantities supplied are associated with higher prices to patients.[9] These higher quantities result in higher costs per unit because of the principle of diminishing returns. Given the fixed sizes and facilities of the hospitals, the application of more and more variable resources (nurses, medical personnel, supplies) will eventually result in smaller and smaller increases in output. These smaller increases in output associated with given increases in variable resources or inputs mean higher costs per unit. Higher costs of hospital services may be eventually encountered, also, if hospital size increases. A wider range of services and, thus, more costly services are often associated with large hospitals. In addition, there may be diseconomies connected with larger outputs, due to increasing complexities of management.[10]

Factors affecting the supply of hospital services

Investment. An increase in hospital investment, that is, the construction of new hospitals, the expansion of existing hospitals, and the purchase of new equipment, increases the capacity of the hospital industry to provide

---

[9] Some statistical studies indicate that the supply curve for hospital services may be perfectly elastic, indicating that additional quantities may be supplied at the same price. See Klarman, *The Economics of Health,* p. 105.

[10] Ibid., p. 107.

hospital services. Hospital investment is a way to increase the supply of hospital services to meet the growing demand for these services.

Technology. Technological advancements increase the quantity and quality of hospital services. As a result of new technology, a greater quantity of the same services may be provided at lower prices, or new and better services may be provided. New medical technology (procedures and techniques such as open-heart surgery, cobalt therapy, and intensive care) usually result in both improved hospital care and higher hospital costs to patients. Between 1971 and 1973, hospital costs per patient day increased 11.5 percent and 49 percent of the increase was due to the improvement in hospital services.[11]

Wages and other costs. Hospitals are buying greater quantities of labor and medical supplies and are having to pay higher prices for these inputs. Wages paid to hospital employees and prices paid for drugs and medical supplies increased per patient-day 5.9 percent between 1971 and 1973.[12] This growth in the cost of hospital inputs accounted for 51.3 percent of the growth in the hospital cost per patient-day. Unless higher wages and prices paid by hospitals are offset by increases in productivity, these increases represent the added cost incurred in producing the same amount of hospital services. With reference to supply, this means that the supply curve of hospital services shifts to the left, illustrating that the same quantity may be supplied, only at higher prices.

EVALUATION OF THE U.S. HEALTH-CARE SYSTEM

The U.S. health-care system is under severe criticism. Herman M. Somers describes the system of health care in this country "as a technically excellent product thrown into a Rube Goldberg delivery contraption which distorts and defeats it, and makes it more expensive than it need be."[13] A committee reported to the Secretary of the Department of Health, Education, and Welfare that "the key fact about the health service as it exists today is the disorganization . . . fragmentation and disjunction that promote extravagance and permit tragedy."[14]

The health-care industry is not performing very well for two reasons: (1) entry into the industry is restricted and (2) the industry is inefficiently organized.

---

[11] U.S. Department of Health, Education and Welfare, Social Security Administration, *Medical Care Costs and Prices: Background Book* (September 1975), p. 39.

[12] Ibid., p. 39.

[13] Herman M. Sommers, "Economic Issues in Health Services," in Neil W. Chamberlain (ed.), *Contemporary Economic Issues,* rev. ed. (Homewood, Ill.: Richard D. Irwin, 1973), pp. 145–46.

[14] Ibid., p. 145.

Reducing entry barriers

Competition in the health-care industry could possibly be restored and certainly encouraged by changing the admission practices of medical schools, by reducing the control of the American Medical Association (AMA) over the medical industry, by breaking up the influence of county medical societies, and by eliminating state licensing and examining procedures.

Admission practices of medical schools. The admission practices of medical schools check the supply of physicians and work to keep supply from catching up with the demand for physicians. Medical schools reject a high rate of *qualified* applicants. It was estimated in 1972 that one half of the qualified applicants to medical schools were turned down.[15] To the extent that the high rejection rate of medical schools is due to limited capacity, a lowering of the rejection rate will require an expansion in medical school facilities.

Monopoly power of the AMA. The AMA virtually controls the supply of physicians. The source of this control is traced to the dominance of the association over medical education.[16] The AMA has controlled the number of medical schools by the use of its power to certify or fail to certify a medical school as a Class A rated school. The effects of its power to certify the quality of medical schools were never more in evidence than between 1906 and 1944, when the number of medical schools in the United States was reduced from 162 to 69. The AMA's dominance over medical education extends, also, to the internship and residency training programs. Its influence and power in this instance is due to the fact that it can approve or disapprove hospitals for administering internship and residency programs. Hospitals strongly favor having interns and residency personnel because these resources are made available at prices below their productivity.[17]

Influence of county medical societies. County medical societies are private clubs which keep a close surveillance on their members. These societies have their own judicial system and may expel physicians from membership or refuse membership to physicians who do not act in the best interest of the group.[18] For example, physicians who reduce prices in order to expand business may be labeled "unethical" and expelled. Expulsion from the society may be tantamount to denying a physician access to the

---

[15] Stewart and Siddayao, *Increasing the Supply,* p. 18.

[16] Reuben A. Kessel, "Price Discrimination in Medicine," in William Breit and Harold M. Hochman (eds.), *Readings in Microeconomics,* 2d ed. (New York: Holt, Rinehart & Winston, 1971), p. 375.

[17] Ibid., p. 378.

[18] Ibid., pp. 379–80.

facilities of a hospital, for hospitals may require and usually prefer their staff to be members of the society.

State licensing systems. Physicians cannot practice in any state solely by virtue of having completed their medical education. Supported by the AMA, states require that physicians be examined and licensed before practicing medicine. Licensing and examining procedures can be an effective way of controlling the supply of physicians coming from abroad. Foreign-trained physicians and other medical personnel may be encouraged or discouraged from practicing medicine in this country by changes in the difficulty of the examinations and other costs associated with getting a license.

Summary. The supply of medical services, especially physicians' services, is kept artificially low by restrictions to entry imposed directly or indirectly by the AMA, county medical societies, and the state. Until barriers to entry are broken down, the supply of medical and health services will not be responsive to competitive market forces, and the services will not be supplied at competitive prices.

Increasing efficiency

Paramedical personnel. Paramedical personnel are medical personnel who have had less training than a doctor. The use of paramedical personnel to do some of the work that doctors usually perform can save the time of doctors, increase their productivity, reduce costs, and increase the supply of medical services.

Although progress has been made in the use of auxiliary personnel, the idea of a lesser trained and lower paid doctor's assistant is not generally accepted.[19] Many patients prefer the expertise and the bedside manner of the licensed physician. This attitude could be changed by an education program pointing out the savings to the patient and the more efficient use of the physician's time. Health service jobs would have to be redefined so that the doctor's assistant could perform the job assigned as competently as the doctor could. One study indicates that the use of paramedical personnel could be doubled and the increase in productivity (output per physician) would be at least 20 percent.[20]

Group practice. The usual way of providing doctor's services is through a solo practice. A doctor receives an M.D. degree, obtains a license to practice medicine in a state, rents office space, buys furniture, supplies and equipment, put up a sign, and goes to work. The chances are that business will be thriving in a short time. In some instances, a young physician may join the practice of an older one.

---

[19] Stewart and Siddayao, *Increasing the Supply,* p. 41.
[20] Ibid., p. 43.

Solo practices are not usually efficient. Modern medical equipment may not be available and, if available, may not be fully utilized. A solo practice does not favor the maximum use of paramedical personnel and does not permit the pooling of human and capital resources. In contrast *group practices* may permit better utilization of human and capital resources, as well as productivity gains from specialization and division of labor.

Group practices vary in size, type of legal organization (partnership, corporation), services provided, method of pricing, and method of financing. The one thing that is usually common to group practices is the sharing of costs and revenues.[21] A type of group practice that has attracted substantial support is a prepaid plan called a Health Maintenance Organization (HMO). Medical services are supplied to people in a certain area at fixed fees contracted for in advance. There is an incentive under the HMO for medical services to be provided at the lowest possible cost, since the net income of the organization varies inversely with the cost of providing medical services.

Hospital-based health center. An extension of the concept of a group practice is the health center. In the health-center concept patients would be tested, classified, and distributed to the area of the center that is best staffed and equipped to treat and cure them. Diagnostic tests could be handled by paramedical personnel. A computer could be used to classify patients as to the type of medical care needed and distribute them to center areas in accordance with their respective health needs.

An important role of a health center is to maintain a check on the quality of health care on its premises and throughout the community it serves.[22] Local health centers, nursing homes, first-aid stations, and clinics would be a part of the organizational structure of the health center. The center could have mobile health teams to provide advice and assistance to local health units and supply health services to areas that are without adequate health-care personnel and facilities.

Health-care centers can be organized and developed around the modern hospital.[23] This is logical, since the hospital is the focal point of health activities today. A hospital-based health center could mean that many hospitals in a given area would be under a single management. Each hospital could provide specialized health services. To cite a living example, in May 1975 eight hospitals in Hartford, Connecticut joined together and formed a health consortium. Each of the eight hospitals that were highly diversified now specialize in cerain services, plan together, share facilities, and permit doctors to treat their patients in any hospital in the group. The benefits that

---

[21] Ibid., p. 44.

[22] Somers, *Economic Issues,* p. 149.

[23] Ibid., pp. 149–50.

are likely and expected from this new hospital group in the Hartford area are better hospital services and lower hospital costs.

Medical training time.   It usually takes about eight years to become an M.D.—four years in college and four years in "med" school. A person who specializes, of course, receives training beyond the M.D. degree. It has been suggested that two years could be saved from the time it takes to become a doctor by admitting candidates to medical schools after three years of college and reducing the medical program to a three-year period.[24] Medical schools could thus turn out more doctors without expanding medical facilities. The supply of physicians would increase, the price of physicians' services would thereby be reduced.

Summary.   The efficiency of the present health-care system could be greatly improved. This could be accomplished through the use of paramedical personnel, the development of group practices and health centers, and the shortening of the period and cost of medical training. The survival of the system of health care as we know it today may depend upon what improvements can be made in the supply and price of health services.

NATIONAL HEALTH INSURANCE

As a possible solution to some of the problems in the health care field, a national health insurance program has been proposed and discussed in and out of government for several decades. National health insurance, at one extreme, is regarded as a panacea; it is regarded as a bad omen at the other extreme. It is certainly no panacea. There are many issues connected with it, and many health care problems won't be completely solved by it. On the other hand, a national health insurance program doesn't necessarily mean "socialized medicine" in the pure sense as, perhaps, illustrated by programs in Sweden and England. The American version of socialized medicine could be uniquely American—a blend of private and public interest and support.

The goals envisoned by proponents of national health insurance can be summarized as follows: (1) to ensure everyone access to "adequate" health care; (2) to eliminate the financial burden connected with the acquisition of health services; and (3) to control and limit rising health care costs.[25] How to fulfill these goals is not clear. The goals may very well be in conflict. For example, it appears difficult, if not impossible, to limit the annual increases in health care costs while at the same time providing comprehensive and universal care. Several basic issues arise.

---

[24] Stewart and Siddayao, *Increasing the Supply*, p. 50.

[25] Karen Davis, *National Health Insurance: Benefits, Costs, and Consequences* (Washington, D.C.: Brookings Institution, 1975), pp. 2–5.

Basic issues

There are many issues involving national health insurance.[26] Among the important issues in question form are: *Who* will be covered? *What* will be covered? *How* will the plan be financed? *How much* will patients pay?

Who will be covered? *Universal coverage* means that the entire population is covered under a national health insurance program. A program that provides incomplete coverage could leave a part of the population without access or much access to health care. A program that provides complete coverage includes both the part of the population that can afford to pay for health care and the part that cannot. The segment of the population that is of major concern is the part that cannot afford to pay for health services either because of generally low income or because of financial hardships associated with exorbitant medical care costs. Persons that can afford to pay for health care without relative financial hardship could be left with the responsibility of providing for their own health care. A difficulty with this approach is that the supply of health services to the poor is interrelated with the supply of services to the nonpoor.[27] Suppliers of health services may prefer and find it more profitable to meet the effective demand of persons not covered under a national health insurance program.

A program of national health insurance that provides universal coverage shifts almost the entire financial burden of health care costs to the government, and redistributes income from taxpayers to the users of health services. Limiting coverage, say, to the poor, in combination with voluntary private health insurance plans for the relative nonpoor is an option to universal coverage. The benefits of this option are in the form of the reduced costs to taxpayers and the costs are in the form of the benefits foregone that could have been associated with universal coverage.

What will be covered? There are many different kinds and a wide range of health services. *Comprehensive insurance coverage* includes almost all of them. In the determination of what will be covered under a national health insurance plan, the following priorities have been suggested: (1) medical services that have high social benefits such as immunizations and mental health care; (2) medical services that can be very expensive to the individual such as hospitalization, fees of specialists, and chronic illnesses; (3) health services that are lower-cost substitutes for covered services, for example, services that could be rendered at the physician's office instead of in a hospital.[28]

It is difficult to draw the line as to the kinds of health services that are

---

26 Ibid., pp. 56–79.

27 Ibid., p. 56.

28 Ibid., p. 58.

essential to good health and that should be covered under national health insurance. Most plans cover a wide range of services. Illustrations of health services that are usually not considered essential and are not covered are some dental services and cosmetic surgery.

How will national health insurance be financed?   National health insurance can be financed from premiums, payroll taxes, and general tax revenues. Unless premiums vary directly with income, premium payments are regressive, that is, they will be a smaller fraction of the income of high income patients than they will be of low income patients. Payroll taxes, as they are currently levied, would be less regressive than a fixed premium payment but they are also regressive on income groups above $15,000.[29] Financing an insurance scheme from state and federal general tax revenues could be made more equitable but would break the connection between individual benefits and costs that might otherwise possibly exist. Most proposals rely on all three sources of revenue in varying degrees. Equity considerations would discourage the use of regressive methods of finance. Efficiency considerations would encourage the use of methods of finance that maintains a relationship between individual benefits and costs.

How much will patients pay?   An important difference in national health insurance schemes is the extent that they vary in regard to direct payments by patients. Under health insurance schemes, direct payments by patients are generally in the form of deductibles and coinsurance provisions. A *deductible* is the amount that the patient pays of the cost up to some figure and *coinsurance* is the fraction of the cost above the deductible that the patient pays. For example, if we assume the deductible is $100 and coinsurance is 10 percent, the total cost of a health care service of $400 would be divided between the patient and insurance as follows:

```
Paid by:
   Patient ........................... $130
      Deductible ($100)
      coinsurance [30 (10% × 300)]
   Insurance ........................   270
         Total cost ..................  $400
```

There are two advantages to patients paying part of the cost. The cost to the taxpayer is reduced and exorbitant use of health services is discouraged. The disadvantage is that deductibles and coinsurance provisions could prevent persons from receiving care that need it. This disadvantage could

---

[29] Joseph A. Pechman and Benjamin A. Okner, "Who Bears the Tax Burden?" (Washington, D.C.: Brookings Institution, 1974), p. 59.

be essentially removed by relating patients' share to the income of the patient. Also, cost ceilings could be established in regard to patients' cost. In a given year, for example, patients' cost could not exceed a given amount, say $500.

Alternative proposals

There have been numerous national health insurance proposals before Congress in recent years. Many more will be forthcoming. President Carter has stressed national health insurance as a priority. Thus, it is likely that the Carter Administration will propose a plan in 1977 or 1978. Various approaches have been taken to national health insurance: (1) tax credit; (2) poor and catastrophic coverage; (3) mixed public and private insurance; (4) and public insurance.[30]

Tax credit approach. This approach would retain the existing Medicare program, and keep Medicaid but in a more limited form. The essence of the approach is a full tax credit against income taxes on private insurance premium coverage of catastrophic illnesses, and a variable credit depending upon tax liabilities against the premium payment for basic benefits. Concerning the variable credit, families with no income tax liabilities would have their full premiums paid; families with income tax liabilities would receive tax credits scaled downward so that families with more income and paying more taxes would receive a credit that would be a lower percent of the premium payment. Deductibles and coinsurance provisions are generally incorporated into the tax credit approach. This approach has appealed to some members of Congress and was at one time supported by the American Medical Association.

Poor and catastrophic coverage approach. Senators Long and Ribicoff proposed a plan in 1973 that illustrates this approach. The Long-Ribicoff Bill has a catastrophic expense provision, a low-income provision, and provisions to encourage the sale of private health insurance policies.[31] The catastrophic expense provision would cover all medical service now offered under the Medicare Program but payments would be made only after large deductions. For example, physician charges over $2,000 would be covered. The low-income provision would take care of the health needs of low income families. This provision would replace the current Medicaid program. Families covered under this provision would pay very little of the cost of their medical care. Under the Long-Ribicoff Bill, private insur-

---

[30] Davis, National Health Insurance, pp. 80–113.

[31] Barry M. Blechman et al., *Setting National Priorities: The 1975 Budget* (Washington, D.C.: Brookings Institution, 1974), p. 227.

ance companies would be encouraged to develop a standard policy that would cover the deductible amounts related to the catastrophic expense provision.

Mixed public and private insurance approach.   Although it was not reintroduced under President Ford, the Nixon Administration introduced a plan that exemplifies a mixed public and private insurance approach. The Nixon Administration's proposal contained three parts.[32] The first part was an employee health care insurance plan for working families. Under this plan, employers would have to offer their full-time employees a health insurance package and health care benefits would be provided by private health insurance companies. Both the employer and employee would share in the cost of the program with the employer's share starting at 65 percent and reaching 75 percent after the third year. The health insurance coverage would be quite broad including hospital care, physician and other medical services, drugs, and a $1,500 ceiling for total family contributions toward medical expenses in a single year.

The second part of the proposal was a health care plan for the poor called an assisted health care insurance plan. This plan was essentially to replace the existing Medicaid program. It would cover families who are poor and families who cannot afford to pay insurance premiums for private health insurance. The health care benefits are the same under this plan as under the employee health care insurance plan. There are differences, however, between the two plans. For example, cost sharing—premiums and other patient costs—under the plan for the poor and near-poor is based on income, with the lowest income families paying nothing or very little.

The third part of the plan revised and improved the current Medicare program—a program designed to provide health care benefits to persons 65 years and older under Social Security. Persons eligible for Medicare would be extended the same health benefit package as provided under the first and second parts of the administration's program. Similar to the plan for the poor, costs to the elderly patient would be related to income. Different than the plans for working families and for the poor, the plan for the elderly would be a federal program administered by the Social Security Administration.

Public insurance approach.   In comparison to the other approaches, this approach transfers a much larger part of the cost of health care to the government to be financed by taxes. Under the public insurance approach, benefits are generally more comprehensive and the coverage more universal. The Health Security Act introduced by Senator Kennedy and Congressman Griffiths illustrates this approach.

---

[32] Ibid., p. 218.

The Health Security Act (Kennedy-Griffiths Bill) would replace the existing systems of private insurance coverage and public programs such as Medicare and Medicaid with a single comprehensive federal health program.[33] The entire population would be covered with a wide range of health services that would be provided at a zero price to the individual demander. In other words, patients would not have to make any direct payments, for the financing of medicare services would be entirely from taxes.

Under the Health Security Act, the quantity and price of health care services would be determined through budgetary controls and regulatory devices. Each year a budget would be determined and allocated on a regional basis. Providers of health services would have several options as to how they would be paid. Physicians, say, could elect to be paid by a fixed salary, or by a fee for services rendered, or on a capitation basis. The act would encourage the establishment of HMOs (Health Maintenance Organizations), organizations that would agree to supply health services to a given population on a fixed per capita fee basis.

The Kennedy-Griffiths plan is the most thorough and far-reaching of the health proposals to date. The plan attempts to fulfill all three goals of national health insurance; namely, that of assuring everyone access to medical care, that of eliminating the financial burden associated with the purchase of health services; and that of limiting health care costs. But, the plan has basic drawbacks—the huge cost of health services that would have to be financed from taxes and the government controls and regulations that would be established to implement the plan.

What plan will the Carter Administration propose?

It is hazardous to guess what national health insurance plan the Carter Administration will propose. It is not likely to be as extreme as the Kennedy-Griffiths plan. It is more likely to be a mixed public and private insurance approach. It will be of interest to see what will develop.

After Carter's first five months in office, the only development is the suggestion by the President that the costs of hospital services be restricted to about a 9 percent increase a year. This would be significantly below the 15 percent annual rise of recent years. It is difficult to see how a government decree like this can be an effective way to slow down hospital inflation. Behind the rising prices for units of health services including hospital services is the rising demand for these services increasingly paid for by third parties—private and public insurance. Thus, the solution is to slow down demand and/or to increase the supply of health services. The former

---

[33] Davis, *National Health Insurance,* pp. 109–10.

solution is not an attractive one according to some people for it means less health care for people. The latter solution (increasing supply) is more attractive but is difficult to bring about without fundamental changes in the structure of the health care industry.

SUMMARY

The recent spectacular rise in the cost of medical care reflects growth in demand, slow response of supply, improvements in the quality of medical services, and the inefficient organization of the health-care system. The growth in demand for health services is primarily due to the rise in per capita income in our society and the development of third-party payments. There are more people with more income who desire greater quantities of health-care services and are willing to pay higher prices for them. Third-party payments, that is, payments for health care made by government and private health insurance companies on the behalf of people, have extended health care to more people and have encouraged the utilization of health services. Government payments for medical services have increased demand by providing the means of payment to people covered under Medicare and Medicaid. Prepaid voluntary health insurance reduces the out-of-pocket costs of medical care to the consumer and, consequently, increases the use of health services.

The impact of more people, higher income, and third-party payments on prices of health services would be minimized if the supply of health services responded quickly to the rise in demand. However, supply has been slow to respond. It takes time to construct new hospitals and to train doctors, nurses, and other medical personnel. In addition, human resources cannot move freely into the health field because of restrictions on entry.

Medical services have improved in quality. New and better medical equipment has been introduced. New medical procedures and treatment are being used. A part of the rising cost of medical care, then, is due to the technically better product being supplied.

Increases in productivity can offset in part or entirely an increase in cost. Although the health-care systems have had some increases in productivity, the system in general is inefficient. A great deal of progress cannot be made toward increasing the efficiency with which health services are supplied without major changes in the organization and structure of the health-care system. A hospital-based health center is one type of organization within which health services may be supplied more efficiently.

It will be difficult to achieve all of the goals envisioned by the proponents of national health insurance which are (1) to insure everyone access to adequate health care; (2) to eliminate the financial burden connected to the acquisition of health services; and (3) to control and limit the rise in health care costs. There are many national health insurance issues to be worked out such as: who will be covered? What will be covered? How will the plan be financed? How much will patients pay? The various national health insurance proposals approach these issues in different ways. The Carter administration acknowledges that national health insurance is a priority; however, there has not been a concrete proposal to date.

SUPPLEMENTARY READINGS

Committee for Economic Development. *Building a National Health-Care System.* New York, 1973.

A pamphlet stating the policy recommendations of the C.E.D. concerning a program for national health insurance. This reference could be distributed and used as a basis for class discussion.

Davis, Karen. *National Health Insurance: Benefits, Costs, and Consequences.* Washington, D.C.: Brookings Institution, 1975.

A thorough examination of all aspects of national health insurance.

Fuchs, Victor R. *Who Shall Live?* New York: Basic Books, Inc., 1974.

A well-written and thorough book that covers most all aspects of health care.

Ginzberg, Eli. *Men, Money and Medicine.* New York: Columbia University Press, 1969.

Well-written and easy to understand book. Presents the view that physicians create their own demand. Chapter 6 on the physician and market power and chapter 7 on the physician shortage are interesting contrasting reading.

Klarman, Herbert E. *The Economics of Health.* New York: Columbia University Press, 1965.

An economic analysis of the demand and supply of health care is presented in chapters 2, 4, and 5. Economic concepts and principles are introduced throughout the analysis of health. A background in economic theory would be helpful in comprehension of the analysis.

Lambert, Richard D., ed. *The Annals of the American Academy of Political and Social Science,* vol. 399 (January 1972).

The entire volume is devoted to health issues. Articles by Irving Levesin, "The Challenge of Health Services for the Poor," and by Anne R. Somers, "The Nation's Health: Issues for the Future," are suggested supplementary readings.

Schultze, Charles L., et al. *Setting National Priorities: The 1973 Budget,* chap. 7. Washington, D.C.: Brookings Institution, 1972.

Chapter 7 provides coverages of major issues in health insurance and national health insurance proposals.

Stewart, Charles R., Jr., and Siddayao, Corazon M. *Increasing the Supply of Medical Personnel.* Washington, D.C.: American Enterprise Institute, 1973.

The main theme is that government subsidies to medical students are unnecessary, since there is a surplus of qualified medical students. This is a good general reference. Chapter 4 is especially recommended to supplement the section above on the health-care system.

PART TWO

Distribution of income

Chapter 9

POVERTY PROBLEMS

CHECKLIST OF ECONOMIC CONCEPTS

Income inequality
Demand for labor
Supply of labor
Wage rate determination *workers are paid what they're worth*
Determinants of income distribution
Ownership pattern of resources
Negative income tax

9

Poverty problems

Is poverty necessary?

The young today are just play-acting in courting poverty. It's all right to wear jeans and eat hamburgers. But it's entirely different from not having any hamburgers to eat and no jeans to wear. A great many of these kids—white kids —seem to have somebody in the background they can always go to. I admire their spirit, because they have a strong sense of social justice. But they them- selves have not been deprived. They haven't experienced the terror. They have never seen a baby in the cradle crying of hunger. . . .

I think the reason for the gap between the black militants and the young white radicals is that the black kids are much more conscious of the thin edge of poverty. And how soon you can be reduced to living on relief. What you know *and what you* feel *are very different. Terror is something you* feel. *When there is no paycheck coming in—the absolute, stark terror.*[1]

"Poverty amidst plenty" is a striking feature of the American scene. Our nation is the richest in the world, yet millions of people are poor, and millions more that do not live in poverty are poor relative to others. This is not the American dream; it is the American paradox.

Poverty may be a more serious problem in our society than in societies with much less income and wealth. Poverty amidst poverty is easier to understand and even condone. But, in a land of abundance it is difficult to comprehend why some people are inadequately fed, clothed, and sheltered.

---

[1] Quote from Virginia Durr in Studs Terkel, *Hard Times* (New York: Random House, 1970), p. 462.

Poverty is a reality that needs to be studied, understood, appreciated, and then eradicated.

Our study of poverty in the United States will be approached in two ways. First, poverty will be examined in reference to *absolute* income levels. This approach permits the identification of people who live below a designated poverty level of income. Second, it will be studied in terms of *relative* incomes, that is, the share or percent of national income that people receive.

POVERTY IN TERMS OF ABSOLUTE INCOME LEVELS

The poverty problem in the United States is essentially an income distribution problem. There is enough income to go around so that no one would have to live in poverty. But enough income does not go to everyone, and some people do live in poverty.

Median family income in the United States was $13,720 in 1975. As Figure 9–1 shows, more people and families move out of poverty each year due to growth in family income. This is the good news. The bad news is that 25.9 million persons were poor in 1975.

FIGURE 9–1
Poor persons in 1960 and 1975

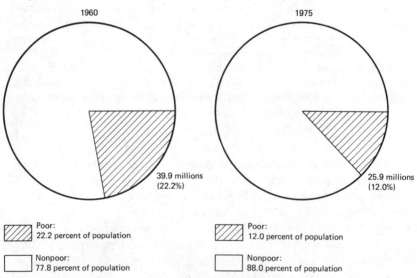

The number of poor persons decreased from 39.9 million (22.2 percent of the population) in 1960 to 25.9 million (12 percent of the population) in 1973.

Source: U.S. Department of Commerce Bureau of the Census, *Consumer Income,* Current Population Reports, series P–60, no. 103 (September 1976).

What is poverty?

Poverty is not easily defined. Yet, a precise definition has been implied in the statement that many Americans are poor. We shall use the definition of poverty developed by the government.

Poverty is concerned with the relationship between the minimum needs of people and their ability to satisfy these needs. The difficulty with any definition of poverty involves the meaning of "minimum needs" and the amount of money required to satisfy these needs. The approach taken by the government is essentially, first, to determine a minimum food budget and the money cost of that budget. Second, the cost of the food budget is multiplied by three because the cost of food represents about one third of consumers spending, according to studies of consumer spending patterns. For an illustration, $1,833 represents the cost of the minimum food budget for an urban family of four. The cost of food times three equals $5,500, the official poverty level for this type of family in 1975. Poverty levels as defined for different family sizes are listed in Table 9–1.

TABLE 9–1
Poverty levels in 1975

Family size	Urban	Rural
2	$3,506	$2,955
3	4,293	3,643
4	5,500	4,695
5	6,499	5,552
6	7,316	6,224

Poverty levels as defined vary by family size and residence of family. For example, a family of four living in an urban area in 1975 had a poverty level of $5,500.

Source: U.S. Department of Commerce, Bureau of the Census, *Consumer Income*, Current Population Reports, series P–60, no. 103 (September 1976).

Who are the poor?

Table 9–2 lists family groups that have a high incidence of poverty. Note that some of these groups overlap with others.

Blacks and other minority groups. Blacks and other minority groups have a very high incidence of poverty. The poverty rate among black families is about four times that of white families. For example, 27.1 percent of black families were poor in 1975, as compared to 7.7 percent of white families. The incidence of poverty may be as high or higher among some

TABLE 9–2
Selected characteristics of families below the poverty level in 1975

Selected characteristics	Total families	Families below poverty level	
		Number	Percent
All families	56,245,000	5,450,000	9.7%
White families	49,873,000	3,838,000	7.7
Black families	5,586,000	1,513,000	27.1
Age of family head			
14–24 years	4,042,000	850,000	21.0
65 years and over	8,163,000	728,000	8.9
Size of family			
2 persons	21,280,000	1,784,000	8.4
4 persons	11,276,000	939,000	8.3
7 or more persons	2,296,000	589,000	25.6
Educational attainment of family head			
Less than 8 years	5,784,000	1,293,000	22.4
High school, 1–3 years	7,964,000	1,118,000	14.0
High school, 4 years	17,550,000	1,090,000	6.2
College, 1 year or more	15,930,000	470,000	3.0
Employment status of family head			
Employed	41,078,000	2,154,000	5.2
Unemployed	2,378,000	505,000	21.2
Not in labor force	12,788,000	2,761,000	23.0
Nonfarm families	54,045,000	5,148,000	9.5
Farm families	2,200,000	302,000	13.7

Source: U.S. Department of Commerce, Bureau of the Census, *Consumer Income,* Current Population Reports, series P–60, no. 103 (September 1976).

other minority groups, such as Indians and Chicanos (Mexican-Americans), than among blacks. It was estimated that the unemployment rate among Indians was 40 percent when the national average was 3.8 percent in 1966.[2]

The young. The incidence of poverty is very high among young families. Some families headed by young persons, say under 25 years old, have difficulties making ends meet because the family head frequently lacks education and work experience. About one out of every five families headed by young persons is poor.

The aged. Families headed by persons of 65 years of age and over frequently have low levels of family income due to retirement or illness of the family head. Most of the aged poor are couples or widows attempting to live on private or public retirement payments such as social security payments. Some own their homes, but many live in rented rooms and apartments. Among the poor, about one out of every eight poor families is headed by an aged person.

---

[2] Gustav Schachter and Edwin L. Dale, Jr., *The Economist Looks at Society* (Lexington, Mass.: Xerox College Publishing, 1973), p. 27.

The uneducated. Poverty rates vary inversely with the level of education. Low poverty rates are associated with high education levels and high poverty rates with low education levels. Only 3 percent of families headed by persons with one or more years of college are poor. In contrast, 22.4 percent of the families headed by persons with less than eight years of schooling are poor.

The unemployed. Heads of families who are unemployed for any significant period of time are normally forced to draw on their savings to support their families. After their savings are depleted, a drastic cut in their living standard occurs. In 1975, there were 2,378,000 families headed by unemployed persons. Almost one out of every five of these families lived in poverty.

The working poor. A job is no guarantee that a person or a family will not be poor. In 1975, there were 2,154,000 poor families that were headed by persons with jobs. These poor families headed by working persons represented 39.5 percent of all families that lived in poverty.

The nonworking poor. The sick, disabled, aged families that lose hope, give up, and live on welfare are not included in the labor force. There were approximately 12.8 million families like this in 1975. About 23 percent of these families, or 2,761,000, lived in poverty in 1975. This group of families represents about one half of the families living in poverty.

Rural people. Poverty is widespread among families that live in rural areas. In some instances poverty in rural areas may not be as visible as it is in an urban environment. Poverty rates are almost one and a half times higher among farm families than among nonfarm families. For example, the poverty rate was 13.7 percent among farm families as compared to 9.5 percent among nonfarm families in 1975. Job opportunities and family incomes are higher in urban areas than in rural ones.

POVERTY IN TERMS OF INCOME DISTRIBUTION

The second approach to poverty considers the distribution of income in the United States. We have said that the poverty problem in this country is mainly one of income distribution. This means that the level of income in our country is high enough so that a more equal distribution of income should mitigate the poverty problem and reduce its significance.

Income equality

Economists usually explain income equality and income inequality by reference to a curve called a Lorenz curve, after M. O. Lorenz. Income equality among families means that any given percent of families receive an equal percent of family income; 10 percent of families receive 10 percent of income, 20 percent of families receive 20 percent of income, and

100 percent of families receive 100 percent of income. In Figure 9–2, equal percentages of families and incomes can be measured along the two axes. Income equality is shown by a 45-degree line starting at the origin. At any point on the 45-degree line, the percent of families shown receive an equal percent of total family income.

FIGURE 9–2
Lorenz curve plotted with data on U.S. family income, 1975

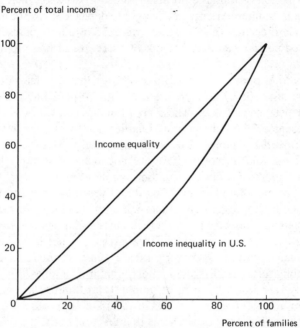

Percent of total income

Income equality

Income inequality in U.S.

Percent of families

The Lorenz curve shows the existing degree of income inequality. The horizontal axis measures the percent of families, starting with the poorest. Thus the 20 percent mark represents the lowest earning fifth of the population. In 1975, the lowest 20 percent earned 5.4 percent of the total income, and the lowest 40 percent earned 17.2 percent of total income. This means that the second quintile (the families included between the 20 percent and the 40 percent marks), earned 11.8 percent of the total income (17.2—5.4). If perfect income equality existed, the Lorenz curve would be the 45-degree line.

Source: Data from U.S. Department of Commerce, Bureau of the Census, *Statistical Abstract of the United States, 1976*, p. 406.

Income inequality

Income inequality can be illustrated graphically by lines that deviate from the line of income equality. A Lorenz curve derived from actual data on income distribution will usually lie to the right of the line of income equality (the 45-degree line). The further to the right of the 45-degree line it lies, the greater the inequalities in income distribution. Lorenz curves are useful in making income distribution comparisons in a given year among different countries or in the same country over time.

Table 9–3 divides U.S. families into five numerically equal groups, or quintiles, and indicates the distribution of personal income among these groups. The table also shows the income share of the top 5 percent of families. It can be observed that income is very unequally distributed. The highest 20 percent of families received over 41 percent of income in 1975, and the lowest 20 percent received 5.4 percent. The top 5 percent of families received 15.5 percent of income. These data on income inequality are shown by the Lorenz curve in Figure 2–2.

TABLE 9–3
Percent of income received by each fifth and top 5 percent of families in selected years, 1950–1975

Quintile of families	1950	1955	1960	1965	1970	1975
Lowest fifth	4.5%	4.8%	4.9%	5.3%	5.5%	5.4%
Second fifth	12.0	12.2	12.0	12.1	12.0	11.8
Third fifth	17.4	17.7	17.6	17.7	17.4	17.6
Fourth fifth	23.5	23.7	23.6	23.7	23.5	24.1
Highest fifth	42.6	41.6	42.0	41.3	41.6	41.4
	100.0%	100.0%	100.0%	100.0%	100.0%	100.0%
Top 5 percent	17.0%	16.8%	16.8%	15.8%	14.4%	15.5%

Source: U.S. Department of Commerce, Bureau of the Census, *Statistical Abstract of the United States, 1972*, p. 324; *Statistical Abstract of the United States, 1976*, p. 406.

Income inequality was reduced during the 1930s and the years of World War II. The share of income received by the top 5 percent and the highest 25 percent decreased between 1929 and 1944, while the share received by the lowest 25 percent of families increased. It is generally agreed that the two main reasons for this trend toward greater income equality were that property income fell drastically during the Great Depression of the 1930s, and the gap between low-paid and high-paid workers was reduced when full employment was reached during World War II.[3]

Since the 1950s, the trend toward greater income equality has not been so pronounced. The shares of income received by the top 5 percent and top 20 percent have decreased slightly, from 17 percent and 43 percent, respectively, in 1950 to 15.5 percent and 41 percent, respectively, in 1975. The share of income received by the lowest one fifth of families increased from 4.5 percent in 1950 to 5.4 percent in 1975. The shift in in-

---

[3] Joseph A. Pechman, "The Rich, the Poor and the Taxes They Pay," *The Public Interest,* no. 17 (Fall 1968).

come since 1950 has been away from the upper income groups and toward
the lower income ones. The striking feature concerning the distribution of
income during the past two decades is the stability of the income distribution pattern, especially the share of income received by middle-income
families.

THE ECONOMIC CAUSES OF POVERTY

Determinants of resource prices and employment

Family incomes depend on the quantities of resources that families can
place in employment and the prices received for those resources. To understand poverty, then, it is important to understand what determines the
prices paid for human and capital resources and what determines the quantities that can be employed.

Wage rate determination.   Under competitive market conditions, the
basic principle of wage rate determination is that units (person-hours) of
any kind of labor tend to be paid a price equal to any one worker's (hourly)
contribution to an employer's total receipts. In other words, workers are
paid about what they are worth to employers. What a worker is worth to
an employer is referred to by economists as the worker's marginal revenue
productivity. Suppose the marginal revenue productivity of the worker is
$4 per hour; that is, an hour of labor is contributing $4 to the receipts of
the employer. Then the worker is worth $4 an hour to the employer and
would be paid that amount under competitive conditions. If a worker were
paid less than what she or he is worth to an employer, the worker would
also be paid less than she or he would be worth to *other* employers. Consequently, other employers would bid for the worker's services, driving the
worker's wage rate (hourly wages) up to what she or he *is* worth. On the
other hand, rather than pay $5 an hour, an employer would lay a worker
off.

This principle can be seen more clearly with reference to Figure 9–3.
The demand curve for labor (DD in the figure) shows what employers are
willing to pay at different quantities of labor (man-hours per month), or,
alternatively, how much a unit of labor is worth at different possible employment levels. The supply curve for labor (SS in the figure) shows the
quantity of labor that will be placed on the market at different wage rates.
Labor is paid less than it is worth at the wage rate w_0. Only q_0 units of
labor want to work at this wage rate. However, at this employment level,
labor is worth w_2 to any employer. Thus, a shortage exists; that is, at the
wage rate w_0, the quantity of labor demanded is greater than the quantity
supplied, the wage rates will be driven up to w_1. Labor is paid about what
it is worth to any employer at w_1. At a wage rate above w_1, however, the

FIGURE 9-3
Wage rate determination under competition

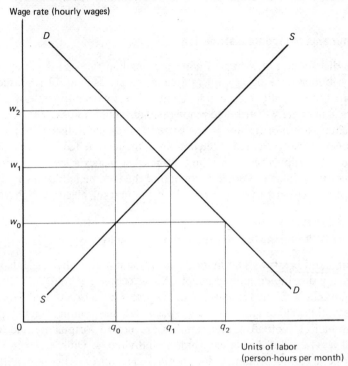

Wage rate (hourly wages)

quantity of labor supplied is not worth that wage to employers. A surplus exists; that is, the quantity of labor supplied is greater than the amount demanded. Thus the wage rate will return again to w_1.

The price of capital. In a competitive market the price of a unit of capital, say a machine, is determined in a way similar to the price of a unit of labor. The price of any kind of capital depends upon the demand for and supply of units of capital and, at market equilibrium, the price of capital equals what that capital is worth to its employer.

Determination of individual or family income

The income of a person depends upon the *price* he or she receives for his or her resources, labor and capital, and the *quantities* of resources he or she can place in employment. For example, the monthly family income from labor equals the quantity of its labor employed, multiplied by the wage rate. From capital, its income equals the quantity of capital employed, multiplied by the price of each unit of capital. Total monthly family income, then, is a summation of the two monthly income flows.

Determinants of income distribution

The distribution of income among persons and families depends upon the distribution of resource ownership and the prices paid for resources of different kinds in different employments. The ownership pattern of resources is unequally distributed among persons and families. This unequal ownership pattern of resources gives rise to an unequal distribution of income in our society. People at the bottom of the income ladder own a small share of the nation's resources, and the market places a low value on the resources they do own. People at the top of the income ladder own a large share of the nation's resources on which the market places a high value.

Causes of differences in labor resource ownership

Brains and brawn. The inheritance of mental and physical talents is not equally distributed among people. Some people have greater capabilities than others. Some families' labor resources have exceptional learning abilities; others' labor resources have special talents—acting, singing, playing baseball or football. Other families are not so fortunately endowed.

Skill levels. Skill levels vary among individuals. Differences in skills among persons are primarily due to differences in inherited capabilities, training opportunities, and discrimination. Some persons inherit specific abilities to do certain tasks better than others. Most often people with high skill levels have acquired them from their training and education. In some instances, people have low skill levels because they have been discriminated against and have not had equal opportunities for training and education. Even with the same training, certain groups, say females, may not receive the same pay as others, although they perform the same tasks. In general, persons with highly developed skills are worth more and, therefore, are paid more in the market than are unskilled or semiskilled workers.

Causes of differences in capital resource ownership

Inheritance. Some persons and families inherit real property and claims on real property such as stocks and bonds. These people have a head start on those who do not begin with inherited capital resources.

Luck. Luck is not evenly distributed among the population. Some families may be at or near the bottom of the income pyramid because of bad luck. A business failure caused by a depression, a prolonged illness, a fatal accident, or a natural disaster may leave persons and families without income or the ability to earn an adequate income.

Propensities to accumulate. People vary as to their propensities or tendencies to save and accumulate capital resources. Those who are strongly motivated are willing to forego consumption today in order to enjoy greater income in the future. Others are more concerned about their current consumption standards. They do not save and do not accumulate capital resources.

Summary of the causes of poverty

Several things are clear about the poor and about low-income families. They have small quantities and low qualities of resources. The market places a low value on the services they provide in the market. The low productivity and, therefore, the low pay of the poor are due to low levels of training and education, misfortune, relatively small inheritances, and discrimination. The poor are in a vicious circle which is difficult to escape. What they need in order to move out of poverty they do not have and cannot afford to acquire. So they remain poor.

GOVERNMENT ATTEMPTS TO ALLEVIATE POVERTY

Two approaches to poverty are suggested by the foregoing analysis. First, the productivity of the employable poor can be increased. This can be accomplished through subsidized education of the children of the poor, adult training and education programs, counseling and guidance, job placement programs, and the elimination of discrimination. Second, a minimum annual income can be guaranteed. This is essential if no one is to live in poverty. Some people, such as the very young, the very old, the disabled, and the ill, are poor because they cannot produce at all, and others are poor because they cannot produce enough. Income-support programs are required to aid persons who are unproductive and those who have low productivity.

Government measures to increase productivity

The federal government has a variety of programs designed to increase the quality of human resources. These may be classified as personnel programs and the provision of goods and services, such as education and health, which will enhance productivity. Many of these programs are not exclusively for the poor and, therefore, benefit the rich as well.

Personnel programs were launched in a big way in the 1960s. They can be grouped into training programs, job creation programs, and information services.[4] Training programs include vocational education, adult education, vocational rehabilitation, and special training programs for technologically displaced and disadvantaged persons and those on welfare. To complement the training programs, other programs were designed to create jobs for the poor. The aim of the job creation programs is to pave the way for jobs in private industry and in government for the poor and disadvantaged. In addition, the productivity of the poor has been increased through the services of the U.S. Training Employment Service, which provides information to the poor concerning employment opportunities and training programs.

Government income-support programs

Government programs to support the income of individuals and families are numerous and large in dollar amounts (approximately $177 billion estimated in fiscal year 1977). They were developed in a piecemeal fashion over a number of years and vary as to purpose, benefits, eligibility requirements, and method of financing. Most government income-support programs are not restricted to families who live in poverty; they are designed to assist any family who happens to fall in a specific category, such as the disabled, the blind, the aged, the female heads of families with dependent children. In some income-support programs, benefit payments are related to previous contributions (social security) or past services (veterans' payments). In other income-support programs, such as public assistance, individual benefits are not related to individual costs or contributions.

There are two kinds of federal assistance for the support of incomes of persons and families—assistance in the form of cash payments and assistance in-kind, that is, in the form of goods and services. The growth and the current levels of both kinds of federal assistance are shown in Table 9–4.

Cash income assistance. Most federal assistance is in the form of cash payments to the aged and disabled. For example, the first six cash income assistance programs listed in Table 9–4 are directed toward supporting the income of the aged and disabled. These six programs represented 82 percent of the $130 billion expected to be spent for cash income assistance in fiscal year 1977. The largest cash income assistance program, social security, is self-financing, that is, it is financed from social security taxes, and is designed as a retirement income and disability plan for persons who contributed to the program while they were working. Public assistance to the aged, blind, and disabled, on the other hand, is financed out of general tax

---

[4] Sar A. Levitan, *Programs in Aid of the Poor for the 1970s* (Baltimore: Johns Hopkins Press, 1969), pp. 50–61.

TABLE 9–4
Federal outlays on programs for cash income assistance and in-kind assistance, selected fiscal years, 1960–1977 (in millions)

Program	1960	1970	1973	1975	1977 (estimate)
Cash income assistance					
Social security	11,018	29,685	48,288	64,351	83,393
Public assistance to aged, blind, and disabled	1,449	1,979	2,000	25	—
Supplemental security income	—	—	41	4,770	5,369
Veterans' compensation and pensions	3,312	5,229	6,401	6,548	8,350
Federal civilian retirement	1,821	4,192	6,954	10,229	9,662
Benefits for disabled miners	—	10	952	879	982
Aid to families with dependent children	612	2,163	3,922	4,322	6,306
Unemployment compensation	2,375	3,369	5,362	7,065	16,380
Total	20,587	46,927	73,920	98,189	130,442
In-kind assistance					
Medicare	—	7,149	9,479	14,191	21,991
Medicaid	—	2,727	4,600	6,508	10,229
Food stamps	—	577	2,208	3,926	4,754
Other food	324	833	1,433	1,744	3,385
Housing	279	1,279	1,420	2,292	2,952
Higher education student aid	498	1,625	3,880	4,556	3,283
Total	1,101	14,190	23,020	33,217	46,594

Source: Barry M. Blechman et al., *Setting National Priorities: The 1975 Budget* (Washington, D.C.: Brookings Institution, 1974), p. 168; *The Budget of the United States Government Fiscal Year 1978*, pp. 144, 156, 166, 179.

revenues and is aimed primarily at assisting the poor that fall in these adult categories. With the introduction of a new federal program called supplemental security income (SSI), public assistance to the adult categories (aged, blind, and disabled) is a federally financed program, providing a uniform minimum income to all eligible persons. States can continue, however, to make supplementary payments over and above the federal amount.

Two cash income assistance programs not aimed at the aged and disabled are public assistance in the form of aid to families with dependent children and unemployment compensation. Aid to families with dependent children provides cash payments to poor families headed by a woman. Although small in comparison to all of the programs assisting the aged and disabled, this program is growing rapidly and is a target for much criticism. Unemployment compensation payments are estimated to be $16 billion in fiscal year 1977, which were very high due to the high unemployment rates. Unemployment compensation provides income support for persons who have temporary loss of income due to unemployment.

In-kind assistance.   In-kind assistance programs grew rapidly in the 1960s and have continued to grow rapidly in the 1970s. The main reason for this growth has been the expansion of medical care services to the elderly, many disabled persons, and the poor. Medicare provides medical care services to the elderly who are covered under social security, and Medicaid does the same for persons on public assistance. The cost of the Medicare and Medicaid programs in fiscal year 1977 is estimated to be $20.6 billion, representing about three fourths of the cost of in-kind assistance. The fastest growing in-kind assistance is the food stamp program. The cost of this program increased from about one half billion dollars in fiscal year 1970 to approximately $4.7 billion in fiscal year 1977. The food stamp program has twin objectives. One objective is to improve the diets of low income families, and the second one is to increase the demand for food products. Any family is eligible for food stamps if their income and assets fall below prescribed limits. The remaining in-kind assistance programs—other food, housing, and higher education student aid—provide assistance to a limited number of families. Some of these families may be poor and some may not be.

Evaluation of government programs

Government measures to increase the productivity of labor resources, particularly those of the handicapped, disadvantaged, and other poor, are an essential part of any antipoverty program. Most people agree that close and continuous scrutiny of these programs is necessary to improve their efficiency, that it is especially important for these programs to concentrate on the young, and that the long-run solution to alleviating poverty among the employable poor is through personnel training programs of some sort.

Opinion is divided with respect to what constitutes equity and what constitutes efficiency in income-supporting programs. However, there is some common ground. For one thing, it is agreed that income-support programs, both cash assistance and in-kind assistance, are in need of reform because they are aimed at persons and families who fall in certain demographic groups, not all of whom are poor, and omit or provide very little assistance to some poor families. In addition, there is growing acceptance that the income of the poor may be best supported through a negative income tax plan—a guaranteed annual income plan based on the idea that when you have taxable income you pay money to the government (positive taxes), and when you have negative taxable income the government pays you (negative taxes).

NEGATIVE INCOME TAX PROPOSALS

In this final section two alternative proposals for income support are presented. The negative income tax is the major feature in both.

The two proposals differ in the degree in which the negative income tax replaces existing income support programs. Before discussion of these proposals, including the pros and cons of each, we shall look into the essential features of a negative income tax.

The negative income tax

There are three variables common to every negative income tax scheme, as noted in Table 9–5. These variables are the guaranteed level of income, the negative tax rate, and the break-even level of income. In the example in Table 9–5, the guaranteed level of income is $4,000, and the negative tax rate is 50 percent. The break-even level of income, that is, the level of earned income at which negative taxes or government subsidies are zero, is $8,000.

TABLE 9–5
Negative income tax plan for a family of four

Minimum guaranteed income	Earned income	Negative tax or subsidy ($4,000–50% of earned income)	Disposable income (earned income plus negative tax)
$4,000	$ 0	$4,000	$4,000
4,000	1,000	3,500	4,500
4,000	2,000	3,000	5,000
4,000	3,000	2,500	5,500
4,000	4,000	2,000	6,000
4,000	5,000	1,500	6,500
4,000	6,000	1,000	7,000
4,000	7,000	500	7,500
4,000	8,000	0	8,000

The relationship among these variables may be seen from the formulas $Y = rB$, $r = Y/B$, or $B = Y/r$, where

$$Y = \text{guaranteed annual income}$$
$$r = \text{negative tax rate}$$
$$B = \text{break-even level of income}$$

In the example of a negative income tax plan in Table 9–5, the guaranteed annual income and the negative tax rate are given. Thus, the break-even level of income may be calculated—$B = \$4,000/0.5 = \$8,000$.

Under the plan a family of four earning $2,000 would have a disposable income of $5,000. This family would receive negative taxes of $3,000 (4,000 − 50 percent of earned income), plus $2,000 in earned income. (Before going further, examine Table 9–5 carefully in order to be certain that you understand this illustration of a negative income tax plan.)

The level of income that will be guaranteed to every family, along with negative tax rate, will be determined by whatever society believes to be acceptable. It should be pointed out, however, that the costs of negative income tax plans vary directly with the guaranteed level of income and inversely with the negative income tax rate. For example, an increase in the guaranteed level of income increases the cost of a scheme, given the negative tax rate; and an increase in the negative tax rate, given the guaranteed annual income, decreases the cost of a plan.

The negative income tax scheme is simple and easy to administer, and incentives to earn income are built into the program. Under a negative income tax plan, people are always better off if they earn income than they are if they do not earn it, and the more they earn, the better off they will be. Two alternative proposals concerning the negative income tax will be considered in the sections below.

Alternative 1

One alternative is to replace public assistance and related programs with a negative income tax plan, keeping the other income-support programs essentially as they are. Under this approach, income-support programs are viewed as having multiple objectives. For example, retirement programs are considered on their own merits as "rights to retirement income" that people have built up over their lifetimes. Similarly, benefit payments to veterans are thought of as payment for past services and past contributions to society.

A rough estimate of the cost of moving all poor families to a poverty level of income of $5,000 is $27 billion. This estimate assumes that families living in poverty have no income. The 1977 fiscal year estimate of the cost of federal programs aimed exclusively to help the poor—supplemented security income, food stamp program, Medicaid, and aid to families with dependent children—is $20.4 billion (Table 9–4). The added or marginal cost of alternative plan 1 can be estimated, then, to be no more than $6.6 billion ($27 − 20.4).

Alternative 2

A second alternative is to replace all income-support programs with a negative income tax plan, that is, a plan based on the single objective of eliminating poverty. The underlying idea of this alternative is that the only justification for income support is poverty. A person who is over 65 years old, who is disabled, or who is a veteran may or may not be poor. A person who is a farmer may or may not be poor, and so on. In this view, the sole purpose of government income support programs is to increase the purchasing power of the recipients, at the expense of the purchasing power of those who pay taxes. The presumption is that the alleviation of poverty by transfers from those above the poverty line to those below it is the primary legitimate use of income support payments.

It has been stated that the cost of moving all persons to the poverty line is $27 billion. Thus, if an income support program aimed only at eliminating poverty replaced the current income-support programs, there would be substantial savings to society.

Advantages and disadvantages

Several advantages are claimed for alternative 2. One, inequalities in present antipoverty measures would be eliminated by concentrating transfer payments on the poor. Two, the coverage of the poor would be universal, and payments to the poor would exceed in many instances what they receive from present transfer programs. Three, special-interest groups such as veterans, farmers, and the aged are not subsidized unless they are poor. Four, the cost of this alternative is substantially less than the cost of current transfer programs.

There are also disadvantages associated with alternative 2.[5] In the first place, this alternative will encounter strong political opposition. The idea of a negative income tax is simple but novel, and it represents a fundamental departure from providing transfer payments based on specific categories such as the aged to providing transfer payments based strictly on financial need.

Second, it is argued that providing cash benefits on the basis of need is not an adequate substitute for many social service programs. The mere payment of money may not solve all the problems of the poor. Many social service programs for the poor, such as child health and maternity programs, services to crippled children, medical aid, and vocational rehabilitation, may need to be improved and expanded.

Third, a negative income tax plan, as other subsidization programs, may discourage persons who are working and earning low incomes. Suppose that in the absence of such a plan a person is earning $4,000 a year and receives no public assistance benefits. After personal deductions this

---

[5] Joseph J. Klos, "Public Assistance Family Allowances, or the Negative Income Tax?" *Nebraska Journal of Economics and Business,* Spring 1969, pp. 26–28.

individual is likely to pay a tax at a rate of 14 percent on taxable income, which is the lowest present personal income tax rate. Under a negative income tax plan, earned income is likely to be taxed (the subsidy is likely to be reduced) at a much higher rate, such as 50 percent. However, the disposable income of a person or family will still be directly related to earned income under a negative income tax plan; that is, the more you earn, the better off you are in terms of disposable income.

The main advantage of alternative 1 over alternative 2 is that the former is more likely to receive political support. The disadvantage of alternative 1 in comparison with alternative 2 is that there would still be many income-support programs not directly related to aiding the poor.

SUMMARY

Progress has been made in the United States toward the reduction of poverty. There are fewer persons and families living below the poverty line, and income inequality has been reduced. Still, more progress is needed. Too many persons and families remain poor, and the distribution of income remains very unequal.

The incidence of poverty is extremely high among blacks, the young, the aged, the uneducated, the unemployed, the working poor, the non-working poor, and farm families. One out of four to one out of five families with any of these social characteristics is living in poverty.

A program to alleviate poverty should (1) increase the productivity of the poor and (2) guarantee a minimum annual income to families who cannot work and those who cannot earn that minimum when they do work. Government measures to increase the productivity of the poor have, in part, been successful.

A guaranteed annual income plan in the form of a negative income tax scheme would appear to be more efficient than our current public assistance program. Two important aspects of a negative income tax scheme are that (1) only the poor receive negative taxes (subsidies) from the government and (2) the recipients of government subsidies are encouraged to earn income.

SUPPLEMENTARY READINGS

Barth, Michael C.; Carcagno, George J.; and Palmer, John L. *Toward an Effective Income Support System: Problems, Prospects and Choices.* Madison: University of Wisconsin Institute for Research on Poverty, 1974.

This is a very good study of our welfare system, including the major issues and options.

Green, Christopher. *Negative Taxes and the Poverty Problem*. Washington, D.C.: Brookings Institution, 1967.

The idea of the negative income tax is fully developed (chapter 4), and the common features of negative income tax schemes are presented (chapter 5).

Kershaw, Joseph A. *Government against Poverty*. Chicago: Markham Publishing Co., 1970.

Discusses different types of income maintenance problems. The advantages and disadvantages of the negative income tax scheme are covered in chapter 6, which could be used to supplement the section above on the negative income tax.

Levitan, Sar A. *The Great Society's Poor Law*. Johns Hopkins Press, 1969.

Chapter 3, "Programs for the Employable Poor," is suggested to contribute to the understanding of personnel programs designed to increase the productivity of the poor.

Report of the Subcommittee on Fiscal Policy of the Joint Economic Committee, Congress of the United States. *Income Security for Americans: Recommendations of the Public Welfare Study*. Washington, D.C.: U.S. Government Printing Office, 1974.

This report describes in detail public welfare programs and the defects in the existing system.

Sackrey, Charles. *The Political Economy of Urban Poverty*. New York: W. W. Norton & Co., 1973.

A critical analysis of the way poverty is usually studied. Chapter 3, "Economics and Black Poverty," attacks the methodology and theories of economists concerning poverty.

Scoville, James G. *Perspectives on Poverty and Income Distribution*. Lexington, Mass.: D. C. Heath & Co., 1971.

A selection of readings. Some of the readings in part 3, which covers the incidence and causes of poverty, can be used effectively to supplement the sections above on the economic causes of poverty.

Thurow, Lester C. *Poverty and Discrimination*. Washington, D.C.: Brookings Institution, 1969.

Extent of poverty is covered in chapter 2, and the income distribution patterns for whites and blacks are examined. Chapter 3 is good on the causes of poverty.

Chapter 10

DISCRIMINATION

CHECKLIST OF ECONOMIC CONCEPTS

Market discrimination
Wage discrimination
Employment discrimination
Occupation discrimination
Price discrimination
Nonmarket discrimination
Monopoly power
Exploitation
Tastes for discrimination
Economic cost of market discrimination

10

Discrimination

The high cost of prejudice

Outfielder King is going to be taught a lesson. Outfielder King is not going to mess up the exact extent of children's rights as the Little League, in its own infinite adolescence, knows them to be. Outfielder King is going to be the reason all of Ypsilanti, Michigan, blows its Little League charter.

Parents can act like idiots in the grandstand and on the coaching lines, kids can have psyches bent, bruised and embarrassed. But no girl is going to set foot on a Little League diamond and that's that.

Carolyn King is 12 years old and, given her choice, she doesn't feel that nature has preordained her to a recreational life of jacks and jump ropes.

She went out for and earned a place on a Little League team in Ypsilanti, Michigan. Somebody pulled out the Little League charter and found a clause barring girls from competition. The 10 coaches voted and it came up 8–2 in outfielder King's favor.

Yesterday Bob Taylor, the Ypsilanti Little League Vice President, was advised by telephone that Ypsilanti could play gorillas, iguanas and even girls if it chose to do so from here on in because the deep thinkers at national headquarters wouldn't have to deal with Ypsilanti as it was then constituted any more. Ypsilanti was being kicked out of the league.

"People," Taylor reported, "are being sent out here from national headquarters to organize a new franchise."

"Listen kid, they tell me you're pretty quick with the bat. Have a fresh slice of bubble gum, kid. That's O.K., there's plenty where that came from. Now listen, we got the old, established Little League, kid. I mean a guy makes it. Well, he wants to make it against the best."[1]

---

[1] Jerry Izenberg, "Little League Faces a Major Crisis in Ypsilanti," *Daily Oklahoman*, May 10, 1973, p. 64.

Discrimination shows its ugly face through varied expressions. At its worst, discrimination attacks heart and soul, takes away all or large chunks of freedom and rights, robs people of human dignity and, in the end, enslaves them. In its milder form, discrimination is an unintentional by-product of decision making. For example, a famous restaurant in the French Quarter in New Orleans will not take a reservation unless there are at least four persons in the party. Parties with three or less persons are denied access to a service because of the decision of the restaurant to exclude or discriminate. However, the decision of the restaurant to restrict reservations to parties based on size was undoubtedly motivated not by the desire to discriminate but by desire to use its facilities efficiently. Also, this form of discrimination leaves open access to the restaurant to everyone in a party of four or more.

WHAT IS DISCRIMINATION?

The public view

Most people relate discrimination to what they consider to be unfair treatment of some sort. Discrimination is viewed as the opposite of social justice. A person who is discriminated against is one who is treated unjustly.

There is nothing wrong in relating discrimination to unfair treatment. The shortcoming of this view is that it does not go far enough. It leaves unanswered the vital question: What is unfair treatment?

A working definition

Discrimination as we use it means that equals are treated unequally or that unequals are treated equally. More specifically, discrimination exists in a labor market when persons with equal productivity are paid different wages or persons with differences in productivity are paid equal wages. Discrimination exists in the product market when consumers pay different prices for the same product.

Market discrimination exists, then, when the terms on which market transactions are based are not the same for all persons. A seller who charges different prices to different consumers for essentially the same product or service is practicing price discrimination. A buyer who pays different wages for identical units of labor provides another illustration. Sellers who cannot sell in a certain market and buyers who cannot buy in a certain market for reasons other than price provide examples of complete market discrimination.

ECONOMIC ANALYSIS OF DISCRIMINATION

Sources of market discrimination

Market discrimination may be traced to two primary sources. These are the power to discriminate in the market and the desire to discriminate.

Monopoly power. Monopoly power may exist on the selling and buying sides of markets. In Chapter 2 we defined a monopolistic market as one in which the seller is able to manipulate the product price to his own advantage and can keep potential competitors out of the market. A monopsonistic market was defined as a market in which the buyer is able to control resource prices. This *monopoly* control over price and impediments to entry in markets which are not competitive makes it possible for consumers and workers to be *exploited*. Consumers are exploited when the price of a product is above the cost per unit of producing it, and workers are exploited when the wage rates paid are below their marginal productivity—below their contributions to the receipts of their employer.

Exploitation may exist without discrimination. For example, both blacks and whites with the same productivity may be paid equal wages that are below their productivity. However, monopoly power is a source of discrimination. In the exercise of monopoly power, a seller may segregate the market and charge consumers different prices for the same product. A monopsonistic buyer may segregate the job market and practice discrimination by paying workers on bases other than merit or productivity.

Taste for discrimination. Some people have a taste for discrimination and strive to satisfy this taste or desire. An employer who has a taste for discrimination acts as if nonmoney costs were connected with hiring women, blacks, Chicanos, Indians, or Puerto Ricans.[2] The result is that resources are allocated on bases other than productivity, and the incomes of minority groups are reduced.

Kinds of market discrimination

There are different kinds of market discrimination. The major ones are wage, employment, occupation, and price discrimination.

Wage discrimination. The U.S. Census Bureau reported that in 1975 the average income of males ($10,429) was over twice that of females ($4,513).[3] Is this evidence of wage discrimination by sex? Differences in

---

[2] Douglass C. North and Roger Leroy Miller, *The Economics of Public Issues* (New York: Harper & Row, Publishers, 1971), p. 136.

[3] U.S. Bureau of the Census, *Consumer Income,* Current Population Reports, series P–60, no. 103 (September 1976), pp. 20–21.

wages and incomes of males and females may arouse the suspicion that discrimination exists, but they are not by themselves evidence that discrimination does exist in fact. Wage and income differences among people may reflect differences in productivity. Wage differences between males and females would indicate discrimination, then, only if both sexes were contributing the same to the receipts of their employers.

The meaning of wage discrimination can be elucidated further by the slogan "equal pay for equal work." Suppose a male and female complete their Ph.D. degrees at the same time and place, have identical records and recommendations, are hired by the same university to teach speech, and differ in only one respect—the male is paid $14,000 a year and the female is paid $12,000 a year to teach. This is a case of discrimination. Two workers have the same productivity but are paid unequal wages.

It is often difficult to be sure that wage discrimination exists because the person who discriminates may deny it, and the relative productivities of labor may be difficult to measure. A discriminator may say that qualified blacks cannot be found or that females are paid less than males because their productivity is less. In some instances, the discriminator may be right; in others, one may only be trying to hide discriminatory behavior.

The meaning of wage discrimination is clear enough—unequal pay for equal contributions. But the proving of discrimination depends upon being able to distinguish among individuals on the basis of individual efforts and productivity. Generally speaking, human resources, like any other resources, are paid approximately what they are worth in a competitive economy. Thus, wage differences where competition exists reflect differences in labor productivity. Wage discrimination that does exist in the economy means that the market is not working perfectly in allocating resources among alternative uses.

Employment discrimination. Employment discrimination means that some persons are not hired because of noneconomic characteristics such as race or sex. Two persons with the same training, education, and experience apply for a job. One is black and one is white. If both do not have the same chance of getting the job, discrimination has entered into the decision-making process.

Employment discrimination, like wage discrimination, is difficult to identify positively. Differences in unemployment rates among whites and minority groups and between males and females may suggest discrimination but do not prove that it exists. However, when you consider all low-productivity families and discover that unemployment rates are much higher among blacks than whites, or when you look at families with identical education levels and find unemployment rates higher among black families than white families, the evidence of employment discrimination becomes more conclusive.

Occupation discrimination. There is a growing belief that discriminatory differences in pay, especially sex differences in pay, occur largely because of occupational segregation. In general, men work in occupations that employ very few women, and women work in occupations that employ very few men. Barbara Bergman points out that the economic results of occupational segregation for women are low wages.[4] She observes that women are relegated to occupations where productivity and experience have little to do with their status as they advance in age.[5] Another study confirms the concentration of women in low-paying occupations and points out further that women are found in occupations where opportunities for overtime and premium pay are limited.[6]

Why do women fail to enter the high-paid occupations? Male prejudice has been an important factor, but in some cases women have imposed discrimination upon themselves along occupational lines. Women are usually taught early in life to believe that their economic role will be unimportant. "They are socialized to expect that they will spend their lives as housewives and mothers—for toys they are given the tools of their trade: dolls, tea sets, frilly dresses, and so on."[7] Until women begin to think in terms of careers, prepare themselves for them, and break completely away from self-imposed economic exile, the male-female pay gap is likely to remain sizable.

The women's liberation movement has probably had little impact thus far in changing the distribution of women among occupations. Clare Booth Luce entitled her article in the *1973 Britanica Book of the Year,* "Woman: A Technological Castaway." She states that men make all important decisions and there are not 100 women who occupy critical policy-making positions. "The only institution in which women appear in equal numbers with men is our institution of monogamous marriage."[8]

Price discrimination. A shopping study in New York City revealed that an Admiral 19-inch screen, portable television set varied in price from $179 to $200 on the lower east side and that an identical set was sold in a downtown discount house for $139. Three different prices were quoted for a set by one lower east side store—$125 for a white law student,

---

[4] Barbara R. Bergman, "The Economics of Women's Liberation," *Challenge,* May–June 1973, p. 12.

[5] Ibid.

[6] Mary Hamblin and Michael Prell, "The Incomes of Men and Women: Why Do They Differ?" *Monthly Review,* Federal Reserve Bank of Kansas City, April 1973, p. 10.

[7] Marilyn Power Goldberg, "The Exploitation of Women," in David Mermelstein (ed.), *Economics: Mainstream Readings and Radical Critiques,* 2d ed. (New York: Random House, 1973), p. 52.

[8] Elsie Shoemaker, "Famous Woman Has Full View of Liberation Movement," *Stillwater (Oklahoma) News Press,* April 4, 1973, p. 28.

$139 to a Puerto Rican housewife, and $200 to a black housewife.[9] Is this evidence that the lower east side consumers are discriminated against?

The price differential for the identical TV set between the lower east side store and the downtown discount store does not by itself indicate price discrimination. The price difference between the lower east side store and downtown discount store may reflect costs differences. The former may have higher costs in the form of higher insurance rates, higher bad-debt rates, higher theft rates. It may be an inefficient supplier of TV sets.

There is evidence of price discrimination on the part of the lower east side store because different prices were quoted to different customers for the same set. Even here more information is needed about the payment record of each customer. We have defined price discrimination as charging different prices to different consumers for the same product or service. We need to qualify this definition of price discrimination. We must add the assumption that costs in the form of risks of payment are constant or do not account for the differences in price.

Price discrimination may take the form of preventing a person, because of race, from having access to a given market. The housing market has been mentioned in this regard. Another illustration is the refusal to allow blacks equal access to the capital or credit markets. The purchase of real capital—equipment, machinery, buildings—is usually financed from borrowed money. The complete or partial barring of blacks from the credit market may result in low ratios of capital to labor for blacks and, consequently, low productivity. Their production efforts are thus limited to products and services where high ratios of labor to capital are required.

Economic costs of discrimination

The economic costs of discrimination are both individual and social in nature. The individual costs of discrimination are those imposed on individuals or groups who lose one way or another because of discrimination. The social cost of discrimination is in the form of a reduction in total output in the economy due to discrimination.

Individual losses and gains.   Individual losses and gains flow from discrimination. Individuals discriminated against, or the discriminatees, suffer losses in the form of reduced living standards. They tend to be paid less for what they sell, to pay higher prices for what they buy, to have fewer employment opportunities, and to be segregated in low-paying occupations. Individuals who discriminate, the discriminators, may gain and may lose.

---

[9] Warren G. Magnuson and Jean Carper, *The Dark Side of the Market Place* (Englewood Cliffs, N.J.: Prentice-Hall, 1972), p. 37.

An employer-discriminator may gain if a female worker can be sired at a lower wage than a male worker, assuming both are equally productive. The wages of whites may be kept artificially above blacks if blacks are shut off from jobs and occupations because of race. Discriminators, however, may lose by having to forfeit income in order to satisfy their taste for discrimination. For example, an individual who refuses to sell a house to a black may end up selling the house at a lower price to a white. Or, an individual who refuses to hire a woman may end up paying a higher price for a male with the same productivity.

Output reduction. We have said that the cost to society of discrimination is the reduction in the nation's output of goods and services resulting from discrimination. In the *Economic Report of the President,* the President's Council of Economic Advisors estimated in 1966 that if the unemployment rate and average productivity of blacks were equal to those of whites, total production in our economy would expand by $27 billion.[10] Lester Thurow argues that discrimination causes a large reduction in the potential level of output of the American economy and that losses caused by discrimination against blacks amount to approximately $19 billion per year.[11] Add to this discrimination against females, Chicanos, Puerto Ricans, and Indians, and you have a huge annual loss of goods and services to the American society.

Discrimination causes losses of goods and services to society because it results in unnecessarily low levels of economic efficiency. Without discrimination, resources would tend to be allocated on the basis of their productivities. Units of any given resource would tend to be used where their productivity is the greatest.

The production possibilities curve shown in Figure 10–1 illustrates the impact of discrimination on production of goods and services in the economy. Point *D* represents the combination of goods *X* and *Y* produced in the economy when discrimination exists, with its resultant inefficiency. Without discrimination, the quantities of goods *X* and *Y* may be expanded to points like *B* and *C*.

Discrimination prevents the efficient use of resources, causing the combination of goods and services that is produced to lie below the production possibilities curve. The elimination of discrimination makes possbile the producton of those combinations of goods and services that lie on the curve. The social cost of discrimination is equal to the difference between the gross national product represented at point *D* and that represented by points on the production possibilities curve, such as points *B* and *C*.

---

[10] *Economic Report of the President, 1966,* p. 10.

[11] Lester C. Thurow, *Poverty and Discrimination* (Washington, D.C.: Brookings Institution, 1969), p. 158.

FIGURE 10–1
Production possibilities with and without discrimination

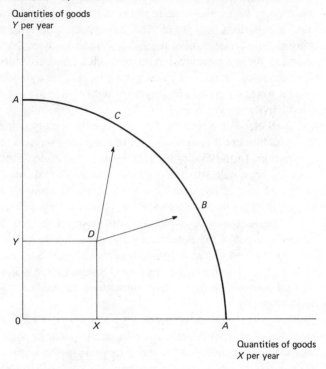

Quantities of goods
Y per year

Quantities of goods
X per year

Point *D* = combination of *X* and *Y* with discrimination.

Points *B* and *C* = combination of *X* and *Y* without discrimination.

Line *AA* = production possibilities curve.

NONMARKET DISCRIMINATION

Social discrimination

Social tastes and attitudes, customs, and laws are the bases for social
discrimination. Social discrimination may take the extreme form of preventing certain persons or groups from engaging in social interaction. The
direct quote at the beginning of this chapter concerning a Little League
rule that prevents girls from playing baseball in Little League games provides an illustration. Fraternities and sororities that have rules limiting
membership to certain races provide another. Segregated schools are examples of discrimination based on customs and laws. Societies such as the
Deep South and South Africa are structured along lines of social dis-

crimination. Under these arrangements, discrimination by race is a way of life, sanctioned by custom and frequently enforceable by law. Deviations from the legal segregated manner of behavior are crimes, and severe punishment may be handed out to offenders.

Social discrimination is difficult to root out, since it is based on deep-seated beliefs and customs often supported by law. In contrast to market discrimination, it is difficult to associate monetary costs with social discrimination. Persons who may with joy vote to keep certain persons from joining their country club often with the same joy sell products to them in the market. Although the source of much market discrimination is social discrimination, the self-interest motive in the market tends to overcome and reduce the effectiveness of discrimination in the marketplace.

Educational discrimination

It is generally believed that if everyone had equal access and opportunity to training and education, many of the major issues in our society, such as poverty and extreme income inequality, would be significantly alleviated, perhaps even eliminated. Unfortunately, however, inequality and discrimination exist in our public school system.[12]

A great deal of the inequality in public education is due to the way it is financed. The public school system is a highly decentralized system composed of thousands of school districts charged with the responsibilities of providing education. School districts pay for education with revenues from the local property tax and grants-in-aid, primarily from the state. Variations in the market value of property give rise to variations in per pupil expenditures on education within a given state and among states. A poor district (one with low property values) within a state and a poor state will have low per pupil expenditures and may have high property tax rates. This regional and state inequality in the allocation of resources for the purpose of public education has led to court decisions opposing the way public education is financed. In the meantime, however, resources are unequally distributed and the rich receive better education than the poor.

Discrimination in the public school system is indicated by the allocation of experienced and highly paid teachers.[13] The worst teachers, the least experienced and the lowest paid, are concentrated in the ghettos. Also, there is a regional bias to discrimination. Effective discrimination in public schools is more evident in the South; in some cases it reaches complete

---

[12] John D. Owen, "Inequality and Discrimination in the Public School System," in David Mermelstein and Robert Lekachman (eds.), *Economics: Mainstream Readings and Radical Critiques* (New York: Random House, 1970), pp. 137–44.

[13] Ibid., p. 141.

segregation, "with all black students taught by black teachers and all white students taught by white teachers."[14]

WHAT CAN BE DONE ABOUT DISCRIMINATION

Markets and humans are not perfect. Perfection may be beyond reach. However, movements in the direction of perfection are possible. What courses of action can be taken to move in the right direction? What policy implications can be drawn from our analysis?

Reduce tastes for discrimination

If discrimination resulting from tastes is to be reduced, people must be persuaded that they should alter their views and behavior. Tastes for discrimination may be reduced by education, by legislation, and by the use of government subsidies to discourage discrimination.

Education. A task of education is to teach people to understand one another and to be unprejudiced. Unfortunately, this task of education is hampered by discrimination in education itself, especially in regard to the allocation of resources for primary and secondary education. Although not a panacea, a more equal distribution of resources for public education would reduce inequality in per pupil educational services, and it could contribute toward reducing tastes for discrimination.

Legislation. It is difficult to change the tastes of people by coercion, that is, by passing laws. Laws are usually effective only when they are supported by or coincide with people's beliefs. However, the framework for reducing tastes for discrimination can be established by laws. The Civil Rights acts of 1964 and 1965 make certain acts of discrimination illegal. They provide the legal basis for protecting the rights of people who may be treated harmfully—for example, denied employment or opportunities for advancement because of race, sex, or religion. These laws have reduced discrimination by imposing greater risks and higher costs on discriminators. A person who satisfies a taste for discrimination by refusing to sell a house to a black breaks the law and risks prosecution.

Government subsidies. If the sole goal is to eliminate discrimination, government subsidy payments may be used to encourage employers not to discriminate. Subsidy payments would be made to employers who do not practice discrimination in hiring, wages, and promotions. Employers who discriminate would be sacrificing subsidy payments. Thus an incentive is provided not to discriminate. The alternative cost of discrimination is equal to the subsidy payment. Government subsidy payments will reduce dis-

---

[14] Ibid., p. 144.

crimination if the subsidy payments are equal to or greater than the non-monetary gain the discriminator receives from discrimination.

Reduce market imperfections

Market defects such as scarce labor market information, imperfect competition, and immobility of labor constitute a major source of market discrimination. Some people receive low wages, that is, wages below what they could earn in alternative employments, because they are unaware of other job openings. Improved job information would make it less necessary for one to receive income below what he would be paid on a similar job.

The market for goods and the market for resources may not work well at all if there is little competition in these markets. In imperfect markets, discrimination may be prevalent. A seller or a buyer has control over the price of what he sells or buys in highly monopolized markets. Other potential sellers or buyers are shut out of the market. Price, wage, employment, and occupational discrimination may remain unchallenged in the absence of competitive forces and in the presence of monopolistic controls. Antitrust action to strengthen competition and reduce barriers to entry into markets would be an important way to eliminate or at least lessen discriminatory market behavior.

The government has an important role to play in the elimination of discrimination when it is due to the use of monopoly power. First, it is the responsibility of the government to reduce monopoly power and restore competition in markets where competition is lacking through the vigorous use of antimonopoly laws. Second, a great deal of monopoly power is derived from and granted by government. Thurow noted that "The institutions of government are an important link in implementing discrimination. Either directly through legal restrictions or indirectly through harassment and expenditure decisions, the coercive power of the white community flows through local, state, and federal government institutions."[15]

Reduce discrimination in development of human capital

Investment in human capital, that is, spending on education, training, and health, provides a high rate of return in the form of increased productivity and income. Blacks and other minority groups generally do not and cannot invest enough in human capital, and public investment in human capital is unequally distributed. The elimination of human capital discrimination would tend to make most forms of market discrimination, such as wage and employment discrimination, less effective. The reason

---

[15] Thurow, *Poverty and Discrimination,* p. 158.

for this is that it is difficult to treat human resources unequally if they are productive and have access to other jobs. Thurow, who believes human capital investment holds the key to nondiscrimination, states, "Attacking human capital discrimination will not raise Negro incomes by itself, since wage, employment, and occupational discrimination would also have to be eliminated, but eliminating human capital discrimination would make the enforcement of these other types difficult in the absence of government discrimination."[16]

Reduce occupational segregation

Women, blacks, and other minority groups have been pushed into low-wage occupations. The effect of segregation by occupations is two-fold. First, the supply of labor is increased in those occupations restricted to minority groups, depressing wages in those occupations. Second, the supply of labor is decreased in those occupations closed off to minority groups, thus increasing wages in those occupations. The result of these effects is to create a wider gap between low and high wage occupations.[17]

In addition, if a member of the minority group crosses over into segregated occupations usually closed to members of the group, he or she has typically not received equal pay for equal work. For example, a black male with a Ph.D. in chemistry who works as a research chemist for an oil company may be discriminated against in wages and opportunities for advancement because he has a position typically reserved for whites. In recent years this situation has been reversed in many cases by the Equal Opportunities Act. Employers are virtually required to bid for minority group personnel. The small supplies available of these workers who are qualified assure they will receive salaries *above* those of white employees.

However, segregation by occupations would be difficult to maintain if minority groups were relatively well educated and well trained. Education and training open up job opportunities. Those who have job opportunities cannot easily be forced into designated occupations; they are mobile and can cut across occupations. Providing improved job opportunities for minority groups is one way to break up segregation by occupations.

SUMMARY

Market discrimination means that people with the same economic characteristics are not treated equally. For example, workers who have

---

[16] Ibid., p. 138.

[17] Daniel R. Fusfeld, *The Basic Economics of the Urban Racial Crisis* (New York: Holt, Rinehart & Winston, 1973), pp. 64–68.

the same productivity receive different wages, and consumers are charged different prices for the same product.

Discrimination comes from two sources—market and human imperfections. Market imperfections are due to imperfect knowledge, immobility of resources, and imperfect competition. Human imperfections are revealed in the tastes and preferences that some people have for discrimination. Market discrimination exists in the form of wage, employment, occupation, and price discrimination.

Discrimination is costly both to individuals and to society. There are individual welfare gains and losses from discrimination. It is difficult to say who gains and who loses. Sometimes the discriminator can lose. It is certain that there is a loss to society from discrimination, in the form of a reduction in output.

The economic analysis of market discrimination stresses two related points: (1) the observed differences in wages and prices may reflect differences in productivity and (2) market discrimination exists only to the extent that wage and price differences cannot be explained on the basis of productivity. Competitive markets tend to minimize the extent and degree of discrimination. Occupational segregation explains to a large extent differences in wages and income, and social discrimination, especially in the field of public education, is the source of much inequality.

Several policy conclusions may be drawn from our analysis. One, tastes for discrimination have to be reduced. This can be done by changing the tastes of people concerning discrimination through education, preventing by law the fulfillment of tastes for discrimination, and encouraging people not to discriminate by the payment of subsidies to employers who refrain from discriminating. Two, the source of exploitation and much discrimination—the exercise of monopoly power—has to be reduced. The way to reduce the use of monopoly power is to reduce that power itself through vigorous antimonopoly laws. A great deal of market discrimination is primarily due to human capital discrimination. If there were no discrimination in regard to investment in human capital (education, training, and health), segregation by occupations would be dealt a serious blow. It is difficult to discriminate in the market against people who are productive and have job choices.

SUPPLEMENTARY READINGS

Fusfeld, Daniel R. *The Basic Economics of the Urban Racial Crisis.* New York: Holt, Rinehart & Winston, 1973.

> Presents an economic theory of discrimination that is different from the two theories presented in this chapter: the crowding theory. This theory holds that minority groups are forced into menial occupations, which

causes an increase in the supply of labor and a decrease in wage rates for these occupations. Chapter 5 is the relevant one.

Magnuson, Warren G., and Carper, Jean. *The Dark Side of the Market Place.* Englewood Cliffs, N.J.: Prentice-Hall, 1968.

Easy reading and personalized in style. Many illustrations of market imperfections are presented. There is a bibliography at the end of the book, but footnoting is not used.

Mermelstein, David, ed. *Economics: Mainstream Readings and Radical Critiques.* 2d ed. New York: Random House, 1973.

Includes several good essays on discrimination, particularly "The Structure of Racial Discrimination," by Raymond Franklin and Solomon Resnick, and "The Economic Exploitation of Women," by Marilyn Power Goldberg.

Schiller, Bradley R. *The Economics of Poverty and Discrimination.* Englewood Cliffs, N.J.: Prentice-Hall, 1973.

Primarily treats the poverty problem, but chapter 9 would be a good supplement to the section above on discrimination in education.

Thurow, Lester C. *Poverty and Discrimination.* Washington, D.C.: Brookings Institution, 1969.

Covers the economic theories of discrimination. In chapter 7, various kinds of market discrimination are presented and analyzed.

PART THREE

Stabilization

Chapter 11

UNEMPLOYMENT ISSUES

CHECKLIST OF ECONOMIC CONCEPTS

Potential GNP
GNP gap
Involuntary unemployment
Frictional unemployment
Structural unemployment
Cyclical unemployment
Circular flow of production and income
Leakages
Injections
Aggregate demand
Aggregate supply
Monetary policy
Fiscal policy

11

Unemployment issues

Why do we waste our labor resources?

I'd get up at five in the morning and head for the waterfront. Outside the Spreckles Sugar Refinery, outside the gates, there would be a thousand men. You know dang well there's only three or four jobs. The guy would come out with two little Pinkerton cops: "I need two guys for the bull gang. Two guys to go into the hole." A thousand men would fight like a pack of Alaskan dogs to get through there. Only four of us would get through. I was too young a punk.

So you'd drift up to Skid Row. There'd be thousands of men there. Guys on baskets, making weird speeches, phony theories on economics. About eleven-thirty, the real leaders would take over. They'd say: O.K., we're going to City Hall. The mayor was Angelo Rossi, a dapper little guy. He wore expensive boots and a tight vest. We'd shout around the steps. Finally, he'd come out and tell us nothing.

I remember the demands: We demand work, we demand shelter for our families, we demand groceries, this kind of thing. . . .

I remember as a kid how courageous this seemed to me, the demands, because you knew that society wasn't going to give it to you. They'd demand that they open up unrented houses and give decent shelters for their families. But you just knew society wasn't yielding. There was nothing coming.[1]

SOME EFFECTS OF UNEMPLOYMENT

Both economic and social effects are associated with unemployment. The economic effects are related to the impact of unemployment on the

---

[1] Studs Terkel, *Hard Times* (New York: Random House, Pantheon Books, 1970), p. 30.

nation's production of goods and services, that is, the GNP. The social effects of unemployment are more difficult to pin down and measure, but they are just as real as the economic effects.

Effects on GNP

Idle human resources represent a waste, a loss of goods and services, and, therefore, a loss of real income. Unemployed resources could have contributed to society's well-being; the economic value of this lost contribution of goods and services is the economic cost of unemployment. The difference, then, between what may be produced at full employment and what is produced at less than full employment measures the total cost of unemployment. In 1975, the total or aggregate cost of unemployment, or, as shown in Figure 11–1, the gap between actual and potential GNP, was in excess of $100 billion.

FIGURE 11–1
Actual GNP and potential GNP

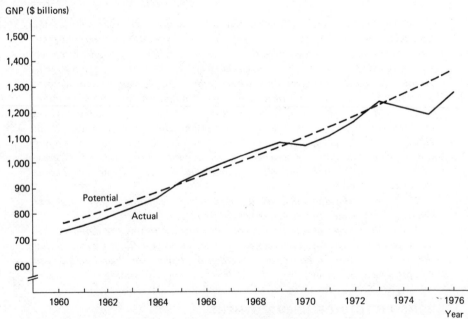

Potential GNP is what the GNP would be if the economy was operating at full employment. In calculating the potential, two benchmarks are used—the Department of Commerce's manufacturing capacity utilization index of 86 percent and the unemployment rate of 4.9 percent. Under this definition of full employment, the average annual growth rate in the potential GNP is estimated to be 3.5 percent between 1962 and 1976.

Source: *Economic Report of the President, January 1977,* pp. 52–55.

Unemployment may affect not only current production of goods and services but also future production. During periods of unemployment, machines as well as men are idle. Capital goods, plant and equipment, become obsolete and are not replaced. The productivity of labor and the overall ability of the economy to produce in the future are reduced during periods of unemployment.

Effects on social relations

Unemployment threatens the stability of the family as an economic and social unit. Without income or with a loss of income, the head of the family cannot play the role in which he or she was cast. Family wants and needs are not fulfilled, and family relationships suffer as a consequence. Economic and social dependency and important family ties may be in jeopardy and may eventually be severed by prolonged unemployment.

Human relationships outside the family are also seriously affected by unemployment. An unemployed person loses self-respect and influence among the employed, may be rejected by working companions and lose pride and confidence. In the end, the unemployed may become spiritually disabled persons.

Although there may be a few families who are economically and socially prepared for unemployment, it tends to strike families who are least capable of withstanding either its economic or its social effects. Also, the incidence of unemployment, like family instability and crime, is high among low-income groups.

The social and economic effects of unemployment extend beyond the period in which it occurs. During a period of high unemployment, consumption and savings are reduced, debt is incurred, and, for many unemployed persons, home and auto loans may be defaulted. Afterwards, when work is available and income is earned, debts must be paid and savings replenished. It may take a long period before the living standards that prevailed prior to the unemployed period can be reattained and even longer before self-esteem is restored.

WHAT IS UNEMPLOYMENT?

It would seem that unemployment could be easily defined. However, there are many complexities and ramifications concerning its meaning. The first thought about unemployment may be that the unemployed are people without jobs. This may be true, but many people without jobs are not considered unemployed. What about a person who prefers leisure to work? Are persons over 65 to be considered unemployed? Is a college student included in the unemployment count?

Our approach to unemployment in this section is, first, to give a general definition of unemployment, and, second, to elucidate the meaning of *involuntary* unemployment—the unemployment that is of major economic concern. The subsequent section probes deeper into the meaning of unemployment.

General definition

In general, unemployment may be defined as a situation in which persons who are qualified for a job, willing to work, and willing to accept the going wage rate cannot find jobs without considerable delay. There are three important aspects to this definition.

First, a person has to be qualified for a job. A person is not involuntarily unemployed if one seeks jobs which one is precluded from obtaining because of a lack of training, experience, and education. For example, one cannot be considered an unemployed truck driver if unable to drive a truck.

Second, a person is not considered unemployed if one is not seeking a job and willing to work at the market wage rate. Some may decide to withdraw their labor services because they prefer leisure to work at the market rate. These persons represent a type of unemployment, but not the kind that usually presents a problem.

Third, it may take time to find a job that a person is qualified for and is willing to accept at the going wage rate. However, the delay in finding a job should be of a short duration. The time delay should probably not extend beyond a 30- or 60-day period for most occupations. Some may believe that this time period is too long for people to be without jobs.

Involuntary unemployment

The economic aspect of unemployment originates from a situation in which the quantity of labor demanded is less than the quantity supplied at the market wage rate. This results in involuntary unemployment. Involuntary unemployment occurs when wage rates are too high, that is, above competitive levels. The solution to involuntary unemployment is to expand demand or, if competitive forces are operating, to rely upon automatic market forces to drive wage rates down to the level at which the amount of labor demanded equals the amount supplied.

Figure 11–2 is shown to clarify the meaning of involuntary unemployment in a competitive economy. DD and SS are the demand and supply curves for labor. The wage rate is w_1. The amount of labor demanded at this wage rate is e_0, and the amount of labor supplied is e_1. The difference between e_0 and e_1 is equal to the distance $AB,$ which is the excess of the

FIGURE 11-2
Involuntary unemployment in a competitive market

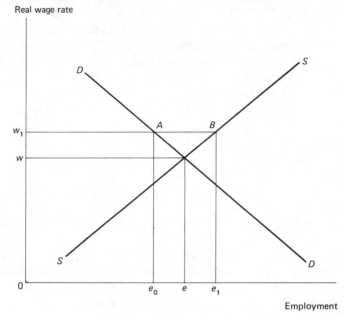

DD = Demand curve for labor.
SS = Supply curve for labor.
e_0 = Amount of labor demanded at w_1.
e_1 = Amount of labor supplied at w_1.
$e_1 - e_0$ = Involuntary unemployment.

amount of labor supplied over the amount of labor demanded. In a purely competitive situation, wage rates would be forced downward to w, and involuntary unemployment would disappear.

ANALYSIS OF THE UNEMPLOYMENT PROBLEM

Types of unemployment

The meaning of unemployment may be elucidated further by distinguishing among different types of unemployment. Three major types are frictional, structural, and cyclical unemployment.

Frictional unemployment. Frictional unemployment is transitional or short run in nature. It usually originates on the labor supply side; that is, labor services are voluntarily not employed. A good illustration is the unemployment that occurs when people are changing jobs or searching for new jobs. The matching of job openings and job seekers does not always take place smoothly in the economy and, as a consequence, people are without work.

The important thing about frictional unemployment is that it does not last. Frictional unemployment may exist at all times in the economy, but for any one person or family it is transitional. Therefore, frictional unemployment is not considered a significant economic problem. It can be reduced by improvements in the flow of information concerning job openings.

Structural unemployment. Structural unemployment is usually long run in nature and usually originates on the demand side of labor. Structural unemployment results from economic changes that cause the demand for specific kinds of labor to be low relative to its supply in particular markets and regions of the economy.

·A relatively low demand for labor in a given market may be due to several factors. Technological change, although expected to reduce costs and expand the productive capacity of the overall economy, may have devastating effects in a particular market. Changes in consumer preferences for products expand production and employment in some areas but reduce them in others. Immobility of labor prolongs the period of unemployment which may have originated due to technological change and changes in consumers' tastes. A reduction in job opportunities should induce the unemployed to move, but immobility may prevent this from taking place.

Cyclical unemployment. Unemployment caused by economic fluctuations is called cyclical unemployment. Cyclical unemployment is due to reductions in aggregate or total demand for goods and services in the overall economy. A decline in aggregate demand in the economy reduces total production and causes general unemployment throughout the economic system. Cyclical unemployment is usually the culprit when the unemployment rate goes above 4 percent.

Further dimensions of the unemployment problem

The unemployment rate. The unemployment rate (UR) equals U/L, where U equals the number of persons included in the labor force who are unemployed and L equals the number of persons in the labor force. The unemployment rate underestimates the number of persons without work. Only those who are in the labor force are considered to be unemployed when they are without jobs. Those who have withdrawn from the labor force, that is, persons who are not actively seeking employment, are not included in the labor force.

Full employment is often defined for economic policy purposes in terms of a maximum acceptable unemployment rate. An unemployment rate of 4.9 percent is now being arbitrarily used as the dividing rate to determine whether the economy is at full or less than full employment. Using this definition of full employment, the economy was operating at less than full employment in five of the ten years during the 1960s and in five years of the present decade. With a labor force of 96 million people, a 4.9 percent unemployment rate means that 4.7 million people are unemployed when the economy is said to be at full employment.

Who are the unemployed? Unemployment rates vary by age, sex, and color. The highest unemployment rates are among the young between the ages of 16 and 19 (Table 11–1). These rates of unemployment are usually about two and a half times higher than the rates among all workers. For example, in 1976 the overall unemployment rate was 7.7 percent, as compared to 19.0 percent among young people. Men 20 years and older have an unemployment rate lower than women in the same age bracket. Also, the unemployment rate among whites is usually half the unemployment rate among blacks.

TABLE 11–1
Unemployment rates by sex, age and color, 1960–1976

Year	All workers	Both sexes, 16–19 years	Men 20 years and over	Women 20 years and over	White	Black and other races
1960	5.5	14.7	4.7	5.1	4.9	10.2
1961	6.7	16.8	5.7	6.3	6.0	12.4
1962	5.5	14.7	4.6	5.4	4.9	10.9
1963	5.7	17.2	4.5	5.4	5.0	10.8
1964	5.2	16.2	3.9	5.2	4.6	9.6
1965	4.5	14.8	3.2	4.5	4.1	8.1
1966	3.8	12.8	2.5	3.8	3.4	7.3
1967	3.8	12.8	2.3	4.2	3.4	7.4
1968	3.6	12.7	2.2	3.8	3.2	6.7
1969	3.5	12.2	2.1	3.7	3.1	6.4
1970	4.9	15.2	3.5	4.8	4.5	8.2
1971	5.9	16.9	4.4	5.7	5.4	9.9
1972	5.6	16.2	4.0	5.4	5.0	10.0
1973	4.9	14.5	3.2	4.8	4.3	8.9
1974	5.6	16.0	3.8	5.5	5.0	9.9
1975	8.5	19.9	6.7	8.0	7.8	13.9
1976	7.7	19.0	5.9	7.4	7.0	13.1

Source: *Economic Report of the President, January 1977*, p. 221.

The overall unemployment rate does not reflect, of course, this wide variation in unemployment rates among people of different age and socioeconomic backgrounds. The unemployment rate was 7.7 percent in 1976. Yet, in the same year 19.0 percent of the young people in the labor force and 13.1 percent of nonwhites were unemployed. A full-employment economy, as now defined by a 4.9 percent unemployment rate, fails to provide ample job opportunities to all groups.

WHAT CAUSES PEOPLE TO LOSE THEIR JOBS?

People lose their jobs in a recession when production in the economy is falling. But what causes the recession? What causes a decline in production? Economists have searched for a single answer and have found many —not enough spending, too much saving, wages too high, and so forth. Thus the answer is neither simple nor single. There are many contributing causes; we shall try to explain those that seem to be the most important.

Circular flow of economic activity

To understand why people lose their jobs it is necessary to understand how jobs are created. This is not difficult in terms of the forces of supply and demand pertaining to products in individual markets. We have established an understanding of equilibrium prices and quantities for individual commodities like wheat, automobiles, dresses, television, ice cream, necklaces, and all other commodities produced in our economy—and demanded. We will move now from demand and supply curves for individual products to a demand and supply curve representing all commodities. This will be done by presenting an overview of the operation of the economy which economists call the *circular flow of economic activity.*

The circular flow is illustrated in Figure 11–3. The relationships it shows are important in understanding the operation of the economy. (Look at this figure and study it carefully.)

FIGURE 11–3
Flow of production and income in a stationary economy

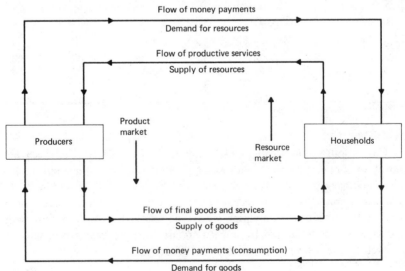

Income and jobs are created in a society when goods and services are produced. Owners of resources—labor, capital, and natural resources—sell their productive services to producers who, in turn, pay them money in the form of wages, interest, rent, and profits. The flow of productive services to producers represents the supply of resources, and the flow of money payments from producers represents the demand for resources. Producers transform productive services or resources into goods and services through the production process and sell the goods and services to households. They receive a flow of money payments from households in exchange. The flow from producers to households represents the aggregate supply of goods and services, and the flow of money payments from households to producers represents the aggregate demand for them.

There are several points to remember about the circular flow. First, there are two markets—a resource market and a goods market. The prices of resources and employment are determined in the resource market, and the prices of goods and production are determined in the goods market. Second, the resource and goods markets are interrelated. The demand for goods creates a demand for the resources that are used to produce goods. The costs of producing goods depend upon the prices paid and the quantities of resources used in production. Third, there are two circular flows involved in the economy—a real flow of productive services (labor, capital, and natural resources) and goods (autos, dresses, medical services), and a flow of money payments to owners of resources for productive services and to producers for goods and services. Fourth, real income is determined by the physical goods and services produced, and money income is the money value of the physical goods and services produced.

The circular flow of economic activity shows in a simple way how the overall economy operates. It emphasizes the interdependency of economic variables—the dependency of income on production, production on spending, spending on income, demand for resources on the demand for products, and so on. Now we shall turn to the products market in order to find possible reasons why people lose their jobs.

Aggregate demand

Aggregate demand is a schedule showing output demanded in the economy at different prices. Since we are concerned with the prices of all goods and services, we must view prices as an average, or as a price level. Since we are also concerned with the quantities of all goods and services, we must view the quantities demanded as composite units of goods and services—each unit composed of shirts, tables, food, fuel, and other items that comprise the real output of the economy.

Aggregate demand is illustrated in Figure 11–4. At the price level p_1, 200 units of goods and services are demanded; at the price level p, output

FIGURE 11–4
Aggregate demand

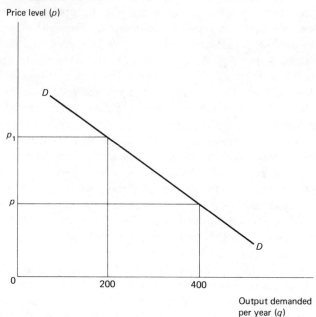

DD is an aggregate-demand schedule which shows the output demanded at different price levels. For example, at price
level p_1, 200 units of goods and services are demanded.

demanded is 400 units, and so on. The output demanded of goods at any
price level is the summation of the outputs of goods and services purchased
by *consumers,* such as shoes and steaks, the outputs purchased by *investors,* such as new plant and equipment, and the outputs purchased by
government, such as highways and recreational services. A change in the
output demanded at a given price level by these groups—consumers, investors, and government—will change aggregate demand. For example, if
consumers begin to buy greater quantities of consumer goods at all prices
than they did previously, aggregate demand will increase—shift to the
right, indicating that greater outputs are demanded at all prices.

The distinction between a change in demand and movement along a
given demand curve is as important to remember in reference to aggregate
demand as it is in the case of an individual demand curve. In a movement
along the aggregate-demand curve, output demanded is inversely related
to the price level—at a low price level output demanded is greater than it
is at a high price level. This is the principle of demand. A change in aggregate demand refers to a shift in the entire aggregate-demand curve.

This discussion of aggregate demand leads to the question of why people lose their jobs. Suppose aggregate demand becomes deficient; that is, total spending in the economy has become too low to buy all the goods and services that have been produced at the current price level. The effect of this on jobs can be seen most easily in an individual market. Toward the end of 1973 automobile manufacturers were having trouble selling all the cars they were producing—especially the big ones. As the energy crisis hit, demand for automobiles with poor gasoline mileage decreased. Consumers no longer desired the gas eaters that Detroit produced. Simultaneously, surpluses occurred in the recreation vehicle industry, the steel industry, and many other industries throughout the economy. People lost their jobs because of those surpluses—at the current price level, quantity demanded was less than quantity supplied, so production levels were decreased.

Once a surplus appears in a market—watch out! It does not always spread to other markets, but it can. Every job loss is a loss in someone's income and results in a cut in spending for many products. General surpluses in the economy lead to losses of many jobs, reducing national income.

Aggregate supply

Aggregate supply is a schedule showing the output supplied at different prices. In discussing the role of aggregate supply in the unemployment picture, we shall consider prices as a price level and quantities in terms of composite units of goods and services.

Unemployment is closely linked to aggregate supply. New jobs are created when the level of goods and services produced expands, and existing jobs are destroyed when it contracts. Producers hire more people to produce goods and services when profits increase. When profits decrease and losses are incurred, production is cut and jobs are lost.

To illustrate what causes changes in profits and losses, we shall use the resource of labor to see how a change in labor costs affects profits and hence aggregate supply. In general, labor is paid what it is worth to the employer. Now, if the contribution of a unit of labor to the receipts of employers does not change, higher wages will lead to a decrease in profits and a decrease in aggregate supply. By the same reasoning, if wages stay the same, and workers begin to contribute more to the receipts of employers, profits increase and aggregate supply increases.

The relationship between wages, profits, and prices is complex. It may be helpful to remember that producers are trying to make money, and therefore they will tend to produce more at higher prices and less at lower prices. They will also produce more if costs are lower and less if costs are higher.

Aggregate demand and supply

Employment and job opportunities depend upon both aggregate demand and aggregate supply. Figure 11–5 shows aggregate supply, *SS*, and two aggregate demands, *DD* and D_1D_1. Given *DD* and *SS*, output demanded and output supplied are equal at an output of *q* and at a price level of *p*. The price level, *p*, and the output, *q*, are the equilibrium levels of price and output. Can aggregate demand be deficient at an equilibrium price and output?

Full-employment output is represented by q_f in Figure 11–5. This is the output where production is at its maximum and cyclical unemployment is zero. You can see that aggregate demand, *DD*, is deficient. A deficient aggregate demand in this instance means that at the equilibrium price level, output demanded falls short of the full-employment output.

FIGURE 11–5
Unemployment equilibrium and full employment output

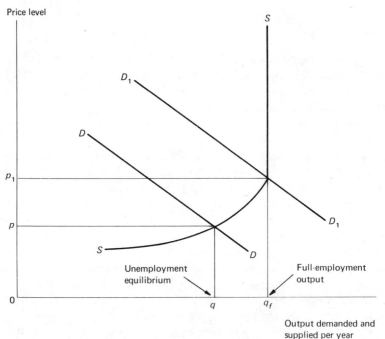

Unemployment equilibrium is an output level (*q*) where output demanded and output supplied are equal at less than the full-employment output (q_f). Full-employment output is the output level where production in the economy is at its maximum and cyclical unemployment is zero.

Now look what happens when aggregate demand increases to D_1D_1. The price level increases to p_1, and the output demanded and output supplied are equal at the full-employment output. People who were thrown out of work when aggregate demand was deficient now have jobs at D_1. At the higher price level p_1 it is profitable to produce more goods and services, and output supplied increases to the full-employment output, q_f.

What would happen if aggregate demand increased to D_1D_1 but the price level were not permitted to rise because of government controls? There would be no incentive for producers to increase output supplied. Output supplied would stay at q and shortages would appear. People would remain out of work because at the controlled price level it would not be profitable to employ more labor.

Reasons for deficient aggregate demand

We have said that producers may not produce an output that represents full employment because it may not be profitable to do so. But aggregate demand may fail to provide full employment, for a number of reasons.

Saving and investment. The circular flow of economic activity shows that income is created in the process of production, and income created in production may return to producers in the form of spending for the products produced. However, there may be breaks in the circular flow.

These breaks are called *leakages* and *injections*. Figure 11–6 shows the leakages and injections in the circular flow of economic activity.

Leakages, or withdrawals from the flow of economic activity, may be offset by *injections, or additions to the flow of economic activity.* An example of a leakage is *saving,* and an example of an injection is *investment.*

FIGURE 11–6
Breaks in the circular flow of economic activity: Leakages and injections

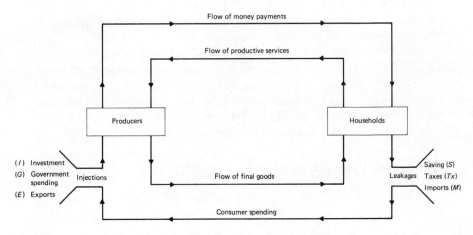

Saving means that people are not spending part of the income created in production on the purchase of consumer goods such as radios, apples, cigarettes, ties, or refrigerators. This may turn out all right. Saving is required for the economy to invest in new plant and equipment and to grow. If the rate of saving at full employment returns to the circular flow of economic activity through investment (that is, the purchase of investment goods such as plant and equipment), aggregate demand will be sufficient to buy all of goods and services produced. If full-employment saving is greater than full-employment investment, then aggregate demand will be deficient unless other injections into the circular flow happen to be greater than other leakages by the amount of difference between saving and investment. When aggregate demand is deficient, part of the income created by production does not return to producers in the form of spending. This results in surpluses at current market prices and employment levels. Producers respond to a surplus market situation by reducing production (and, therefore, income), which causes people to lose their jobs.

Taxes and government purchases.   Another example of a leakage is government *taxes,* and the corresponding example of an injection is *government purchases.* Taxes are similar to saving in the sense that they represent a withdrawal from the circular flow of economic activity. Taxes reduce private spending and, therefore, reduce aggregate demand. Government purchases of goods and services increase aggregate demand. Aggregate demand may be deficient because taxes are too high in relation to government purchases.

Imports and exports.   Do you know why we have been so concerned about the *deficit* in the U.S. international balance of payments? A deficit in international trade means we are buying more products and services from other countries than they are buying from us. An *import* is a leakage from the circular flow of economic activity, and an *export* is an injection. A deficit, an excess of imports over exports, tends to decrease aggregate demand and contributes to the difficulty of reaching the level of aggregate demand required for full employment.

Summary.   Aggregate demand may be deficient for a number of reasons. The cause may be that saving is greater than investment, taxes are greater than government purchases, and so on. There are more questions we could ask, such as: Why do people save? What determines investment? But the temptation will be resisted because we might begin to lose sight of the major issue—the wastes of unemployment.

COMBATING UNEMPLOYMENT

The type of unemployment must be identified before policies can be designed to cope with it. Among the three types of unemployment—frictional, cyclical, and structural—the first does not present a serious problem because of its transitional nature. Cyclical and structural unemployment do present problems, and policies must be designed to deal with them.

Cyclical unemployment

Government fiscal policy. Cyclical unemployment, which is unemployment caused by a deficiency in aggregate demand for goods and services, may be controlled by the appropriate use of government fiscal policy in its tax-expenditure policy. An increase in government spending relative to tax collections will increase total spending in the economy. The relative increase in government spending may be in the form of an increase in the level of government spending, holding tax rates constant, or in the form of a decrease in tax rates, holding government spending constant. In the former case, aggregate demand increases primarily due to an increase in government demand, and in the latter the increase in aggregate demand is due primarily to the increase in private demand made possible by tax cuts. In both cases, a relative rise in government spending and a relative decline in tax collections, aggregate demand is stimulated and cyclical unemployment is reduced.

Federal Reserve monetary policy. Aggregate demand for goods and services is influenced by changes in the growth of the money supply. An increase in the money supply tends to increase aggregate demand, and a decrease in supply tends to decrease demand. The money supply is controlled largely by Federal Reserve monetary policy. The Federal Reserve System and the tools used to control the money supply are covered in the following chapter. However, it is important to indicate here that Federal Reserve monetary policy may play an independent or positive role in stimulating aggregate demand. It must play at least an accommodating role if government fiscal policy, such as an increase in government spending, is to have its maximum effect in stimulating aggregate demand and reducing cyclical unemployment.

Structural unemployment

Additional measures are needed to cope with structural unemployment. Expansionary monetary and fiscal actions, assuming structural unemployment, will tend to increase resource and product prices without significantly reducing unemployment. Structural unemployment may be reduced by government policies designed to (1) relocate human resources from surplus labor areas to those where jobs are available, (2) foster wage and price flexibility, and (3) improve job opportunities of people who have a high incidence of unemployment.

It is difficult to design government policies which will successfully foster the voluntary movement of labor from depressed economic areas. There are social as well as economic costs involved in a human resource relocation program. Monetary incentives may be provided in the form of "free" transportation, low-cost housing, and job assurances. However, the social cost of moving and the government programs designed for different purposes, such as a guaranteed income program, may discourage the mobility of resources.

Government policies designed to foster competition and manpower training programs are more likely to reduce structural unemployment and to encourage resource mobility. In competitive labor and product markets, wage-price adjustments take place which tend to eliminate unemployment. Unemployment is much lower among the skilled and the highly trained and educated because of their relative scarcity and adoptability to technological changes and demand changes. Government policies designed to remove price fixing, whether by labor, business or government, and personnel training programs may contribute significantly toward alleviating the problem of structural unemployment.

SUMMARY

There are economic and social effects of unemployment. The economic effect involves the waste and loss of goods and services when resources are unemployed. The social effect involves the breaking up of human relationships within the family and outside it.

Involuntary unemployment, in a competitive framework, means that some people want to work but cannot find jobs because the amount of labor supplied is greater than the amount demanded at existing wage rates. The general solution to involuntary unemployment is a reduction in real wage rates until the amount of labor demanded equals the amount supplied. In a competitive market, the reduction in real wage rates would take place automatically.

There are three types of unemployment—frictional, cyclical, and structural. Frictional unemployment is not a serious economic issue, but cyclical and structural unemployment are. Cyclical unemployment may be kept under control by the appropriate use of monetary and fiscal policy. Structural unemployment may be reduced by policies designed to foster competition and to improve the long-run job prospects of persons who are not adaptable to a changing economy.

The economic forces operating in the economy which determine the levels of production and employment were analyzed with the help of concepts such as the circular flow of production and income and demand and supply curves. Employment rises and unemployment falls when injections into the circular flow are in excess of the leakages or, alternatively, when aggregate output demanded is greater than output supplied at current levels of prices and production. Employment falls and unemployment rises when injections into the circular flow of production and income are less than leakages or, alternatively, when aggregate output demanded is less than output supplied at current price and production levels.

SUPPLEMENTARY READINGS

Economics '73–'74. Guilford, Conn.: Dushkin Publishing Group, 1973.

An especially well-written book. Unit 20 would be an excellent supplement to the chapter above.

Hutchinson, Harry D. *Economics and Social Goals.* Chicago: Science Research Associates, 1973.

Analytical tools are developed in a lucide manner in this one-semester principles text. Chapters 7 and 8 are suggested as supplementary reading.

Miller, Roger L. *Economics Today.* San Francisco: Canfield Press, 1973.

Readings and issues are integrated with text materials in this well-organized two-term principles text. Chapter 7 and issue VII are suggested readings.

Phillips, James, and Pearl, Carl. *Elements of Economics.* New York: Macmillan, 1973.

A one-term principles text written primarily for nonmajors in economics. Chapter 11, "What Are Inflation and Depression?" and chapter 12, "What Is Fiscal Policy?" are suggested readings.

Rogers, Augustus J., III. *Choice.* Englewood Cliffs, N.J.: Prentice-Hall, 1971.

Aggregate economic analysis is developed with the use of aggregate demand and aggregate supply curves in chapter 6, which examines the determinants of national income using the same approach taken in the chapter above.

Chapter 12

INFLATION

CHECKLIST OF ECONOMIC CONCEPTS

Inflation
Price index numbers
Equity
Efficiency
Demand-pull inflation
Cost-push inflation
Money supply
Equation of exchange
Quantity theory of money
Legal reserve requirement
Open market operations
Discount rate
Inflation-unemployment dilemma
Wage-price controls
Recession
Recovery and expansion

12

Inflation

How to gain and lose at the same time

We had sold out almost our entire inventory and, to our amazement, had nothing to show for it except a worthless bank account and a few suitcases full of currency not even good enough to paper our walls with. We tried at first to sell and then buy again as quickly as possible—but the inflation easily overtook us. The lag before we got paid was too long; while we waited, the value of money fell so fast that even our most profitable sale turned into a loss. Only after we began to pay with promissory notes could we maintain our position. Even so, we are making no real profit now, but at least we can live. Since every enterprise in Germany is financed in this fashion, the Reischsbank naturally has to keep on printing unsecured currency and so the mark falls faster and faster. The government apparently doesn't care; all it loses in this way is the national debt. Those who are ruined are the people who cannot pay with notes, the people who have property they are forced to sell, small shopkeepers, day laborers, people with small incomes who see their private savings and their bank accounts melting away, and government officials and employees who have to survive on salaries that no longer allow them to buy so much as a new pair of shoes. The ones who profit are the exchange kings, the profiteers, the foreigners who buy what they like with a few dollars, kronen, or zlotys, and the big enterpreneurs, the manufacturers, and the speculators on the exchange whose property and stocks increase without limit. For them practically everything is free. It is the great sellout of thrift, honest effort, and respectability. The vultures flock from all sides, and the only ones who come out on top are those who accumulate debts. The debts disappear of themselves.[1]

---

[1] Erich Maria Remarque, *The Black Obelisk* (New York: Harcourt, Brace and Co., 1957), pp. 54–55.

Inflation is considered by most people as equal to or second only to unemployment among the nation's major aggregate economic problems. In almost every presidential campaign, candidates call inflation a bad thing and vow to control it once elected. The rising cost of groceries, auto repairs, medical services, clothes, travel, and everything else is a main topic of conversation among consumers. Business firms realize that higher prices for materials, labor, equipment, and other things they buy will reduce business profits unless they are successful in passing these higher costs on to the consumer in the form of higher consumer prices. Inflation is a prime bargaining consideration in labor union negotiations. A stated national goal of government economic policy is to stabilize the price level. All groups comprising the population—consumers, unions, business firms, and government—are concerned about inflation.

MEANING AND MEASUREMENT OF INFLATION

Most people have a good idea of what is meant by inflation. They know that it causes a sack full of groceries to cost more money. They know that buying Christmas presents costs more. They know that it is more expensive to eat out, to go to a movie, to take a vacation, or to buy a car. They know they will be generally worse off in the future unless their pay can keep up with inflation.

Inflation defined

Inflation means that the general level of prices is rising. That is, enough commodity prices are rising so that, on the average, prices in general are rising. During inflation some commodities may be falling in price and some may be rising, but the commodities rising in price are dominant, and they exert an upward force on the general price level.

Further aspects of inflation

Dynamic aspects.   An aspect of inflation that needs to be stressed is its dynamic and self-sustaining properties. Increases in the price level induce economic groups to react to rising prices, causing further increases in prices. For example, consumers expecting increases in prices may increase current consumer spending, causing current market prices to rise. During periods of rising prices, producers are not inclined to resist increases in wages and other costs, since higher production costs may be shifted forward to consumers in the form of higher prices. These increases in prices, however, become the basis for further increases in production costs and still higher prices.

Inflation without rising prices. Inflation is not always observable in the form of rising prices. It may be suppressed; market prices may not reflect the inflationary forces operating in the economy. *Suppressed inflation* is usually associated with an attempt on the part of the government to control prices. For example, the government decreed a 90-day price freeze period beginning August 15, 1971. During the freeze period prices remained about the same. Inflationary forces, however, continued to exist. The reason is that the government did not do anything to alter the relationship of demand and supply. Inflation existed in the economy because aggregate output demanded exceeded aggregate output supplied at existing market prices.

Measurement of inflation

Inflation is measured by price index numbers. Price index numbers indicate the general level of prices in reference to a base year. For example, the consumer price index in 1975 was 161.2 using 1967 as the base year. This means that prices on the average were 61.2 percent above prices in 1967. The consumer price index increased further, to 170.4, in 1976. What was the rate of inflation between 1975 and 1976? The answer is 5.7 percent. This was derived as follows:

$$\text{Rate of inflation} = \frac{170.4 - 161.2}{161.2} = 5.7\%$$

Consumer and wholesale price indices. Table 12–1 shows the behavior of consumer and wholesale prices between 1929 and 1976. The U.S. Bureau of Labor Statistics computes both of these series of price indices. The consumer price index, sometimes referred to as the cost-of-living index, includes commodities which city wage earners and clerical workers buy, such as food, housing, utilities, transportation, clothing, health, and recreation. The wholesale price index includes hundreds of commodities such as farm products and processed foods, as well as industrial commodities, such as textiles, fuels, chemicals, rubber, lumber, paper, metals, machinery, furniture, nonmetallic minerals, and transportation equipment.

Construction of a price index. Since inflation is measured by price index numbers, it is important to understand how price index numbers are derived. A simple illustration can point out the essential principles underlying their construction. Suppose a family spends $10,000, $10,500, and $11,000 in 1970, 1971, and 1972, respectively, for identical baskets of goods. If 1970 is used as the base year, the index number for the goods for that year is 100. It is 105 for 1971, calculated by dividing the cost of the basket in the base year ($10,000) into the cost in 1971 ($10,500) and

TABLE 12–1

Consumer price index and wholesale price
index in selected years, 1929 through the
first quarter of 1975 (1967 = 100)

Year	Consumer price index	Wholesale price index
1929	51.3	49.1
1940	42.0	40.5
1950	72.1	81.8
1960	88.7	94.9
1962	90.6	94.8
1964	92.9	94.7
1966	97.2	99.8
1968	104.2	102.5
1970	116.3	110.4
1971	121.3	113.9
1972	125.3	119.1
1973	133.1	134.7
1974	147.7	160.1
1975	161.2	174.9
1976	170.4	182.9

Source: *Economic Report of the President, January 1977*, pp. 242, 247.

multiplying by 100 in order to remove the decimal. Using the same procedure, the index number in 1972 is 110, or

$$\frac{\text{Cost of market basket (1972)}}{\text{Cost of market basket (1970)}} \times 100 = \frac{\$11,000}{\$10,000} \times 100 = 110.$$

The basket of goods used to compute price index numbers is a representative sample. The quantities of each good in the basket—the number of dresses, shirts, loaves of bread, gallons of gasoline, movie tickets, TV sets, autos, and so forth—bought during the year are specified. The summation of the price times the quantity of each good in the basket gives the value of the basket. After the value of the basket is calculated, the final step in the construction of a price index is to select the base year and compute the index numbers as illustrated.

A set of price index numbers is not a perfect measure of inflation. Only a sample of commodities is included in the index. What constitutes a representative sample is difficult to determine, and it changes over time in response to changes in tastes and preferences of people. It is also difficult to account for changes in the quality of goods that occur over time; for some goods and services, higher index numbers reflect higher costs for a better commodity rather than higher cost for the same commodity. Despite these imperfections, price index numbers still provide useful indicators of trends in the level of prices.

ECONOMIC EFFECTS OF INFLATION

Inflation affects the distribution of income, the allocation of resources, and the national output. The effects of inflation on the distribution of income are referred to as the *equity* effects, and its effects on resource allocation and national output are called the *efficiency* and *output* effects of inflation, respectively.

Equity effects (distribution)

The impact of inflation is uneven. Some people benefit, and some are worse off due to inflation. Because inflation alters the distribution of income, a major concern is the degree of equity or fairness in the distribution of income.

Anyone who is on a fixed income is hurt by inflation, since it reduces real income. For example, a person who earns $10,000 a year during an inflationary period in which there is a 25 percent increase in the price level suffers a cut in real income equivalent to the rate of inflation—$2,500 in this illustration. Examples of those whose incomes often do not rise as fast as the price level are retired persons on pensions, white-collar workers, civil servants, persons on public assistance, and workers in declining industries.

People who hold assets in the form of money and who have fixed claims on money may be worse off by inflation. Suppose a person deposits $1,000 in a savings account and receives a 5 percent interest rate, or $50 during the year. If the rate of inflation is in excess of 5 percent, the real value of the original savings of $1,000 plus the $50 earned on the savings for a year is reduced to less than the original $1,000. Creditors and owners of mortgages and life insurance policies are hurt by inflation, since the real value of their fixed money claims is reduced. People who bought government savings bonds for $18.75 and were paid $25.00 at maturity ten years later have sometimes discovered that the $25.00 would not buy the same quantity of goods and services as the $18.75 would have bought ten years earlier.

Inflation benefits people who have income that rises faster than prices and those who hold assets whose values rise faster than the price level. Wages and salaries of workers in rapidly growing industries are likely to rise faster than the price level. Teachers' salaries grew faster than the price level during the 1960s; therefore, teachers enjoyed absolute and relative real income gains during the period, due to the relative expansion in the demand for education. Strong unions are sometimes successful in bargaining for wage increases that are greater than the increases in the price level. People who depend upon income in the form of profits—owners of stocks and business enterprises—may have increases in real income, depending upon the rate of increase in profits in comparison to prices. The value of land and improvements on land may rise during inflation; if they rise in value faster than the rate of inflation, owners of property will benefit.

In summary, inflation alters the distribution of income and wealth.[2] Inflation is like a tax to some people and like a subsidy to others. Persons whose real incomes are reduced by inflation are those who have fixed incomes and hold assets in the form of money. Persons whose real incomes are increased by inflation are those who have money income that increases faster than prices and hold real assets that appreciate in value faster than inflation. The arbitrary manner in which inflation may change the pattern of income distribution gives support to the claim that inflation is inequitable.

Efficiency effects (effects on resource allocation)

Inflation tends to change the pattern of resource allocation. In a competitive market the prices of different goods and services reflect differences in consumer valuations of the quantities made available. Inflation causes demands for different goods and services to increase, but demands for some increase more rapidly than those for others. Increases in demands evoke supply responses, the extent of which varies from product to product. Thus inflation changes relative demands, relative supplies, and relative prices of different goods and services. The pattern of resource allocation, then, is not the same pattern that would exist in the absence of inflation. It is not certain that the pattern of resource allocation with inflation is less efficient (that is, results in lower economic welfare) than the pattern without inflation.[3] However, many economists argue that inflation distorts the pattern of resource allocation, implying a less efficient pattern when inflation occurs.

Inflation encourages economic groups to spend time and resources in an attempt to adjust to inflation. For an example, since inflation reduces the purchasing power of money, it encourages everyone to economize or minimize their money balances, that is, assets which are held in the form of money. The time spent and the resources used in adjusting to inflation could have been used to produce goods and services. Thus, inflation, by encouraging everyone to make adjustments and divert time and resources away from production, reduces economic efficiency.

---

[2] It is assumed that inflation is unanticipated. A fully anticipated inflation may not alter the distribution of income and wealth.

[3] Frank G. Steindl, "Money Illusion, Price Determinancy and Price Stability," *Nebraska Journal of Economics and Business,* 10 (Winter 1971), pp. 26–27.

Output effects *(effects on nat'l. output)*

The preceding discussion of the equity and efficiency effects of inflation was presented on the assumption of levels of real output and production that lie on the economy's production possibilities curve. This was done in order to focus attention on how inflation may alter the distribution of real income among people (equity effects) and the allocation of resources (efficiency effects). To state this simply, a certain size pie was assumed in the previous discussion, and the concern was how inflation altered the slices of pie and how inflation affected the use of resources in making the pie. Now we consider what the effects of inflation are on the size of the pie. What are the effects of inflation on the level of output of goods and services?

Inflation may have a stimulating effect on production and employment in the economy. The argument in support of this proposition can be presented as follows: During inflation money wages lag behind price increases. Thus, real profit income is increased. Under the stimulus of higher profits, producers expand production and employ more people.

The argument that inflation may stimulate production and employment should be qualified. Runaway or hyperinflation may depreciate the value of money so drastically that it loses its acceptability as a medium of exchange. Under these circumstances a barter economy develops, accompanied by lower production levels and higher unemployment. If the economy is operating at full capacity and full employment, then, of course, inflation cannot stimulate them further. Inflation at full employment is referred to usually as *pure* inflation.

The impact of inflation differs depending upon whether or not inflation is associated with increases in production and employment. As long as production is rising, there is a check on inflation since, although lagging behind demand, supply is increasing, thus tending to mitigate inflationary forces. Also, the equity effects of inflation are minimized if production and employment are rising. However, as the economy approaches full employment, the seriousness of inflation increases. The possibility of an accelerated rate of inflation is nearer, and the possible beneficial effects of inflation on prdouction and employment are remote.

ROLE OF MONEY IN THE INFLATIONARY PROCESS

It is important to understand the role of money in the inflationary process. After a discussion of the meaning and functions of money, we shall discuss the significance of money as an economic variable. This discussion centers around a development of the so-called equation of exchange and the quantity theory of money.

Meaning and functions of money

Money serves three basic functions: a medium of exchange, a measure of value, and a store of value. We use it first as the *medium of exchange;* goods and services are paid for in money, and debts are incurred and paid off in money. Without money, economic transactions would have to take place on a barter basis. Thus money facilitates the exchange process. Second, the values of economic goods and services are measured in money. Money as a *measure of value* makes possible value comparisons of goods and services and the summations of quantities of goods and services on a value basis. Concerning this last point, it is not possible to add apples and oranges, but it is possible to add the *values* of apples and oranges. Third, wealth may be held in the form of money. Money balances held by people in demand deposits at banks or at home in a sock are noninterest-bearing assets. Money serves as a *store of value.*

Economists use the words *money supply* to mean the quantity or stock of money in the economy. The nation's money supply is composed of demand deposits (checking accounts) and currency in circulation (paper currency and coins). Table 12–2 shows the breakdown of the money supply between demand deposits and currency and the growth in the money supply since 1960.

TABLE 12–2
Movements in the money supply in selected years
1960–1976 ($ billions, seasonally adjusted)

Year (Dec.)	Total money supply	Currency	Demand deposits
1960	144.2	29.0	115.2
1962	150.9	30.6	120.3
1964	163.7	34.3	129.5
1966	175.7	38.3	137.3
1968	202.2	43.4	158.7
1970	219.6	49.1	170.5
1971	233.8	52.6	181.3
1972	255.3	56.9	198.4
1973	270.5	61.5	209.0
1974	283.1	67.8	215.3
1975	294.8	73.8	221.0
1976	311.9	80.7	231.2

Source: *Economic Report of the President, January 1977,* p. 253.

The equation of exchange

A simple way of establishing the relationship between the money supply and the price level is provided in the following equation: $MV = PT$, in which M is the money supply, V is the velocity of circulation or the number of times the average dollar is spent per year, P is the price level or price index, and T is the physical volume of goods and services traded per year. The equation states that the supply of money times the velocity of money equals the price times the quantity of goods traded. Another way of looking at the equation is that the amount of money spent (lefthand side of the equation) equals the value of the goods sold (righthand side of the equation). Surely no one doubts that the monetary value of purchases must equal the monetary value of sales. Then what is the importance of the equation of exchange?

Quantity theory of money $MV = PT$

The equation of exchange is the starting point for the understanding and development of the *quantity theory of money*. This theory places prime importance on changes in the money supply. It states that the price level and output tend to move in the same direction as the money supply. Now return to the equation. If the money supply increases and the velocity of money stays the same, prices and output must rise. In these circumstances, if the economy were at full employment, an increase in the money supply would bring a proportionate rise in prices. This is the same conclusion arrived at in the preceding chapter in the discussion of aggregate-demand analysis. An increase in aggregate demand, assuming full employment, will increase prices only. The quantity theory of money is an alternative way of explaining and understanding the economic forces determining prices, output, and employment in the economy.

The quantity theory of money stresses a couple of points that may have been overlooked in the previous analysis. Inflation due to a demand pull is possible only if the money supply expands or the velocity of circulation increases, or both. It is usually correct to say that behind every great inflation there is a relatively great expansion in the money supply. In the section to follow on the causes of inflation, it is assumed that the money supply increases with increases in demand for money.

CAUSES OF INFLATION

Before policies can be designed to deal with inflation, the causes of inflation must be understood. We know from the quantity theory of money that a *basic* cause of inflation is *excess* aggregate demand generated by expansions in the money supply. Are there other causes?

Demand-pull inflation

Economists agree that most inflations are demand-pull inflations. This type of inflation is initiated by an increase in aggregate demand and is self-

enforcing by further increases in aggregate demand. A demand-pull inflation is associated with increases in production and employment until the
economy reaches full employment. Once full employment is reached,
further increases in demand increase prices only.

Figure 12–1 depicts a demand-pull inflation. Beginning at the price level
p and production q, an increase in aggregate demand to D_1 means that all
of demand cannot be satisfied at p. Thus, the price level rises to p_1, and
production rises to q_f. Then demand increases to D_2, causing the price level
to rise further to p_2. This inflationary process continues as long as aggregate demand increases, since all of demand can be satisfied only at higher
prices. Pure inflation, an increase in the price level without an increase in
output, is shown when aggregate demand increases to D_2.

FIGURE 12–1
Demand-pull inflation

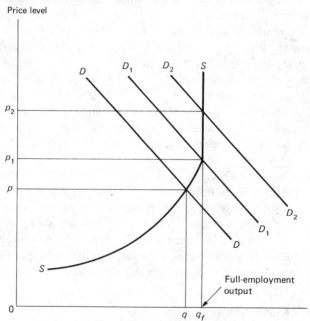

Demand-pull inflation is due to increases in aggregate demand from DD to D_1D_1 to D_2D_2.

Cost-push inflation

It is difficult to explain some of the inflationary periods in the 1960s
and 1970s only on the basis of a demand-pull inflation. The economy ex-

perienced both inflation and recession together at certain times. How can this be? A demand-pull inflation is characterized by *rising* prices and *rising* production until full employment is reached. Inflation and recession at the same time mean *rising* prices and *falling* production.

The only way the economy can experience simultaneous inflation and recession is for inflation to be initiated by a decrease in aggregate supply. This type of inflation is called a *cost-push inflation*. Increases in costs cause aggregate supply to decrease, which reduces the quantity of goods produced and increases prices.

Figure 12–2 illustrates a cost-push inflation. Beginning at price level p and production q_f, aggregate supply decreases to S_1. Now all of demand cannot be satisfied at p, that is, aggregate output demanded is greater than aggregate output supplied. As a consequence, the price level rises to p_1. Aggregate supply decreases further, to S_2. Again, all of demand cannot be satisfied, and prices rise to p_2. This inflationary process continues until there are no further decreases in aggregate supply. It can be observed in Figure 12–2 that a cost-push inflation is characterized by rising prices and falling production.

FIGURE 12–2
Cost-push inflation

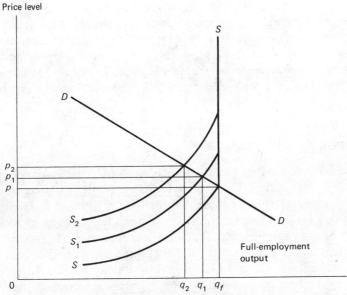

Cost-push inflation is due to a decrease in aggregate supply from SS to SS_1 to SS_2.

A demand-pull inflation is explained in terms of theory—aggregate-demand theory and the quantity theory of money. A cost-push inflation is explained in terms of the market power possessed by unions and producers in certain industries. In highly monopolized industries, unions and management may use their market power to determine wages and prices independently of market forces. One explanation is that unions increase wages in excess of productivity increases. The effect of this is to increase labor cost per unit of output. With control over price and production, producers respond by decreasing supply and shifting higher unit labor costs to consumers in the form of higher prices.

Demand-pull and then cost-push inflation

It may be misleading to look upon demand-pull and cost-push as two separate inflationary processes. They may be part of the same one, in that a single inflationary period may consist of both demand-pull and cost-push pressures.[4] Increases in aggregate demand start the inflationary process. Prices, production, and employment rise in response to the pull of demand. Money wages rise, but with a lag behind prices. Unions realize eventually that wages have lagged behind prices and begin to try to catch up by demanding wage increases in excess of productivity increases. Once this happens, cost-push pressures begin to reenforce demand pressures.

The end of an inflationary process may not coincide with the moment that demand-pull pressures no longer exist. Prices may continue to rise for a period because of cost-push pressures. These pressures operating alone sustain the inflation temporarily, even though production and employment are falling. However, without demand-pull pressures, inflation eventually stops.

CONTROL OF INFLATION

With reference to the equation of exchange—$MV = PT$—inflation results when MV is rising faster than T. Consequently, it should be controllable if one or more of these variables can be controlled. During an inflationary period M almost invariably is expanding, causing an increase in MV, or aggregate demand. The velocity of circulation, V, is also likely to be expanding, reflecting a decrease in people's desires to hold onto their money when it is going down in value. The volume of trade, T, reflecting primarily the total output of the economy, tends to increase if there are

---

[4] Samuel A. Morley, *The Economics of Inflation* (Hinsdale, Ill.: Dryden Press, 1971), pp. 4–6.

unemployed resources in the economy. However, its rate of increase will be impeded if the factors underlying cost-push inflation are present. In this section we shall consider how these variables can be controlled by means of monetary policy, fiscal policy, and the antimonopoly policy of the federal government.

Monetary policy

Monetary policy refers to the control exercised over the money supply, M, by the federal government. Demand deposits are far and away the largest component of the money supply—in 1976 the average amount of demand deposits in existence was $231.2 billion, while the average quantity of the currency was $80.7 billion. Therefore they represent the immediate target of control measures. How is control of the amount of demand deposits available for use accomplished? To answer this question, we must sketch out the structure and operation of the U.S. banking system.

Creation of demand deposits. The hundreds of commercial banks in which we have our checking accounts and do our borrowing generate the demand deposit component of the money supply. Demand deposits come into existence in two ways. First, when we deposit currency in our banks the demand deposits of the banking system are increased by the amount deposited. Second, when we borrow from our banks, they give us the loans in the form of additions to our checking accounts, thus generating new demand deposits.

Deposits arising when we take currency to the banks do not increase the total money supply, M. The currency turned over to the bank is no longer in circulation, so M is decreased by that amount. The deposits generated are equal in amount to the currency turned over to the bank. The whole process is a straightforward exchange of currency for demand deposits, with no net change in M.

Deposits arising from borrowing are a different story. When we borrow we give our banks promissory notes—which are not money. In exchange, the banks increase our demand deposits—our checking accounts—by the amount borrowed. These additions to demand deposits are money, so the lending activities of banks serve on balance to increase M.

The deposit component of the money supply is decreased by the inverse of the process discussed above. When we need currency we write checks to "cash." Our banks give us the currency and reduce our bank accounts by the same amount. Note that this does not change M, however. When we repay bank loans, we write checks to our banks—thus reducing our demand deposits. They give us nothing in return but our cancelled promissory notes! So this process operates to reduce M.

Three fundamental principles characterizing the effects of commercial bank operations on M emerge from the foregoing discussion. First, when commercial banks are making new loans in greater amounts than old loans are being paid off, demand deposits and, consequently, M will be expanding. Second, when the amounts of new loans being made are less than the amounts of old loans being paid off, M will be contracting. Third, when the amounts of new loans being made are just equal to the amounts of old loans being paid off, M is neither expanding nor contracting.

Unfortunately, when banks are left to follow their own individual interests, their actions augment inflationary forces. It is precisely when economic expansion and inflation are occurring that it is most profitable for banks to expand their loans. Business firms want to borrow, and their demands for loans raise the interest rates that banks can charge. The dangers of defaults by borrowers are minimal. The resulting increases in M add fuel to inflationary fires.

Federal reserve control of demand deposits.   The federal government has sought to limit this economically perverse tendency of commercial banks by means of the Federal Reserve System established by the Federal Reserve Act of 1913. Under the act 12 Federal Reserve banks were established—one in each of the Federal Reserve Districts into which the United States is divided. These act in a coordinated way as the central bank of the United States, with their activities controlled by a seven-man Board of Governors. A central bank acts as a banker's bank. Commercial banks themselves hold deposits at Federal Reserve banks and may also borrow from them. A second function of a central bank is to control the demand deposits that exist in the economy.

The bulk of the total demand deposits of individuals and businesses at commercial banks is held in banks that are members of the Federal Reserve System. Many commercial banks are national banks, receiving their charters from the federal government. All of these are required by law to be members of the system. The rest are state banks, chartered by individual states. Membership in the Federal Reserve System is optional for them, but it offers sufficient advantages so that many elect to join.

The feature of commercial banks that enables the Federal Reserve Board of Governors to exercise control over their total demand deposits is the reserves that they hold against their deposits. Reserves are in the form of commercial bank deposits at Federal Reserve banks, but they may also be held in the form of currency. The historical purposes of reserves are twofold. They serve to take care of both current routine needs of customers for currency and any extraordinary demands for currency that customers may have. The larger the ratio of a bank's reserves to the total demand deposits of its customers, the safer the bank is thought to be. Before the Federal Reserve Act was passed, experience indicated that prudent banking called for ratios of reserves to deposits—called *the reserve ratio*—of somewhere between 5 and 20 percent.

The Board of Governors can influence the quantities of reserves available to commercial banks and can set the minimum reserve ratio below which member banks of the Federal Reserve System cannot go. Both of these are indirect controls over the total volume of demand deposits in the economy.

To combat inflation, the Board of Governors can bring about reductions in the reserves of commercial banks through *open market operations* in government securities. Both commercial banks and Federal Reserve banks own large quantities of government bonds and treasury bills. By offering to sell at extraordinarily low prices, the Federal Reserve authorities can induce commercial banks to buy quantities of the securities from the Federal Reserve banks. Commercial banks use their reserves (deposits held at a Federal Reserve Bank) to buy them. As their reserves are reduced, so are their capacities to make new loans and to expand M.

A second means available to Federal Reserve authorities for reducing member bank reserves is elevation of the *discount rate*—the rate of interest charged commercial banks when they borrow from Federal Reserve Banks. At any given time some part of total commercial bank reserves consists of such borrowing. When a member bank borrows from a Federal Reserve Bank it receives the loan in the form of a deposit at the Federal Reserve Bank; such deposits serve as reserves for member banks. Consequently, when Federal Reserve authorities raise the discount rate, making it more expensive for member banks to borrow, the total amount of member bank borrowing shrinks, making the total reserves of member banks smaller. This in turn reduces the capacities of member banks to make new loans and expands M.

A third method of reducing the tendency of commercial banks to expand demand deposits during periods of inflation is Federal Reserve control of the *minimum required reserve ratio* that member banks may hold. Suppose, for example, that the minimum required reserve ratio of member banks is 10 percent, total reserves are $50 billion, and total demand deposits are $250 billion. The actual reserve ratio of all banks together is 20 percent—$50 billion/$250 billion. If inflation is occurring, member banks could expand their total deposits to $500 billion, thus contributing to further inflation. However, if the Federal Reserve authorities increase the minimum required reserve ratio to 20 percent, the $50 billion in reserves will permit no expansion at all in new loans and demand deposits.

We should note that all of the three means available to Federal Reserve authorities for controlling demand deposit expansion during inflation can operate in reverse to encourage expansion of demand deposits during recession. Open market purchases of government securities by Federal Reserve banks will increase member bank reserves. So will decreases in the discount rate. Further, decreases in the minimum required reserve ratio will permit demand deposit expansion.

Fiscal policy

Fiscal policy refers to federal government decision making with respect to its tax receipts and its expenditures. The relative magnitudes of these factors have important effects on aggregate demand and, therefore, on the price level of employment in the economy. Given the level of government expenditures, increases in tax collections will reduce aggregate demand, whereas decreases in tax collections will increase it. On the other hand, given the level of tax collections, increases in government expenditures will increase aggregate demand, while decreases in government expenditures will reduce it. Thus changes in either or both tax collections and expenditures should provide means of attacking either inflation or unemployment.

When the economy is experiencing a period of inflation, the government can combat it by raising taxes, reducing expenditures, or both. To the extent that rising aggregate demand is causing demand-pull inflation, such measures will serve to slow or stop it. If, however, cost push is the primary cause of inflation, fiscal policies of this sort acting on aggregate demand will serve to increase unemployment at the same time that they slow down the rate of inflation.

Output expansion policies

Since inflation occurs whenever MV is increasing faster than T, it follows that anything that increases T or the output of the economy will be helpful in mitigating it. Obviously T can rise most easily when there is slack or unemployment in the economy, as there was in 1960. From 1960 through 1965 aggregate demand was increasing, but inflation was mild because T was increasing rapidly also. Once the economy approaches full employment of its resources, output expansions are difficult to achieve.

One possible way to encourage output expansion is through antimonopoly policies. Business monopolies tend to restrict production and hold prices higher than they would be in a more competitive economy. This can, of course, lead to unemployment of resources or an inefficient allocation of resources among different uses. Similarly, union labor monopolies tend to press wage rates higher, causing the employment level to be lower than it would be in their absence. Both business and labor monopolies tend to keep prices artificially high—higher than they would be under more competitive conditions.

A second way to encourage an expansion of the goods and services available to be purchased is through decreasing the restriction of imports from abroad. With reductions in tariffs and allowable quotas of foreign goods, more foreign goods will be imported and sold. These larger quantities amount to increases in T which help to hold the price level down.

THE INFLATION-UNEMPLOYMENT DILEMMA

A major problem in controlling inflation once it has gotten underway is that effective control measures almost inevitably cause unemployment. This happened as monetary and fiscal policies were tightened to control inflation from 1969 through the summer of 1971. By August 1971 what had been a 6 percent inflation rate was down to approximately 3.5 percent. But over the same period unemployment increased from less than 4 percent of the labor force to over 6 percent. This type of thing has led many people to raise the question: Can aggregate demand be controlled by monetary and fiscal policy so that the economy can operate at a stable price level and full employment?

The trade-off problem

Some economists advance the argument that full employment and a stable price level are incompatible policy goals. They argue that an increase in aggregate demand, at less than full employment, will expand production and employment but will be associated with a cost-push inflation before full employment is reached. Also, they argue that an attempt to reduce inflation by reducing aggregate demand will prevent the economy from reaching full employment or move it away from full employment if it is already there.

Therefore, it is concluded that economic policies designed to control aggregate demand, such as monetary and fiscal policy, cannot achieve both full employment and a stable price level. Instead, there is a policy choice between full employment and some rate of inflation or between a stable price level and some rate of unemployment. This policy dilemma may be referred to as the trade-off problem. How much unemployment should be traded for stable prices, or how much inflation should be traded for full employment?

Possible inflation-unemployment combinations

Paul Samuelson and Robert Solow studied the relationship between changes in the price level and changes in the unemployment rate in this country over a 25-year period and derived a trade-off curve similar to the *TT* curve depicted in Figure 12–3.[5] The trade-off curve shows the various combinations of inflation and unemployment that are possible, given the competitive behavior of buyers and sellers and the market structure of the

---

[5] Paul A. Samuelson and Robert M. Solow, "Our Menu of Policy Choices," in Arthur M. Okum (ed.), *The Battle against Unemployment* (New York: W. W. Norton & Co., 1965), pp. 71–76.

FIGURE 12–3

Possible combinations of inflation and unemployment

Any point on the trade-off curve, *TT,* shows a combination of inflation and unemployment which is possible, given the degree of competition in the economy. For example, point *B* represents a combination of 3 percent inflation and 4 percent unemployment. T_1T_1 shows an increase in the trade-off curve.

economy. Look at points *A, B,* and *C* on the trade-off curve (*TT*). Point *A* shows a combination of a 3 percent unemployment rate and 5 percent inflation. Point *B* shows a combination of a 4 percent unemployment rate and a 3 percent inflation, and point *C* a stable price level associated with a 5.5 percent unemployment rate. Points between *A* and *B* and *C* show other possible combinations of unemployment and inflation.

The trade-off curve indicates the policy choices. Can anything be done to improve these choices, that is, to make stable prices and full employment more compatible? In terms of the trade-off curve, this means a shift of the curve to the left, indicating a reduction in trade-off costs—a lower rate of inflation associated with any given rate of unemployment.

The evidence, however, is that the trade-off curve has shifted to the right since the Samuelson and Solow study. This means that higher rates of inflation are associated with given rates of unemployment or higher rates of unemployment are associated with given rates of inflation. In other words, the cost in the form of unemployment of maintaining a stable price level has increased, or alternatively, the cost in the form of inflation of maintaining a 4 percent unemployment rate has increased. George Perry concluded from his study that at 4 percent unemployment the annual rate of inflation was 1.7 percent higher in the late 1960s than it was in the mid-1950s.[6] This increase in the trade-off curve is shown in Figure 12–3. The 1974 recession casts some doubt that a trade-off exists at all at times since in that year the economy experienced both rising prices and rising unemployment.

The trade-off curve could be shifted to the left and even made to disappear if noninflationary monetary and fiscal policies were pursued and if the economy were perfectly competitive. Some inflation may be necessary to bring us out of a recession in which there is substantial unemployment. But over time, given monetary and fiscal policies that are not inflationary, people will come to expect and depend on stable prices. This in turn will induce them to price their goods and resources so that surpluses and unemployment do not occur. The more competitive the market structures of the economy, the more likely it is that stable prices and full employment will be compatible.

EXPERIENCES WITH WAGE-PRICE CONTROLS

The Nixon Administration became convinced that monetary and fiscal policy could not cope with the economic situation existing in the economy in the summer of 1971. The economy was suffering from a high rate of inflation and unemployment. Although the rate of inflation was slowing down, it was argued that a new course of action was required to deal with both inflation and unemployment. The new course of action turned out to be a policy of wage and price controls.

The four Phases

Phase One. A policy of wage and price controls was initiated by the Nixon Administration on August 15, 1971, with the announcement of a 90-day freeze period. The freeze period, Phase One, has been followed by Phases Two, Three, and Four. During Phase One, plans were developed for the operation of a wage and price control scheme. Wages and prices did not rise much during the freeze period, since by government decree they were not supposed to increase. However, economic forces operating behind demand and supply are not affected by government decrees, and in-

---

[6] George L. Perry, "Changing Labor Markets and Inflation," *Brookings Papers on Economic Activity,* Vol. 3 (1970), p. 433.

flationary forces were continuing to build during the freeze period. In an attempt to explain why the freeze was a mistake, Milton Friedman stated, "Freezing individual prices and wages in order to halt inflation is like freezing the rudder of a boat and making it impossible to steer, in order to correct a tendency for the boat to drift one degree off course."[7]

Phase Two. Phase Two covered a 14-month period from November 14, 1971, to January 11, 1973. The wage and price control scheme was a mandatory scheme, that is, wage and price increases in industries under the controls had to be justified and approved by government. The wage and price guidelines were a 5.5 percent wage increase and a 2.5 to 3 percent price increase. The record during Phase Two was good if judged against these guidelines. During Phase Two food prices rose 6.5 percent, the cost of living increased 3.6 percent, and wages increased 5.9 percent.

Phase Three. Phase Three covered five months from January 11, 1973, to June 13, 1973. Under Phase Three the wage and price control scheme was voluntary. Wage and price guidelines were to be adhered to voluntarily, with the threat of government action in the event that they were not followed. Phase Three proved to be disastrous; wage and price controls completely broke down. This was partly because it was a voluntary scheme but primarily because of the adverse effects of price controls on supply and an increase in demand. The money supply rapidly increased during the period, making it possible for goods and services to be purchased at higher price levels.

Phase Four. A full cycle—from freeze to freeze—was completed on June 14, 1973, with the announcement of a 60-day freeze period. This was a half freeze, since some goods and services were not frozen (food and health) and some were frozen (meat, nonfood products, gasoline). After the 60-day freeze, on August 15, 1973, a system of mandatory wage and price controls was established. This marked the beginning of Phase Four. Phase Four, although a return to mandatory controls like Phase Two, may be remembered by its program of progressive decontrol. The purpose of the decontrol program was to provide for a smooth transition to a free market. By April 1974, when the last wage and price controls were dropped, many industries had already been exempted.

What have we learned from wage-price controls?

Our recent experiences with wage and price controls reflect some important lessons of economics. Lesson no. 1 is that a wage and price freeze does not prevent wage and price increases—it only postpones them. Lesson

---

[7] Milton Friedman, "Why the Freeze Is a Mistake," *Newsweek*, August 30, 1971, p. 22.

no. 2 is that a price control scheme that keeps market prices below market equilibrium prices creates shortages. Lesson no. 3 is that mandatory wage and price control schemes appear more effective than voluntary schemes, but both types of schemes treat the symptoms, not the cause, of inflation. Lesson no. 4, a concluding lesson, is that wage and price controls cannot resolve the inflation-unemployment dilemma.

RECESSION, RECOVERY, AND EXPANSION

The economy began slowing down in the last quarter of 1973—a slowdown that turned into a deep-seated slump in 1974 and 1975. The longest and costliest recession since World War II came to an end during the second part of 1975. Since, the economy has bounced back and is expanding into 1977.

The recession of 1973–1975

The recession started with strong inflationary pressures operating in the economy and what was considered at the time a fairly high unemployment rate of 5 percent. Before the recession was over, the economy experienced an inflation rate of over 10 percent (1974) and an unemployment rate of 8.5 percent (1975). *Both* rising prices and rising unemployment that characterized the economy during the first year of the recession suggest that there were problems on the supply side of the market. Given aggregate demand, about the only way the rates of inflation and unemployment can move together is for there to be decreases in aggregate supply. Scarcities created during the time of wage-price controls and shortages of food and fuel in 1973 were basic causes of inflationary and recessionary forces existing side by side in 1974. This situation was not the inflation-unemployment dilemma that we have previously described. In 1974, there was no trade-off between inflation and unemployment. We had high and rising rates of both.

Gardner Ackley, former chairman of the Council of Economic Advisors to the President, described the 1973–75 recession as a two-stage affair. The first stage, between the third quarter of 1973 and the second quarter of 1974, was characterized by declines in real consumer spending and residential construction. The basic cause of the decline in consumer spending was attributable to a decrease in the disposable income of consumers, primarily due to a $20 billion annual tax levied on them in the form of a unilateral rise in the price of imported oil.[8] During the second stage of the

---

[8] Gardner Ackley, "Two-Stage Recession and Inflation, 1973–1975," *Economic Outlook USA,* vol. 2, no. 1 (Ann Arbor: University of Michigan Survey Research Center, 1975), p. 6.

recession, between the second half of 1974 and the first quarter of 1975, declines in business investment occurred in response to further declines in real consumer spending and residential construction. With declines in business investment, both in the form of spending on plant and equipment and on inventories, a modest recession changed to a severe one.

The end of the recession was in evidence in the late spring 1975 when certain leading economic indicators showed upward trends. Before the end came, recessionary forces slowed down the rate of inflation to about 5 percent. These same recessionary forces caused the highest unemployment since the Great Depression of the 1930s—at one time the unemployment rate was approximately 9 percent (June 1975).

The recovery and the 1975–1977 expansion

With the recovery and the economy expanding in the last half of 1975, two old and familiar questions were asked. Can the unemployment be reduced without causing inflation? Or alternatively, can inflation be prevented without causing unemployment?

There may not be a simple answer to these questions. A review of some basic facts and ideas about the economy can, perhaps, shed light on these questions. One, the economy can recover and usually expand without reviving new inflationary pressures if the pace of the expansion is slow enough. Two, the way to prevent inflation is to control increases in aggregate demand made possible by money supply increases. Three, a slow paced expansion is likely to gradually reduce the rate of unemployment. Concerning this last point, some economists argue that it takes an annual growth rate in the real GNP in excess of 4 percent to reduce the unemployment rate. For example, these economists estimate that a 7 percent real growth rate tends to reduce the unemployment rate one percentage point each year. To summarize, a gradual expansion, say, 5 or 6 percent per year would have a chance of not generating new inflationary pressures and would, at the same time, be working in the direction of lowering unemployment rates.

The 1976 expansion illustrates what can be generally expected in regard to changes in the rates of inflation and unemployment when the economy is growing at a pace of about 6 percent. Between 1975 and 1976, the rate of unemployment was reduced nine tenths of one percent. The inflation rate which had been reduced to a range between 5 and 6 percent by the end of the recession in 1975 remained within this range during the 1975–1976 expansion.

The pace of growth in 1976 was a major issue in the presidential campaign. The newly elected Carter Administration quickly proposed a package of tax cuts and expenditure increases in early 1977 that was intended to stimulate the economy over a two-year period. Some of these proposals were laid aside when it was discovered that the rate of growth increased more than it was expected during the first quarter, 1977, resulting in a reduction in the unemployment rate to 7 percent and a higher rate of inflation. By mid-year 1977, the expansion returned to a slower pace and inflationary forces appeared to have receded at least for the moment. A growth rate between 5 to 6 percent, further reductions in the unemployment rate and a rate of inflation of about 6 percent were the predictions for 1977. What will occur and what lies beyond 1977 are both, of course, uncertain. Past periods of expansions suggest that in the second and third years of an expansion, the expansion slows down and the rate of inflation accelerates.

SUMMARY

Inflation means that the general level of prices is rising. It means that it takes more money to buy the same quantity of goods and services. Inflation may be suppressed. This occurs when quantity demanded is greater than quantity supplied at the current price level, but the price level does not rise because of government price controls.

The three effects of inflation are the equity, efficiency, and output effects. The equity effects involve the impact of inflation on income distribution. The people who lose during inflation are those receiving fixed incomes, holding assets in the form of money, and having fixed money claims. The people who gain during inflation are those whose money incomes rise faster than prices and who hold assets which rise in value more than the increases in the prices of goods and services.

The efficiency effects of inflation involve the impact of inflation on the allocation of resources. Inflation changes the allocating of resources, since inflation alters relative commodity prices. It is not certain that this change in resource allocation is a less efficient allocation. However, some economists argue that the allocation of resources is distorted by inflation and results in a less efficient allocation of resources.

The impact of inflation on national production of goods and services (output effects) may be to encourage production. Before the economy reaches full employment, rising prices tend to go hand in hand with rising production. The same forces that cause prices to rise cause production to rise. However, the continuation of inflationary forces at full employment leads to pure inflation, that is, rising prices not associated with rising production.

It is very important not to allow inflation to get out of hand. Whereas a steady rate of inflation of 5 percent yer year may not be the ideal situation, it does not represent the kind of problem that an accelerated inflation does. The key to controlling inflation is to control the growth in the money supply. The growth in the money supply may be controlled by Federal Reserve monetary policies.

The economic situation in the summer of 1971, rising prices and high unemployment rates, brought on an era of wage and price controls. This era lasted until April 1974. Some important economic lessons learned from the 1971–74 experiment with wage and price controls are (1) wage and price controls only postpone wage and price increases; (2) a price control scheme may create shortages; (3) a mandatory wage and price control scheme appears more effective than a voluntary scheme; and (4) wage and price controls cannot resolve the inflation-unemployment dilemma.

The economy experienced both an inflation and a recession in 1974 and 1975. Shortages in fuel and food, and slumps in the housing and auto markets, were contributing factors. The pace of the inflation slowed down by the summer of 1975, and the economy began to recover from its worse recession in over 30 years. Since the recovery in mid-1975, the economy has been expanding. Thus far, the rate of inflation has stayed within a range of 5 to 6 percent, and the unemployment rate has been reduced to 7 percent. It is uncertain as to what lies ahead; however, it is predicted that the current expansion will last through 1977 and continue into 1978. If it does, a further reduction in the unemployment rate to 6 percent is likely in 1978.

SUPPLEMENTARY READINGS

Economics '73–'74. Guilford, Conn.: Dushkin Publishing Group, 1973.

See especially unit 21, "The Problem of Inflation," and unit 29, "The Current Dilemma: Unemployment and Inflation Together."

Hutchinson, Harry D. *Economics and Social Goals,* chaps. 8 and 9. Chicago: Science Research Associates, 1973.

Levy, Fred D., and Sufrin, Sidney C. *Basic Economics,* chap. 5. New York: Harper & Row, 1973.

Morley, Samuel A. *The Economics of Inflation.* Hinsdale: Dryden Press, 1971.

An intermediate-level treatment of inflation. Chapters 1 and 2 are suggested.

Chapter 13

THE BIG NATIONAL DEBT— IS IT BAD?

CHECKLIST OF ECONOMIC CONCEPTS

Gross federal debt
Primary burden
Secondary repercussions
Balanced budget
Budget deficit
Budget surplus
Monetizing the debt
Debt management policy
Near money
Public investments
Recurrent expenditures
Fiscal rules
The current account
The investment account
The stabilization account

13

The big national
debt—is it bad?

Mythology distracts us everywhere—in government as in business, in politics in economics, in foreign affairs as in domestic affairs . . .

The myth persists that Federal deficits create inflation, and budget surpluses prevent it . . .

Obviously, deficits are sometimes dangerous—and so are surpluses. But honest assessment plainly requires a more sophisticated view than the old and automatic cliché that deficits automatically bring inflation . . .

There are myths also about our public debt. It is widely supposed that this debt is growing at a dangerously rapid rate. In fact, both the debt per person and the debt as a proportion of our gross national product have declined sharply.

Moreover, debts public and private are neither good nor bad in and of themselves. Borrowing can lead to overextension and collapse—but it can also lead to expansion and strength. There is no single slogan in this field that we can trust.[1]

The national debt, the debt of the federal government, is big. For every woman, man, and child, the national debt was $2,887 in 1976. It will be much higher in years to come if history repeats itself.

---

[1] Office of the Federal Register, National Archives and Records Service, General Service Administration, *Public Papers of the Presidents, John F. Kennedy, 1962* (Washington, D.C.: U.S. Government Printing Office, 1963), pp. 471–73.

THE COURSE OF THE NATIONAL DEBT

People probably became very concerned when the national debt topped $1 billion for the first time. It did this about 110 years ago when we were fighting each other over the question of slavery. Can you guess when the Civil War national debt high of $2.75 billion was exceeded? It occurred during the first of the wars designated as World Wars. The debt of the U.S. government reached $27 billion in August, 1919. During the decade of the 1920s, the national debt was reduced, distinguishing this period for decades to come as the decade to reduce the national debt. The national debt shot upward again during the decade of the 1930s. The cause was another war, but a different kind of war. The war was a fight against a domestic enemy known as unemployment. To wage this fight, the government tried spending a lot, at least, for that period, it seemed that way. The part of the spending not paid for by taxes was paid for by government borrowing. This is the way the national debt was increased then and the way it is increased now.

The $32 billion increase in the national debt between 1930 (December 31) and 1940 (June 30) was small in comparison to the increase in the debt of over $200 billion during World War II. The highest World War II debt was $280 billion (February 28, 1946). After reductions in the debt for several years after the war, the debt started climbing again during the 1950s. This story was repeated in the 1960s and to the present time. The national debt reached $633.9 billion in fiscal year 1976, and is estimated to exceed $700 billion in fiscal year 1977.

A major point surfaces in this scenario of the history of the national debt; namely, the growth in the debt is generally associated with wars and economic slumps. The growth in the debt during World Wars I and II, and during the depression of the 1930s, accounts for a major portion of our existing national debt. Significant increases in the debt took place in fiscal years 1975 and 1976 primarily because of the recession in the economy.

THE RELATIVE GROWTH IN THE NATIONAL DEBT

In order to place the historical rise in the national debt in perspective, this section relates the growth in the debt of the U.S. government to the growth in the nation's income, to the growth in private debt, and to the growth in state and local debt.

National debt as a percent of the GNP

The national debt as a percent of the nation's income, the GNP, has declined rapidly since 1945 (Figure 13–1). This means that the ability of the nation to meet principle and interest charges on the national debt has

FIGURE 13-1
Gross federal debt as a percent of GNP

Sources: U.S. Department of Commerce, Office of Business Economics, *Survey of Current Business,* May 1969, p. 12; June 1974, p. 8; August 1976, p. 2; Advisory Commission on Intergovernmental Relations, *Significant Features of Fiscal Federalism* (Washington, D.C.: June 1976), p. 63.

expanded faster than the debt itself. Near the end of World War II, in 1945, the national debt soared to over 100 percent of the GNP. This took place because of the unusually large amount of debt that was incurred during World War II. After this war and during the 1950s, 1960s, and early 1970s, the nation's income grew faster than the national debt with the national debt declining to 35.3 percent of GNP in fiscal year 1974. Large federal deficit spending in fiscal years 1975 and 1976 halted this downward trend in the ratio of the debt to the GNP, at least temporarily. In fiscal year 1976, the debt was 39.8 percent of the nation's income.

The growth in private debt

Private debt, that is, home mortgages, consumer credit, and business borrowing, has increased much more rapidly than the national debt in recent decades. For example, while the national debt was rising on the average of 2 percent and 4 percent yearly in the 1950s and 1960s, respectively, private debt was rising 13 percent and 15 percent yearly. Over the 31-year period, 1945–76, the national debt grew from $279.6 billion to $633.9 billion, or 126 percent, in comparison to the growth of private debt from $154.2 billion to $2,521.1 billion, or 1,535 percent (Figure 13–2).

FIGURE 13–2
Growth in federal debt, private, and state and local debt, 1930–1976

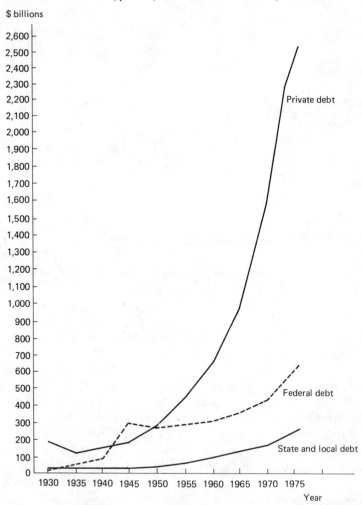

Source: U.S. Department of Commerce, Office of Business Economics, *Survey of Current Business,* May 1969, p. 12; June 1974, p. 8; August 1976, p. 2; Advisory Commission on Intergovernmental Relations, *Significant Features of Fiscal Federalism* (Washington, D.C.: June 1976), p. 63.

The growth in state and local debt

Similar to private debt, state and local governments incurred debt at a more rapid pace than the federal government during the decades of the 50s and 60s. The average annual growth rate in state and local debt was 18 percent in the 1950s and 11 percent in the 1960s. Over the period 1945–76, the growth in state and local debt was from $16 billion to $274.5 billion—a percent growth of 1,446 percent.

WHAT IS THE NATIONAL DEBT?

The data on the national debt already referred to is in reference to the gross federal debt. It includes all securities issued by the federal government—interest bearing and noninterest bearing securities, securities held by citizens of this country and securities held by citizens of other countries, securities held by government agencies and trust funds, and those held privately (individuals, businesses, insurance companies, etc.), securities held by the Federal Reserve and those held by commercial banks. A federal security is a promissory note stating that the federal government will pay the holder or the owner of the note the principle, the amount of money borrowed, plus interest over a specified period of time. It is an obligation of the federal government to pay the holder so much money plus interest for the money borrowed. The government is the debtor or the borrower and the owner of the federal security is the creditor or lender.

Types of federal securities

There are three major types of federal securities. They are marketable securities, nonmarketable securities, and special issues. Marketable federal securities are bought and sold in the market by investors. The price of these securities is determined by market forces similar to those determining commodity prices, such as wheat, in competitive markets. Nonmarketable federal securities are nonnegotiable debt instruments and cannot be bought and sold in the market. However, they may be redeemed in cash or converted to another security. Special federal securities are government securities sold to the various government agencies and trust funds such as the social security trust fund.

Marketable federal securities. Four decades ago the federal debt consisted almost completely of marketable debt. Today (November 1976) marketable securities represent approximately 64.4 percent of the federal debt. The reason for this relative decline has been the growth in the nonmarketable debt and special issues. Various kinds of marketable securities are treasury bills, notes, and bonds. Treasury bills mature or come due in less than a year, treasury notes mature between one and ten years, the treasury bonds are long-term securities normally maturing in over seven years.

Nonmarketable federal securities. Nonmarketable or nonnegotiable federal securities were offered for the first time in 1935. They grew to importance during World War II and represent today (November 1976) about 15.4 percent of the federal debt. The most important kind of nonmarketable security is the U.S. savings bond. Savings bonds are referred to by series such as Series E, H, J, and K. They have generally been issued to attract the savings of the public and are redeemable in cash after specified periods of time.

Special federal securities. Special federal securities, or special issues as they are generally referred to, represent 19.7 percent of the federal debt. These securities are held by U.S. government agencies and trust funds. In the social security trust fund, for example, social security tax revenues flow into the trust fund to pay for social security benefits. In a given year, the social security trust funds may show a surplus or a deficit depending upon the flow of tax revenues to the trust fund and the flow of benefit expenditures from the fund. When a tax surplus occurs, the surplus is transferred to the U.S. Treasury in exchange for special issues which act as a reserve. There has been some concern about the social trust fund in recent years because the current level of benefit payments is exceeding the current level of tax revenues. This means that social security taxes will have to be increased in the future or social security benefits will have to be reduced.

Who owns the national debt?

Federal securities are held by U.S. government agencies and trust funds, Federal Reserve Banks, and private investors. Private investors include commercial banks, mutual savings banks, insurance companies, other corporations, state and local governments, and individuals. Private investors hold U.S. government securities because they represent a relatively safe income-yielding asset.

Most of the national debt is held by individuals and institutions in this country. Approximately 88 percent of the national debt is internally held. The national debt held outside this country has grown from $21 billion in 1970 (December) to $74.6 billion in September 1976. This has resulted primarily from foreign investors buying U.S. government securities with dollar export earnings, especially those from exporting oil to the United States.

PROBLEMS WITH A LARGE NATIONAL DEBT

Now, we know what is meant by the national debt and who owns it. We are, perhaps, in a better position to identify problems associated with it.

Two views will be presented—the views of the general public and the views of economists.

The views of the public

Why is the public aroused and alarmed about a large national debt? The public fears that a large national debt will bankrupt the economy and future generations will have to bear the burden of the federal debt. Are these fears justified?

The bankruptcy argument. The argument that a large national debt will lead to bankruptcy is primarily based on an analogy. An individual or a business that has a large debt may go bankrupt. It happens all the time. It is reasoned, then, that similar to an individual or business, the federal government may be bankrupt.

Unlike individuals and businesses, the federal government cannot go bankrupt in a legal sense. The federal government can always meet its debt obligations. It has the power to tax and the legal right to print money. Individuals and businesses do not have these sources of revenue and therefore are not like the federal government.

Shifting the debt burden. Many people are concerned about the national debt because they are worried about its burden on future generations. They would argue that, when the debt is incurred, the current generation is postponing paying for government goods and services and shifting the cost or burden to the future. This is not entirely untrue as far as it goes. The difference between tax financing and debt financing is that in the former case individual taxpayers pay money today for government goods and services today, while in the latter case taxpayers pay money in the future for government goods and services today. However, is debt financing, which shifts money costs to the future, necessarily a bad deal for future taxpayers? Suppose the government develops an irrigation project for $1 billion and finances it from selling securities. In the future, the government will have to service the debt by raising taxes to pay $1 billion plus interest. But, what about the flow of benefits or income in the future? There is no *net* burden shifted to the future if income from the irrigation project is in excess of the costs of servicing the debt. As a matter of fact, there is a net gain to future taxpayers in this event.

The concern of economists

Economists, like the public, are concerned about a large national debt. Economists don't think much of the argument that a large national debt will bankrupt the government and the economy; however, they have had a great deal to say about the primary burden of the national debt. Unlike the public, economists are generally more concerned about the secondary repercussions of a large national debt; that is, the economic impact of the debt on prices, output, and the distribution of output.

The primary burden of an internally held national debt. Two time periods should be distinguished in trying to locate the primary burden of the national debt—the *present* when the debt is incurred and the *future* when the debt is serviced. Most economists agree that the primary burden of an internally held federal debt is in the present in the form of a sacrifice in private production. Assuming full employment, federal debt or tax financed expenditures withdraw resources from private production. The value of goods and services that could have been produced is the primary burden or real cost. Since these goods are forgone in the present, the burden or real cost is in the present. What about the future when the national debt is serviced; that is, when interest charges have to be paid. Economists have reasoned that there is no primary burden in the future since the reduced incomes of taxpayers having to pay higher taxes are offset by the increased incomes of bondholders who received the interest payments. There is no decrease in private income. Economists realize, of course, that paying interest charges on the national debt may redistribute income. However, the income redistribution effects of servicing the national debt are considered a secondary effect, not a primary effect.

The primary burden of an externally held national debt. Economists do agree that the primary burden of an externally held national debt is shifted to the future. The essential difference is that the sacrifice in private real income and production does not take place until the future in the case of an externally held national debt. For example, suppose the government buys goods and services produced in another country and pays by selling government securities. This is no sacrifice in domestic private real income when the debt is incurred. However, in the future, when the national debt is serviced, a part of domestic private income is reduced since taxes are increased to service the external debt. It is not possible to offset the reduced income of taxpayers with the increased incomes of bondholders as in the case of an internally held national debt, for government securities are held in this case by people outside the country.

Income redistribution effects. The secondary effects of the national debt are the *income redistribution effects,* the *output effects,* and the *inflationary effects.* Servicing a national debt redistributes income and, therefore, alters the distribution of the nation's output among people. The income redistribution impact of servicing the national debt depends upon the distribution of taxes among people and the ownership pattern of the federal debt. Suppose the federal tax system is less progressive than the ownership pattern of federal securities; or, stated more extremely, suppose only poor people pay taxes and only rich people own federal securities. What happens to the distribution of income if the government pays $10 billion in interest by increasing taxes by $10 billion? The answer is obvious; the distribution of income is shifted away from the poor to the rich. It is generally believed that a shifting in income from lower to upper income groups occurs because of the national debt, although the actual degree of redistribution could be determined only after a thorough examination of the relevant data.

Output effects. Our large national debt may reduce productivity and output. Taxes have to be increased in order to meet interest costs on the national debt. In this instance, the economy would be less efficient. It will not produce as much as it would if the national debt did not exist. These disincentive effects of taxes and other distortion effects that taxes may have are a worry.

Real output in the economy may be reduced in still another way by federal debt financing and the ensuing national debt. In the process of creating and servicing the debt, the federal government competes for private saving and, in effect, reduces private saving and private capital formation, that is, the accumulation of real capital assets. The ability of the economy to produce goods and services depends upon its stock of capital. A reduced stock of capital—machines, tools, and plant—associated with the national debt, then, lowers the level of national output or income.

Inflationary effects. There are inflationary woes associated with a large national debt. For one thing, government spending financed from debt is likely to be more inflationary than government spending financed from taxes. This point will be covered more carefully in the next section. In addition, a large national debt like ours gives the economy a great deal of liquidity, that is, assets that are near or like money. This liquidity aspect of the national debt means that people will tend to spend at a higher rate than they otherwise would. The national debt, then, may make it more difficult to control inflation because of the liquidity effect.

Summary in regard to national debt problems

There are problems in connection with the national debt. Some of the fears of the public, however, are unfounded. They are often based on an analogy drawn between an individual and the government—an analogy which is often false. Economists, similar to the public, have their worries about the national debt. But economists differ from the public in that their concerns are more related to the economic effects of the national debt on the operation of the economy. The next section, economic analysis of national debt financing, examines these effects more carefully.

ECONOMIC ANALYSIS OF NATIONAL DEBT FINANCING

The following analysis will, first, include a discussion of the different methods of government finance; that is, the different ways in which the federal government can pay for goods and services. Second, the economic effects of government borrowing will be presented; and third, the effects of tax and debt financing will be compared and analyzed. The analysis will draw upon the aggregate demand and supply framework presented in Chapter 11.

Methods of finance

The U.S. government has three primary ways of paying for goods and services. The government can pay for things out of current tax collections, by borrowing, and by creating money.

Tax finance. The current income of the federal government is primarily derived from its various taxes, such as income taxes, payroll taxes, and excise taxes. Taxes paid out of private income reduce private consumption and saving and, therefore, reduce private demand for goods and services. The government is said to be running a *balanced budget* when tax collections are equal to government expenditures, a *budget surplus* when tax collections are greater than expenditures, and a *budget deficit* when tax collections are less than expenditures. Ignoring the effects of different types of taxes and government expenditures, the net effect of a balanced budget on aggregate demand tends to be neutral, the net effect of a budget surplus tends to reduce aggregate demand, and the net effect of a budget deficit tends to increase aggregate demand. Figure 13–3 illustrates diagrammatically the net effect of a budget surplus and deficit on the price level and output.

Debt finance. The government incurs debt to finance budget deficits and to pay for goods and services over a period of time. Government debt is incurred by government borrowing, that is, by the government selling securities to private investors who desire to buy them. There are differences between tax and debt financing. People have to pay taxes. People do not have to buy government securities. They do so because government securities are an alternative way of holding interest yielding assets. Although tax and debt financing both may reduce private consumption and saving, debt financing does not change the total assets of people. It only changes the composition of assets; whereas, tax financing reduces the assets of people. Lastly, tax financing is a way to pay for government goods and services today; and, as mentioned above, debt financing is a way to pay over a period of time.

Money creation. The federal government may finance budget deficits and pay for goods and services by creating money. Money may be created by the government printing more money and by the government selling securities to banks, assuming banks have excess cash reserves. This latter way is the modern way to create money or to monetize the debt. Let's

FIGURE 13–3
Net effect of a tax surplus and a budget deficit

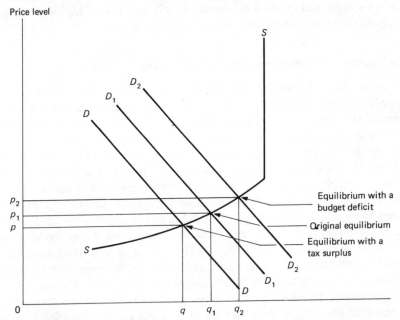

The original equilibrium is at price level p_1 where the output demanded and supplied is q_1. The net effect of a tax surplus is to reduce aggregate demand from $D_1 D_1$ to DD. A tax surplus means that the government is taking more away from the income stream than it is putting into the income stream, thereby causing a reduction in the price level and output. The net effect of a budget deficit is to increase aggregate demand to $D_2 D_2$. A budget deficit means that the government is putting more into than it is taking out of the income stream.

illustrate how this is done. Suppose the government runs a $5 billion deficit and covers it by borrowing from banks. The initial effect of the deficit expenditure is to increase demand deposits and cash reserves of banks by $5 billion. The effect of government borrowing from banks is to reduce cash reserves and to increase government securities held by banks. Then, the net effect of the whole fiscal operation is to increase demand deposits or the money supply by $5 billion. A budget deficit of $5 billion has given rise to an increase in the money supply of $5 billion. Thus, in this instance, government debt has been monetized. Is the federal debt always monetized? The answer is no—only in this case when government securities are sold to banks. The money supply is not increased when government borrowing is from nonbank sources such as individuals, businesses, corporations, and so on. Thus, increases in government debt may or may not lead to increases in the money supply. The method of finance will be referred to as money creation when the money supply increases. This terminology stresses the important fact that the debt is monetized.

Economic effects of government debt financing

Although government debt financing may reduce both private consumption and saving, it is likely to have its major impact on private saving. The part of the nation's income that is not consumed is saved. Saving may flow into noninterest yielding assets such as demand deposits, interest yielding assets such as private securities and government securities, and real investments. Government securities compete with private securities and all other alternative uses for saving. Thus, when the government borrows, that is, sells securities to individuals, businesses, corporations, etc., the government is tapping saving and reduces the amount of saving available for private borrowing and investment. Another way of saying this is that government borrowing increases the demand for saving or loanable funds; and, consequently, upward pressures are exerted on the price paid for loanable funds or the rate of interest. This is shown in Figure 13–4. The effect of a higher rate of interest is to discourage private investment. Therefore, increases in government debt may directly reduce private debt and private investment, and indirectly reduce private investment through exerting upward pressures on the rate of interest.

When the government creates money to finance budget deficits, private saving and investment may not be reduced. In this instance, the money supply is increased and the rate of interest may remain unchanged (Figure 13–4). The difficulty here is that, especially at near or full employment, financing the deficit in this way may lead to a demand-pull inflation. The question as to the best way of financing a deficit depends upon the state of the economy. Government debt financing is preferable during periods of high production and inflation, and creating money is preferable when the economy is in a deep recession or depression.

Differing effects of tax and debt financing

The differing effects of tax and debt financing may be known by now. However, several important points can still be stressed. Both tax and debt financing (borrowing from nonbanks) will reduce private demand. Tax financing does it by reducing consumption and saving, and leaving people with less assets. Debt financing does it by reducing primarily saving and increasing the rate of interest. Which has the greatest downward pull on the economy? Tax or debt financing? Tax financing probably, because

FIGURE 13–4

The effect of government borrowing and money creation on the rate of interest

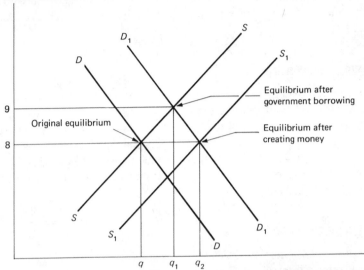

The original equilibrium is at the rate of interest of 8 percent where loanable funds (saving, etc.) demanded equal loanable funds supplied. Government borrowing increases the demand for loanable funds from DD to D_1D_1, causing the rate of interest to rise to 9 percent. Money creation, that is, government borrowing from banks, also increases demand to D_1D_1 and increases supply to S_1S_1. In this case, the rate of interest may remain at 8 percent as shown.

taxes are a direct leakage from the private income stream; but both could have a similar downward impact.

Thus, excluding creating money, finance methods have a contractionary impact on the economy and are offsets to the expansionary impact of government expenditures. Sometimes you may hear people say that government borrowing is inflationary. What they probably mean is that government expenditures may be inflationary and, as compared to tax financing, the net effect of financing budget deficits by incurring debt will tend to be inflationary.

MANAGING A LARGE NATIONAL DEBT

How would you like to be the manager of the national debt? You would be involved in big business. You would have to determine the kinds of government securities to be issued and the amounts of each. You would have to determine how they are to be sold and who is likely to buy them. You would be concerned with the economic effects on the securities market of your decisions, and you would desire to coordinate your decision with decisions made in regard to monetary and fiscal policy which are closely related.

Debt management policy

Debt management policy takes as given the size of the national debt and the cost and availability of money. The size of the national debt is determined by fiscal policy and the cost and availability of money and credit are in the domain of monetary policy. Debt management policy is essentially concerned with the structural characteristics of the national debt; namely, the types of securities, the ownership pattern, and the maturity distribution of the national debt.

Debt management principles

Stabilization role.   Economists differ as to what they believe should be the stabilization role of debt management policy. Some economists argue that debt management policy should be neutral; that is, it should be designed to have no appreciable effect on the economy. Others argue that debt management policy should play a positive role in stabilizing the economy. This would mean, during inflationary periods, that the debt coming due should be funded or refinanced into longer term government securities. The effect of this would be to put upward pressures on the long-term rate of interest and thereby discourage private investment spending. It is the long-term interest rate rather than the short-term rate that is relevant in regard to investment decisions. An alternative to investment is to make loans, especially long-term loans. The long-term rate indicates the cost of acquiring long-term funds for investment.

During recessions and unemployment, the stabilization role of debt management policy would consist of funding the debt coming due into shorter term debt or even money. Since the government's demand for long-term funds would be reduced, this would exert downward pressures on the long-term rate of interest and encourage private investment.

Minimizing interest cost.   A principle of debt management often cited is the idea that debt management policy should be designed to minimize the interest cost of the national debt. This would mean, essentially, funding the debt into short-term securities when the long-term rate is high and funding into long-term debt when the long-term rate of interest is low. The difficulty with this idea is that the effects of such a policy would tend to intensify ups and downs in the economy. The long-term rate of interest is usually low during a recession. If the government increased the supply of long-term securities in a recession, this would tend to drive up long-term interest rates and worsen the recession. Thus, minimizing interest cost on the national debt would be desirable only if it can be done without worsening recessionary and/or inflationary forces.

Lengthening the debt. A major problem with the national debt is that it is concentrated at the short end of the market. This means that a high percent of government securities outstanding is in the form of short-term securities such as U.S. Treasury bills that come due within a year. For example, during 1976, 50.8 percent of marketable securities matured. The uncertainty and impact on the securities market of the government having to enter the market to fund a huge amount of the existing national debt in this brief time span can be significant. Treasury officials and economists alike agree that the maturity distribution of the national debt should be increased. This would enable the government to better manage and plan its debt management operations and would reduce the frequency and the amount of government securities that would have to be refinanced in a given year. (See Figure 13–5.)

WHEN SHOULD THE GOVERNMENT BORROW?

The economic effects of government borrowing, and problems associated with a large national debt, have been examined. An important question, however, still remains unanswered. When should the government borrow, or alternatively, when is government borrowing the best or most efficient method of government finance?

Public investments

Government borrowing may be the efficient way to pay for investment or capital goods. These goods such as bridges, dams, schools, and hospitals provide benefits or real income to society over a period of time. Government borrowing, similar to private borrowing, permits the spreading of the cost of investment goods over a period of time. In this way, costs and benefits can be related over a time span, avoiding the heavy tax claims on private income in a single year.

Government activity of any sort, regardless of how it is financed, should not be undertaken unless it is profitable to do so. In the case of public investments, this means that the present value of the net benefits from the public investment should exceed the present value of the cost of the public investment. After this profitability criterion is met, government borrowing is a legitimate way to distribute the costs of the investment over time.

FIGURE 13–5
Refinancing short-term government debt into long-term debt

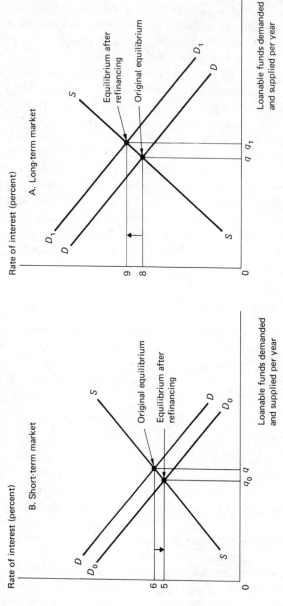

Rate of interest (percent)

B. Short-term market

S

D
*D*₀

Original equilibrium

Equilibrium after
refinancing

D
*D*₀

S

*q*₀ *q*

Loanable funds demanded
and supplied per year

0

6
5

Rate of interest (percent)

A. Long-term market

*D*₁
D

S

Equilibrium after
refinancing

Original equilibrium

*D*₁
D

S

q *q*₁

Loanable funds demanded
and supplied per year

0

9
8

The effect on the rate of interest of refinancing short-term government debt into long-term debt is to put upward pressures on the long-term interest rate and downward pressures on the short-term interest rate. The reason for this is that this debt management operation increases the demand for long-term loans and decreases the demand for short-term loans. Refinancing, that is, paying off long-term government securities tends to have the opposite effects —decreases the long-term interest rate and increases the short-term rate.

If government debt is incurred only to pay for profitable public investments, the growth in the national debt would be limited to the growth in public investment goods. Government debt incurred to finance a given public investment project would be paid off over the lifetime of the project. Thus, for the national debt to grow over time, the stock of public investment goods would have to grow.

Economic instability

If the economy operated at full employment without inflation all the time, the only justification for government borrowing would be to finance public investments. However, this is not the case. The economy experiences ups and downs; that is, the economy experiences economic instability. A responsibility of the federal government is to pursue a fiscal policy that tends to stabilize the economy.

The stabilization responsibility of the federal government suggests three fiscal rules to be followed. First, assuming full or near full employment and a stable or near stable price level, policy designed to stabilize the economy would dictate a balanced budget. In this way, the impact of fiscal operations on the level of aggregate demand would be largely neutral. Second, under the assumption of very high or full employment and inflation, the appropriate fiscal policy would be a budget surplus. The effect of the tax surplus would be to reduce the level of aggregate demand and, therefore, mitigate the inflation. Third, when the economy experiences low levels of production and employment and a decline in the price level, a budget deficit is the appropriate fiscal policy. The effect of the budget deficit would be to stimulate the economy.

Then, the stabilization responsibility of the federal government justifies government borrowing in times of economic recessions. Even if the government does not consciously plan budget deficits, they would likely occur anyway since tax collections automatically decline during recessions.

Is government debt accumulation necessary during war times?

A large part of the national debt arose due to government borrowing during war times. Can this debt increase be defended on economic grounds? The answer is no. During wars, the economy operates at full employment. The economic problem is to transfer resources from private production to war production. This transfer has to be brought about by a decrease in private disposable income and private demand. The best way to do this is through tax financing. Taxes directly reduce private consumption and saving, and are the effective way of releasing resources required to pay for the war.

Next to taxation, the best way for the government to finance war expenditures is to borrow from individuals, business, by paying interest rates high enough to attract saving and reduce consumption. The worst financing alternative during war periods is money creation. This undermines the wage-price control system, which is usually established during major wars, and causes inflation when the war ends.

A budget proposal

A great deal of misunderstanding about budget deficits and the national debt could be clarified by dividing the federal budget into three major accounts—the current account, the investment account, and the stabilization account. The current account would always be kept in balance. This account would include all current costs, including interest costs on the national debt, and current revenues exclusive of government borrowing. The investment account would include spending for investment goods and the debt incurred to finance these goods. The stabilization account would include spending programs designed to stabilize the economy and the methods used to finance these programs. The main reason for separating the budget into three major accounts is to make explicit the various responsibilities of government.

The current account recognizes the government's responsibility to manage its current operations based on principles of business and personal finance. Current costs should be met from current revenues. In the case of the government, this means, essentially, that tax revenues should pay for all current or recurrent expenditures such as expenditures on salaries, providing postal services, recreational services, supplies, interest on the national debt, medical services, welfare services, and so on.

The investment account recognizes that a nonrecurrent expenditure, that is, an investment expenditure, can be financed by government borrowing. This allows for the spreading out of the cost of the investment over a period of time. A $10 billion highway facility could be financed by the government incurring debt. However, the servicing of this debt, and operating and maintaining the highway facility, are current costs and would be paid from tax collections.

The stabilization account recognizes the government's responsibility for economic stabilization. Unemployment represents a waste of human and capital resources. Inflation has undesirable consequences; thus, on the stabilization account, a balanced budget, a tax surplus, or deficit spending would occur, depending upon the state of the economy. The fiscal rules would be: (1) a balanced budget when the economy is at full employment without inflation; (2) a budget surplus when the economy is in a serious inflation; and (3) a budget deficit when the economy is in a recession.

With current federal budget procedures it is difficult to evaluate government activities, since all expenditures are lumped together. Any budget position—a balanced budget, a surplus, or a deficit—is neither good nor bad in and of itself. It would be equally inappropriate for the government to incur debt to finance, say, increases in government employee salaries and not to incur debt to finance a profitable public investment or to promote employment when much unemployment exists.

SUMMARY

Do you now know the answer to the question: Is the national debt bad? You have studied many pages to probe, to understand, and possibly to answer this question. The organization of your answer could be as follows.

The size and growth of the national debt are closely connected to the way wars are financed and the debt incurred during economic recessions. As big as the national debt is, since 1945 it has declined relative to the nation's income and relative to private and state and local government debt.

The national debt, or the gross federal debt, includes all of the securities issued by the federal government. A federal security is a promissory note stating that the U.S. government will pay the owner its face value plus interest over a specified period of time. There are three types of government securities—marketable, nonmarketable, and special issues. Federal securities are primarily purchased and owned by private investors, although federal securities are held also by government agencies and trust funds and Federal Reserve banks. Most of the national debt is held by U.S. investors. However, in recent years, foreign investors have increased the amount they own and, in September 1976, held 11.8 percent of the national debt.

There are problems associated with a large national debt, but not all of the worries of the public are well-founded. Economists are troubled also about a large national debt, especially with regard to the way the national debt may affect the operation of the economy. A large national debt may redistribute income away from low income groups, reduce national output and the stock of capital, and increase prices.

The economic analysis of national debt financing focused on the three methods of financing—tax finance, debt finance, and money creation—and the effects on aggregate demand of each method of finance. Taxes exert a strong downward pull on aggregate demand by reducing private consumption and saving. Government borrowing from nonbanks tends to reduce aggregate demand by reducing saving and increasing the rate of interest. Government borrowing from banks (money creation) usually monetizes the national debt; that is, it increases the money supply.

Managing a large national debt is no easy task. Debt management policy takes as given the size of the national debt (fiscal policy) and the availability of money and credit (monetary policy) and determines the structural characteristics of the debt—types of securities, ownership pattern, and the maturity distribution of the national debt. Some economists believe that debt management policy should play a positive role with regard to economic stabilization while some visualize a neutral role. There is general agreement that debt management policy designed to minimize the interest costs on the national debt is not always a desirable policy, and that the maturity structure of the national debt should be lengthened; that is, the national debt should be composed of less short-term securities and more long-term securities.

Government borrowing is the appropriate method of financing in two circumstances—to finance profitable public investments and to finance programs designed to stimulate employment. Money creation, that is, government borrowing from banks, is the appropriate method of finance when there is much unemployment and no danger of inflation.

Some of the misunderstanding about budget deficits and the national debt could be lessened by dividing the federal budget into three accounts, namely: the current account, the investment account, and the stabilization account. These accounts recognize the various responsibilities of the government, which are: to pay for current expenditures out of tax collections, to pay for investment goods over a period of time, and to prevent both unemployment and inflation. Although not a panacea for government inefficiencies, these accounts would possibly provide a better understanding and a basis for evaluating government deficit spending and the ensuing growth in the national debt.

SUPPLEMENTARY READINGS

Mishan, E. J. *21 Popular Economic Fallacies*. 2d ed., chapter 5. New York: Praeger Publishers, 1973.

One of the 21 popular economic fallacies covered by Mishan is the argument that the primary burden of the national debt is borne by future generations. "First, let us be clear about one thing: that is, that the present generation cannot, in any usual sense, borrow from future generations" (p. 61).

Buchanan, James M. *Principles of Public Debt*. Homewood, Ill.: Richard D. Irwin, Inc., 1959.

James M. Buchanan disagrees with the conclusion of most economists concerning the primary burden of the federal debt, and argues that it is in the future. Pages 48 to 63 in the above reference are recommended for reading in order to study the argument of Buchanan.

Laird, W. P. "The Changing Views on Debt Management." *Quarterly Review of Economics and Business,* Autumn 1963.

This is an excellent review and appraisal of federal debt management policy.

Eckstein, Otto. *Public Finance.* 3d ed. Englewood Cliffs, N.J.: Prentice-Hall, Inc., 1973.

Chapter 7, entitled "The Economics of the Public Debt," covers the growth of the national debt and discusses the burden of the debt.

INDEX

Index

This book has been set in 10 and 9 point Times Roman, leaded 2 points. Part numbers are in 14 point Goudy Bold; chapter numbers are in 36 point Goudy Bold. Part and chapter titles are in 18 point Goudy Bold. The size of the type page is 26 x 44½ picas.